THE MEANING OF PARADOXES AND PARADOXICAL THINKING

This interdisciplinary work offers a comprehensive analysis of paradoxes and paradoxical thinking, exploring their manifestations in philosophy, societal dynamics, personality, and neuroscience. Demonstrating various methods for the augmentation of creativity and improved performance, this book uniquely integrates theoretical perspectives with case studies and practical applications. As such, it elucidates the theory and mechanisms of transforming the apparently impossible into the possible, illustrated by cases of social innovators successfully addressing insurmountable challenges. Aimed at graduate and postgraduate social science students and scholars, with more than 500 bibliographical references, the text remains accessible to a broader audience due to its engaging language. Emphasizing the significance of paradoxes and paradoxical thinking in both professional and everyday contexts, it provides a nuanced exploration of paradoxical phenomena, making it a valuable resource for academic and general readers alike.

RYSZARD PRASZKIER, PhD, is a researcher emeritus at the Institute for Social Studies, University of Warsaw.

CAMBRIDGE SERIES ON POSSIBILITY STUDIES

Edited by Vlad Glăveanu

Possibility Studies are an emerging, interdisciplinary field of study with a long past but a short history. The theme of human possibility is as old as our reflections about human nature and our place in the world. For centuries, answers to questions related to how we discover and explore possibilities have been offered by philosophers, theologians, and natural scientists. From the nineteenth and twentieth centuries onwards, these interrogations came to be placed mostly at the intersection between the humanities, social science, and the arts. Nowadays, calls to take into account themes such as the future, hope, anticipation, creativity, and imagination, among others, are frequent across psychology, sociology, anthropology, and connected disciplines. A paradigm shift is under way in all these fields, built on the background of the multiple emergencies we are faced with, from climate crises to the challenge of "post-truth," and accentuated by the impossibilities brought about by the COVID-19 pandemic.

The Cambridge Series on Possibility Studies welcomes books that aim to expand our theoretical and practical understanding of how individuals and collectives become aware of and explore new possibilities in the realms of the psychological, material, technological, social, cultural, and political. Its volumes showcase and advance current thinking on agency, creativity, innovation, imagination, improvisation, serendipity, wonder, hope, utopias and dystopias, anticipation and futures studies, counterfactual thinking, and all other phenomena that focus on our engagement with what is possible (and impossible) in our existence. The series is particularly open to inter- and trans-disciplinary contributions with high potential for cross-fertilization and, with it, for the development of new theories, methodologies, and practices that can help us study and cultivate human possibility.

A full list of titles in the series can be found at: www.cambridge.org/csps

THE MEANING OF PARADOXES AND PARADOXICAL THINKING

RYSZARD PRASZKIER

University of Warsaw

CAMBRIDGE
UNIVERSITY PRESS

Shaftesbury Road, Cambridge CB2 8EA, United Kingdom

One Liberty Plaza, 20th Floor, New York, NY 10006, USA

477 Williamstown Road, Port Melbourne, VIC 3207, Australia

314–321, third Floor, Plot 3, Splendor Forum, Jasola District Centre,
New Delhi – 110025, India

103 Penang Road, #05–06/07, Visioncrest Commercial, Singapore 238467

Cambridge University Press is part of Cambridge University Press & Assessment,
a department of the University of Cambridge.

We share the University's mission to contribute to society through the pursuit of
education, learning and research at the highest international levels of excellence.

www.cambridge.org
Information on this title: www.cambridge.org/9781009448345
DOI: 10.1017/9781009448321

© Ryszard Praszkier 2025

This publication is in copyright. Subject to statutory exception and to the provisions
of relevant collective licensing agreements, no reproduction of any part may take
place without the written permission of Cambridge University Press & Assessment.

When citing this work, please include a reference to the DOI 10.1017/9781009448321

First published 2025

A catalogue record for this publication is available from the British Library.

Library of Congress Cataloging-in-Publication Data
NAMES: Praszkier, Ryszard, author.
TITLE: The meaning of paradoxes and paradoxical thinking / Ryszard Praszkier, University of Warsaw.
DESCRIPTION: New York, NY : Cambridge University Press, 2025. | Series: CSPS cambridge series on possibility studies | Includes bibliographical references and index.
IDENTIFIERS: LCCN 2024024354 | ISBN 9781009448345 (hardback) | ISBN 9781009448338 (paperback) | ISBN 9781009448321 (ebook)
SUBJECTS: LCSH: Thought and thinking. | Creative thinking.
CLASSIFICATION: LCC BF441 .P735 2025 | DDC 153.4/2–dc23/eng/20240804
LC record available at https://lccn.loc.gov/2024024354

ISBN 978-1-009-44834-5 Hardback
ISBN 978-1-009-44833-8 Paperback

Cambridge University Press & Assessment has no responsibility for the persistence
or accuracy of URLs for external or third-party internet websites referred to in this
publication and does not guarantee that any content on such websites is, or will remain,
accurate or appropriate.

Contents

List of Figures	*page* ix
List of Tables	x
Acknowledgments	xi

	Introduction	1
	Inspiration: Literature, Art, and Music	2
	Inspiration: "Unreasonable" Social Entrepreneurs	5
	Ethnographic Inspiration	7
	Inspirations from the Business Sector	7
	Inspiration: The Paradox of Professional Life	9
	Inspiration: Academic Perspective	9
	The Book: Scope and Plan	10
	Philosophical Disclaimer	12

PART I PARADOXES AND WHAT THEY DO TO US

	Introduction	14
1	Defining the Concepts	15
	Paradoxes	15
	Contradictions and How They Differ from Paradoxes	16
	Examples of Classical Paradoxes	16
2	Mind and Paradoxes	19
	Embracing Contradictions	19
	Conceptual Blending	20
	Constructive Tension	20
	Nonlinear Thinking	21
	Paradoxical Thinking	22
3	The Influence of Paradoxical Thinking and How to Evaluate It	24
	Impact of Paradoxes	24
	Paradoxical Thinking: Evaluation	25
	Discussion and Summary	28

Contents

PART II SUDDEN UNEXPECTED CHANGES

    Introduction   30

4 Abrupt Changes   31
    Introducing the Singularities Concept   31
    Singularities in Different Variations   33
    Singularities: Recapitulation   40

5 Social Movements and Singularities   42
    The Civil Rights Movement, USA, in the 1950s and 1960s   42
    The Peace Process in the Basque Country, Spain, 2011   44
    Polish Underground Peaceful Solidarity Movement, 1980s   46
    Arab Spring   49
    Euromaidan   50

6 Early Indicators of Possible Singularities: The Lessons Drawn from NSMs   52
    Basic Characteristics of Social Movements   52
    The Prognostic Model   56

7 Predicting the Unpredictable   57
    Digital Methods of Predicting Singularities in Social Dynamics   57
    Real-Life Predictive Methods   59

    Discussion and Summary   61

PART III CHALLENGING THE IMPOSSIBLE

    Introduction   64

8 Possibilitivity: Perceiving Insurmountable Challenges as Doable   66
    Relevant Personality Traits   66
    Impossible Yet Possible Paradox   68
    Defining Possibilitivity   69
    Measuring Possibilitivity   70

9 Possibilitivity Heroes   74
    Verónica Abud Cabrera: Public Libraries in Chile   74
    Ani Choying Drolma: The Singing Nun in Nepal   75
    Andrew Kassoy, Bart Houlahan, and Jay Coen Gilbert, USA: B Corps   77

    Discussion and Summary   79

Contents vii

PART IV PEACE AND ITS CHALLENGES

   Introduction   82

10 Peace-Oriented Mindset (POM)   83
   Conflict Transformation   83
   Personality Characteristics of Peacemakers   84
   Constructing the POM Questionnaire   85
   Other Attempts to Measure Peace Attitudes   87

11 POM Heroes   88
   Fatuma Abdulkadir Adan, Kenya   88
   Hahrie Han, USA   89
   Krzysztof Czyżewski, Poland   90

   Discussion and Summary   92

PART V PARADOXES AND CREATIVITY

   Introduction   94

12 Generating New and Useful Ideas   95
   The Paradoxes of Creativity   95
   The Paradoxes of Divergent Thinking   97

13 Brain Plasticity   101
   Synaptic Brain Plasticity   102
   Neurotransmitters   103
   Neurogenesis and Brain Plasticity   105

14 Avenues for Enhancing Neuroplasticity   107
   Physical Exercise Boosts Neuroplasticity   107
   The Feldenkrais Approach to Augmenting Neuroplasticity   108
   Metaphors   110
   Joy   110
   Dancing   111

   Discussion and Summary   113

PART VI PARADOXES IN ACTION

   Introduction   116

15 Turning the Impossible into the Possible   117
   Changers-for-Good   117
   Examples of Doing the Impossible   120
   C4G: Commonalities   127

16	Paradoxes in Psychotherapy	129
	Psychotherapy and Neuroplasticity	129
	Paradox Psychology	131
	The Distance Hypothesis: Paradoxes Open an Outside-the-Box Perspective	137
17	Life and Paradoxes	138
	Paradoxes Are Natural	138
	The Paradox of the Positive Role of Chaos	139
	The Paradox of Synchronization	141
	Artificial Intelligence and Its Paradoxes	142
	Discussion and Summary	144
18	Précis	145
	The Paradox of Generosity	146
	Paradox of Happiness	146
	The Importance of Recognizing Paradoxes	146
	The Wonder	147
	Concluding Paradox	147

References 148
Index 181

Figures

4.1	Function f(x) = 1/(2−x) and its singularity at point x = 2.	page 32
4.2	Liquid–gas–solid phase transitions.	37
4.3	The system over time drifts back to the old attractor; the ball is pushed up by an external force and falls back after the force withdraws.	38
4.4	The new attractor (new hole), built outside the field of confrontation.	39
6.1	Prognostic indications drawn from analysis of New Social Movements.	56
8.1	The three steps into the impossible.	65
8.2	Laying the ground for addressing the impossible.	67
8.3	Possibilitivity: Action paradox.	69

Tables

8.1	The Perception of Doability Questionnaire (PoDQ).	*page* 71
10.1	Final statements identified for the POM questionnaire.	86

Acknowledgments

I want to thank the people who crossed the borderline of the possible, making the impossible happen. They were an essential inspiration for this book.

Thanks to Paige Munnik for her editorial skills, comments, and suggestions, which have added value to the content of this publication. Thank you also to my son, Tom Praszkier, for his professional help in preparing the photos and figures.

The book is assigned to the Robert B. Zajonc Institute for Social Studies, University of Warsaw, Poland, and to the Institute of Advanced Studies Kőszeg (iASK), Hungary.

Introduction

Paradoxes have long existed in human culture. In the sixth century BC, the Chinese Taoist philosopher Lao Tzu demonstrated this when he said (Pheng, 1995):

> A leader is best when people barely know he exists, when his work is done, his aim fulfilled, they will say: We did it ourselves.
> Mastering others is strength. Mastering yourself is true power.
> To the mind that is still, the whole universe surrenders.
> When I let go of what I am, I become what I might be.
> Those who know do not speak. Those who speak do not know.

Additionally, in the fifth century BC, Zeno of Elea, a pre-Socratic Greek philosopher, offered several insights regarding the existence of space, time, and motion. To challenge these concepts, he developed a series of paradoxes illustrating why these ideas are impossible (e.g., the paradox of Achilles and the tortoise, in which although Achilles is faster than the tortoise, he will never catch it, as elaborated later). Richard McKirahan, an American philosopher, noted that Zeno was a master of arguments that reduced things to absurdity (McKirahan, 2001).

An example from our times: Gilbert Keith Chesterton, an author from the nineteenth and twentieth centuries AD, once said that the Bible tells us to love our neighbors, and also to love our enemies; probably because generally they are the same people (Shultz, 2022).

Currently, paradoxes occur prevalently (more examples are given later in this Introduction and in Chapter 1), not limited to philosophy or artistry. Take, for example, physicists, such as the case of Erwin Schrödinger's cat: Is it alive or is it dead? Also, the famous Heisenberg's uncertainty principle. In medicine, there is a known paradoxical reaction to drugs, which is the opposite of what one would expect (such as becoming agitated by a sedative or sedated by a stimulant; see Wilson et al., 2012). In the economy, unpredictable profound upheavals are considered (called "black swan events"; see Chapter 4), and some studies have led to the conclusion that firms guided by paradoxical thinkers are more likely to manage tensions and foster innovative behavior (Ingram et al., 2016).

There are several publications related to the fields in which paradoxes play a role. This book's novelty is that it puts paradoxes into an interdisciplinary perspective, demonstrating their significance in various areas. Along these lines, and using a broader definition of paradoxes (for definitions, see later in this Introduction and Chapter 1), this book presents a variety and a diversity of paradoxical occurrences: philosophical, economic, sociological, dynamical, and psychological. It also delineates the specific approach to paradoxes – that is, the propensity for opening the mind to paradoxes and harnessing them into one's goals (i.e., paradoxicality).

Moreover, this book explores mechanisms enabling this sort of openness of the mind to paradoxical thinking, both on the psychological and the neuroscience levels. Finally, it features diverse case studies of individuals using paradoxical thinking to navigate through challenges. It also presents various practical occurrences of paradoxes – for example, predicting the unpredictable, paradoxes in psychotherapy, and artificial intelligence (AI). This kind of interdisciplinary approach is an original contribution of this book to the science of paradoxes and paradoxicality, opening new research perspectives.

While this book is primarily intended for academic purposes, it draws on inspiration from four distinct sources: One is artistic, another practice, the third stems from the business sector, and the fourth offers an academic perspective. All of these sources are elaborated upon later. The Introduction concludes by defining the scope of this book.

Inspiration: Literature, Art, and Music

It all probably started with Oscar Wilde's aphorisms,[1] such as:

> I can resist anything except temptation.
> Be yourself; everyone else is already taken.
> Always forgive your enemies; nothing annoys them so much.
> Only dull people are brilliant at breakfast.
> The difference between literature and journalism is that journalism is unreadable, and literature is not read.
> I am not young enough to know everything.
> Life is too important to be taken seriously.

---

[1] From Miscellaneous Aphorisms by Oscar Wilde. Oscar Wilde online. www.wilde-online.info/miscellaneous-aphorisms.html. Accessed July 17, 2024.

These "clashes of concepts" were a jolt to the mind: How insightful, how true, though how illogical at the same time! Mark Twain's as well:

> Buy land, they're not making it anymore (McIntyre, 2009).

Not to mention John Lennon's:

> Life is what happens when you're busy making other plans,

which sounds like a koan for meditation.[2]

At some point, I also saw a car bumper sticker that read:

> My convictions are not for public display.

What? They display their convictions, do they not? They do so by implying that they are not for public display.

A more profound inspiration that spurred my mind was Winston Churchill's statement:

> Never let a good crisis go to waste.[3]

These all led me to study the philosophy and psychology of crises and how they can be harnessed into positive development. Another source of inspiration was Yogi Berra's sayings (Berra, 2010):

> Never make predictions especially about the future.
> Always go to other people's funerals, otherwise they won't come to yours.
> No one goes there nowadays, it's too crowded.
> The future ain't what it used to be.
> You've got to be very careful if you don't know where you are going, because you might not get there.

Also singing the same tune, Groucho Marxs' (Marx, 2023):

> I sent the club a wire stating, please accept my resignation. I don't want to belong to any club that will accept me as a member.
> Outside of a dog, a book is a man's best friend; inside of a dog, it's too dark to read.
> I intend to live forever, or die trying.

---

[2] Quotation from John Lennon's song "Beautiful Boy." Might have been inspired by earlier quotations; see Nur, I. (2023). Did John Lennon Create the Phrase, "Life Is What Happens When You're Busy Making Other Plans"?: www.snopes.com/fact-check/john-lennon-life-happens-quote/. Accessed July 17, 2024.

[3] See Gruère, G. (2019). *Never let a good water crisis go to waste*. OECD. Retrieved from: www.oecd.org/agriculture/never-waste-a-good-water-crisis/. Accessed June 16, 2024.

A more visually inspiring string of inspiration came from Banksy's various graffiti works. "Stop me before I paint again," says one of them, featuring a policeman with a dog, standing in front of it.

Finally, listening to various songs was enough to convince me that there must be something mysterious and, at the same time, compelling in contradictions.

The iconic "Oh Susanna"[4] lyrics paint a picture of the hot sun making you freeze (Foster, 1974, p. 177):

> It rained all night the day I left, the weather it was dry
> The sun so hot, I froze to death.

Meanwhile, the "Shut the Door"[5] song suggests that burning fire cools you down:

> I close my eyes so I can see . . .
> I burn a fire to stay cool . . .
> Shut the door so I can leave.

Additionally, "Hot 'n' Cold"[6] indicates that:

> You're hot when you're cold,
> You're yes then you're no,
> You're wrong when it's right.

These aphorisms, drawings, lyrics – all referring to paradoxes, contradictions, impossible collisions of concepts – were not just fun. They constituted a significant source of inspiration for thoughts about human conceptualization: Is it purely logical, smooth, continuous, or, on the contrary, filled with discontinuities, atypical connections, and conceptual clashes? If the latter, what would that mean for our cognition?

I understand that this might all sound a bit abstract. In contrast, the next pillar is embedded in reality: my encounter with social entrepreneurs and their strategies for implementing practical and systemic solutions to address pressing social problems.

---

[4] See Oh! Susanna. Song of America. Retrieved from: https://songofamerica.net/song/oh-susanna/. Accessed June 16, 2024.
[5] See "Shut the Door." Fugazi. https://songmeanings.com/songs/view/38809/. Accessed June 16, 2024.
[6] See Hot N Cold. The Katy Perry Wiki. Retrieved from: https://katyperry.fandom.com/wiki/Hot_N_Cold. Accessed July 18, 2024.

Inspiration: "Unreasonable" Social Entrepreneurs

Working as a consultant for an international organization of social entrepreneurs,[7] I have conducted interviews with more than 200 social innovators across nearly all continents. I was amazed to see how they have successfully addressed seemingly impossible issues. For example, in July 2008, I met Arif Khan, whose idea was to transform the lives of women in remote, mountainous areas of Pakistan. His friends – so-called "realists" – discouraged him from pursuing the idea, considering it dangerous and unattainable. Yet Arif circumvented the conflict surrounding the traditional approach to the role of women by focusing on economic development to underserved communities. He achieved this by elevating the quality of the traditional handicrafts produced by women to a marketable level, along with providing training and education. As a result, he elevated the status of women, as they began generating substantial resources for their families and the community. Their products were proudly sold both locally and abroad.[8] This seemed like a form of wizardry, not only improving the economic prospects of impoverished communities, but also catalyzing a dramatic turnaround: the entire community supporting women's leadership positions, recognizing that women can bring about hope. Long after, I could not stop pondering solutions to seemingly unsolvable yet pressing problems by circumventing looming conflicts, often perilous to life and health, and discovering alternative win–win strategies.

These interviews were each at least three hours long, delving into not only the social innovators' current ideas, but also their historical roots. Were they consistently creative and entrepreneurial throughout their lives? In March 2008, I spoke with Collins Apuyo from Kenya, whose idea was to transform the environmental disaster of mechanics dumping used car oil directly into the soil into a safe and profitable enterprise. Thus far, all attempts to stop this polluting practice had failed. Collins contemplated turning the problem into a profitable business and a means of community development. He paid garage owners for their used oil, either with cash or through microcredit, and then sold the collected oil to producers who used it for machine lubrication. As a side effect, this approach provided jobs in impoverished communities, such as in the form of collecting oil from small, scattered bins and transporting it to larger reservoirs. The

---

[7] Ashoka: Everyone a Changemaker; see www.ashoka.org/en-us. Accessed May 3, 2023.
[8] See www.ashoka.org/en-us/fellow/arif-khan. Accessed May 6, 2023.

microcredits catalyzed the economic development of the community, and many additional benefits emerged, including the provision of protective gear – not to mention soil protection, which was the initial aim. The system generated revenue, enabling its expansion to other areas.[9]

I inquired about Collins' youth: Were there any examples of his early entrepreneurial approach? His answer was affirmative: While he was a high school student, he noticed that students paid little attention to handicraft and technical lessons, merely producing items to pass the classes. He had the idea that if they produced high-quality products, it would enhance their skills, make the teacher happy, and allow Collins to purchase the final products, generating revenue by selling them at the market. He waited until his graduation, then initiated this well-thought-out business plan, contracting students to create products related to technical lessons in several schools, and selling them with special branding. I was astounded by the beautifully circular win–win aspect of both his past and present ideas.

People like Arif and Collins have been labeled "unreasonable" by some (e.g., in the book *The Power of Unreasonable People*, by Elkington and Hartigan [2008], p. ix) because they merge seemingly impossible dreams with successful implementation. At the beginning of the book, the authors quote George Bernard Shaw:

> The reasonable man adapts himself to the world, the unreasonable one persists in trying to adapt the world to himself. Therefore, all progress depends on the unreasonable man.

Indeed, progress is in the hands of social innovators who dream big and who, simultaneously, have a knack for making their visions happen. The change they introduce is not only local (usually the pilot is local), but goes global, as highlighted by David Bornstein (2004) in the title of his book: *How to Change the World: Social Entrepreneurs and the Power of New Ideas*. The author presents various examples, one of them being Mohammad Yunus, the winner of the 2006 Nobel Peace Prize. Yunus proved that in Bangladesh, one of the poorest countries in the world, social innovations can bring hope. He innovated microcredits for groups of poor women (a group guarantees the loan to the bank) in the form of revolving loans, enabling each group member to launch their own small-business venture. Since the mid-1970s, the program has spread globally to rural areas,

---

[9] See www.ashoka.org/en-us/fellow/collins-apuoyo. Accessed May 7, 2023.

changing the lives of millions by introducing a microfinance system.[10] Another author, Beverly Schwartz (2012), emphasizes the global aspect of this approach in her book: *Rippling: How Social Entrepreneurs Spread Innovation Throughout the World*.

The concept of social entrepreneurship is defined and elaborated upon in Chapter 14, and is also mentioned in other chapters of this book.

Ethnographic Inspiration

I found paradoxes in ethnographic research: for example, the dual role of the ethnographer as being both an "insider," exploring the field hands-on, while simultaneously being an "outsider," developing a theoretical framework for the practical findings (Greco & Heucher, 2022; Yeo & Dopson, 2018).

Additionally, some ethnographic examples reveal paradoxes in action, such as the ancient Jewish "slapping" rituals performed at a girl's first menstruation. In the past, when a girl informed her mother that she had experienced her first period, the mother would slap her daughter's face and simultaneously exclaim "Mazel tov!" ("congratulations") (Berliner, 2017). The act of slapping and congratulating simultaneously creates a contradiction conveying a higher-level meaning.

Inspirations from the Business Sector

Some corporate initiatives appear counterintuitive, seemingly contradicting the essence of business, which is profit-oriented. These surprising initiatives go beyond the well-known and widespread concept of corporate social responsibility (CSR).

It is evident that corporations reward employees' innovative initiatives, especially those that have proven to be applicable and effective. However, some companies take the opposite approach: They reward initiatives that have failed. The rationale behind this is that when employees' ideas are not ultimately implemented, they become discouraged and lose their motivation for further innovation. In this context, rewarding unimplemented innovations could sustain creativity-oriented motivation and, in the future, may result in valuable innovations (Baumann & Stieglitz, 2014).

These ideas are supported by practical examples. A business webpage states that rewarding employees for successful, creative ideas is obvious, but

---

[10] See also Yunus (2008).

some companies are taking a different approach, rewarding failures in order to encourage creativity on a broader scale.[11] One of these companies is Google Labs, which actively seeks science fiction-sounding ideas to solve problems. They have received various interesting ideas, such as a frictionless surface that can levitate objects, which obviously was not implemented. However, they believe that one must reward failure, or else people will stop taking risks.[12] Similarly, companies like TATA and Procter & Gamble distribute an annual "Heroic Failure" award to those who take the greatest "intelligent" risk within the company. One of the rationales behind this is the belief that making mistakes is acceptable, but trying to hide them is not.[13]

This approach of rewarding failures made me contemplate the following contradiction: On the one hand, many corporations are profit-driven, promoting workable and applicable innovations, while, on the other hand, some companies "waste" time and resources on recognizing failure – something inconceivable in the education sector.

Moreover, some companies prioritize joy over performance and hard work, which is seemingly detached from their core business mission. An example is Dennis W. Bakke, the founding CEO of the AES company,[14] who rejects workplace monotony as a toxic relic of the Industrial Revolution. He authored a book titled *Joy at Work: A Revolutionary Approach to Fun on the Job* (Bakke, 2006), using the history of his $8.6 billion annual revenue company to demonstrate that joy not only enhances people's well-being, but also serves as a catalyst for creativity and commitment. Similarly, Ricardo Semler, CEO of the successful Brazilian Semco company,[15] believes that the purpose of work is not solely to make money; it is also about making workers feel good about life. One of his books is titled *The Seven-Day Weekend: Changing the Way Work Works* (Semler, 2004).

This complemented my earlier discoveries: Writers, philosophers, painters, and singers have always been fascinated by contradictions and paradoxes, while social entrepreneurs solve seemingly unsolvable problems.

---

[11] See www.cornerstoneondemand.com/uk/resources/article/reward-failures-crush-employees-fear-innovation/. Accessed May 13, 2023.
[12] See BBC report: www.bbc.co.uk/news/technology-25880738. Accessed May 13, 2023.
[13] See www.forbes.com/sites/jacobmorgan/2015/06/02/are-you-embracing-failure-or-encouraging-failure/?sh=fe5cefb32ade. Accessed May 13, 2023.
[14] A Worldwide Fortune 200 company, AES is an energy giant with 40,000 employees across 31 countries and an annual revenue of $8.6 billion.
[15] By 2015, the company had an annual revenue in excess of $240 million per year and employed more than 3,000 workers.

Business is expected to be serious, continuously challenged by a highly competitive market. However, rewarding failures and infusing joy into the workplace are antithetical to the established order.

This exploration led me to delve into what science has to say.

Inspiration: The Paradox of Professional Life

There are also several paradoxes related to professional life and the workplace: for example, the oppositions between efficiency and innovation, short- and long-term perspectives, control and empowerment, and profitability and responsibility (Hauksson, 2023). Professional paradoxes, as well as the positive tension they generate, are also embedded in the author's own professional life. For instance, I wear two hats on my head. The first is practical, such as engaging in identifying and empowering social innovators worldwide: for example, I have conducted interviews with more than 200 social innovators across nearly all continents – most of them in person. As mentioned before, I have been doing this since 1995 on behalf of Ashoka: Everyone a Changemaker, the international association of leading social entrepreneurs.

My second passion is academic: studying and developing the theory and research to understanding the mechanisms of change for good. I have initiated several related research studies and published various academic books and articles.

These two fields are distinct, each having its own methodology (one aggregates knowledge through experience, the other through research) and specific jargon. The best social sector articles might not be accepted in peer-reviewed scholarly journals, and vice versa.

My professional paradox lies in being split between these two worlds, embracing both simultaneously. On the one hand, it seems like quite a tall order; on the other hand, this contradiction continuously clashes and sparks in my head, generating new insights and providing the accompanying thrill of joy.

Inspiration: Academic Perspective

> What we agree with leaves us inactive, but contradiction makes us productive. Johann Wolfgang von Goethe (Cooley, 1918).

The initial literature review revealed several indications that the role of paradoxes and contradictions is worthy of further systematic exploration (see the following chapters). I discovered that a paradox can be defined in various ways, such as a statement contrary to common belief or self-contradictory and thus false; ultimately, it can be a statement that seems contradictory, unbelievable, or absurd, yet may reveal some true understanding (Ackermann, 1991).

It appears that paradoxes exist outside of common belief, contrary to what is initially perceived to be true. This suggests that truth lies beyond the initial perception. Paradoxes may be seen as a gift, as they provide an intriguing capability to reconcile seemingly contradictory truths in order to uncover a greater truth (Lederach, 2005). Some authors emphasize the need for a "science of paradox" to explore the complex psychological and social processes through which contradictions occur (Berliner, 2017).

What appears significant is that contradictions often lead to novel and breakthrough solutions (Heracleous, 2020; Rothenberg, 1996), and leaders who embrace a paradox mindset are more likely to enhance workforce productivity. Moreover, this mindset has a positive influence on workplace innovation (Liu et al., 2019).

The Book: Scope and Plan

These were the inspirations that led me to the decision to write a book demonstrating the positive consequences of paradoxes. There are several definitions of a paradox, such as Merriam-Webster's proposition that it is a statement that is seemingly contradictory or opposed to common sense and yet is perhaps true.[16] It can also be defined as an unacceptable conclusion derived from seemingly acceptable reasoning based on apparently acceptable premises (Sainsbury, 2009), or as a logically self-contradictory statement or a statement that goes against one's expectations (Curry, 2010).

Willard Van Orman Quine – a former Harvard University professor and one of the most respected American philosophers – mentioned the case of Frederic as an example of a paradox: Frederic reached the age of twenty-one after experiencing only five birthdays. Initially shocking and counterintuitive, this paradox finds its solution when one realizes that he must have been born on February 29, in a leap year. Quine concluded that although Frederic's situation is possible, it is paradoxical because of its "initial air of absurdity" (Quine, 1976). Another paradox that he mentioned is Bernard Russell's: Does the barber, who shaves all and only those men in the village who do not shave themselves, shave himself? If yes, then he does not belong

---

[16] See www.merriam-webster.com/dictionary/paradox. Accessed May 18, 2023.

to the set of men in the village who do not shave themselves, and therefore he should not shave himself. If, however, he does not shave himself, he should shave himself, as he is one of those whom he targets to shave. Both paradoxes are similar in the way that they initially appear to sustain absurd conclusions through seemingly valid arguments. In the first case, it is strange to be twenty-one years old having had only five birthdays. In the second case, the conclusion is that no village can contain a man who shaves all and only those men who do not shave themselves. Quine argued that he would not limit the word "paradox" to similar cases (called veridical), as it also encompasses falsidical paradoxes, such as "proving" that $1 = 2$ (some mathematicians engage in this kind of misleading manipulation of numbers) (Quine, 1976, pp. 1–2).

All in all, there seems to be quite a range of understandings of paradoxes: from statements that seem contradictory or opposed to common sense and yet may be true, through logically self-contradictory statements, those running against one's expectations, to, finally, Quine's "air of absurdity."

This book is positioned on the continuum between "a statement that is seemingly contradictory or opposed to common sense and yet is perhaps true" and the broader "air of absurdity," as long as it conveys a higher-level meaning. It addresses seemingly impossible, unpredictable, surprising situations, especially those that are predominantly perceived as inconceivable.

It addresses paradoxes and paradoxical thinking from various perspectives: philosophy (e.g., the paradoxes mentioned by Hellenistic philosophers; Chapter 1), psychology (e.g., how the mind embraces paradoxes; Chapter 2), social psychology (e.g., the dynamics of profound societal transformations; Chapter 5), neuroscience (e.g., the mind's neuroplasticity; Chapter 13), and anecdotal (i.e., cases of individuals achieving the impossible; distributed throughout the book).

Moreover, this book addresses the consequences of applying paradoxes in people's life – mostly positive consequences, though one must be aware that the results may also be negative. On the one hand, paradoxes may promote innovation, while, on the other hand, some paradoxes (i.e., contradictory demands that must be disobeyed to be obeyed) may create paralyzing catch-22 situations (Cunha et al., 2022).

Keeping this reservation in mind, this book presents an overview of paradoxes, especially those raised by ancient philosophers. It also explores the diverse ways of delineating them and discusses the negative and positive consequences of the tension generated by them (Part I). Next, it reviews sudden, unexpected changes, such as Nassim Taleb's black swan events, particularly in the context of profound, peaceful social movements (Part II), as well as the role and importance of perceiving insurmountable, impossible, and seemingly unrealizable challenges as achievable (Part III). The paradoxical embracing of contradictions is demonstrated as especially critical in promoting peace (Part IV). Part V outlines how paradoxes augment creativity, including a touch of neuroscience (i.e., our brains' reaction to maintaining simultaneous contradictions); it delineates the phenomenon of neuroplasticity and the ways of augmenting it. Part VI provides diverse examples of addressing impossible goals in the social arena, especially by social entrepreneurs; moreover, it outlines the use of paradoxes in psychotherapy and AI.

Philosophical Disclaimer

This book does not oppose paradoxes to Aristotle's law of noncontradiction (LNC), which states that opposite assertions cannot be simultaneously true at the same time (Aristotle, 2016; Priest, 2007). It does not endorse Russell's barber paradox; instead, it demonstrates how contemplating whether he shaves himself or not can enhance one's creativity and offer novel perspectives.

In addition to the LNC, Aristotle himself left us various paradoxes. In this regard, one might conclude that, at the meta-level, his legacy suggests that the LNC may coexist, in a person's mind, with paradoxes and contradictions. *The Meaning of Paradoxes and Paradoxical Thinking* adds that this coexistence can lead to various new avenues and discoveries.

PART I

Paradoxes and What They Do to Us

Introduction

The following story reflects the content and spirit of this section well:

> A young actor or actress aspiring to make it to Hollywood discovers a prerequisite: Before being considered for casting, they must possess an appropriate union card. However, upon applying for the card, they find that it cannot be obtained without first being cast in a film.[1] This situation presents a clear contradiction, otherwise known as a catch-22. As a result, a paradox emerges within the system, driven by this contradiction's higher-level meaning: It guarantees that older thespians, regardless of whether younger ones may be better suited, receive casting priority.

This example evokes curiosity: How can paradoxes and contradictions be defined and differentiated?

As the first step, Chapter 1 focuses on defining paradoxes and contradictions, illustrated using a handful of classical examples. Chapter 2 then explores ways of thinking that embrace contradictions. Finally, Chapter 3 centers on the impact of paradoxical thinking and presents relevant evaluation methods.

---

[1] From the Socratic Q&A blog: https://socratic.org/questions/what-is-the-difference-between-a-contradiction-a-paradox-and-irony-can-someone-h. Accessed June 18, 2023.

CHAPTER I

Defining the Concepts

The definitions of and differences between paradoxes and contradictions are considered herein. Furthermore, the concept of specific thinking that encompasses paradoxes and contradictions is introduced. Chapter 1 concludes with a handful of ancient and classical paradoxes.

Paradoxes

Webster's Dictionary defines a paradox as a statement that is seemingly contradictory or opposed to common sense and yet is perhaps true.[2] The first part of the definition, which includes terms such as "contradictory" or "seemingly contradictory," can also be found in other definitions (e.g., Curry, 2010; Dinsdale, 2023; Fletcher & Olwyler, 1997; Quinn, 1998).

The second part of the definition refers to a higher-level meaning: "yet is perhaps true" (Webster[3]), "yet explicable as expressing truth" (Fletcher & Olwyler, 1997, p. 7), "present and operate equally at the same time" (Quinn, 1998), "reveal a previously unknown truth or a deeper truth because, despite being contradictory, a paradox can still be true" (Dinsdale, 2023), or "runs contrary to one's expectation" (Curry, 2010, pp. 3–4).

Decades ago, while observing my overly serious friend and noticing how his seriousness makes him funny, I wrote: "Someone who cannot laugh at himself is just comical." This statement presents a contradiction by juxtaposing seriousness and comicality. The higher-level meaning is that a critical distance toward oneself adds a genuine sense of gravity. Similarly, the phrase "the only thing I know is that I know nothing" (Dinsdale, 2023) imbues contradiction with a higher-level significance.

---

[2] See www.merriam-webster.com/dictionary/paradox. Accessed May 18, 2023.
[3] See www.merriam-webster.com/dictionary/paradox. Accessed July 1, 2023.

Another noteworthy approach to defining paradoxes should be mentioned: An unacceptable conclusion derived from apparently acceptable reasoning based on seemingly acceptable premises (Sainsbury, 2009) – as well as the "air of absurdity" (Quine, 1976) mentioned in the Introduction.

This book incorporates these definitions. As stated in the Introduction, the understanding of paradoxes is positioned here on a continuum between "a statement that is seemingly contradictory or opposed to common sense and yet is perhaps true" and the broader notion of an "air of absurdity," provided that this contradiction or absurdity carries a higher-level meaning.

Contradictions and How They Differ from Paradoxes

A contradiction is a statement, idea, or situation that contradicts itself. It often involves two assertions that cannot logically coexist simultaneously (Dinsdale, 2023). In short, it refers to a statement or phrase whose parts contradict one another.[4]

Examples of contradictory statements include "Never say never"[5] and "Let me say it again: I never repeat myself."[6] Yogi Berra's saying "No one goes there nowadays, it's too crowded" and a bumper sticker that reads "My convictions are not for public display" also demonstrate contradictions.

Contradictions are, simply, conflicting elements within the same system, whereas paradoxes are conflicting elements that reveal a previously unknown truth.[7]

Examples of Classical Paradoxes

The paradoxes of Zeno of Elea (born in 490 BC) present interesting challenges. One of them involves Achilles never catching up with a much slower tortoise. Why? Although Achilles is faster, he gives the tortoise a head start. Every time Achilles reaches the initial position of the tortoise, it moves ahead to a new point, which Achilles then reaches. This cycle continues, with the tortoise always moving slightly further ahead ... da capo al fine (Aristotle, 2018; Clark, 2012; Rescher, 2001).

---

[4] Webster: www.merriam-webster.com/dictionary/contradiction. Accessed June 19, 2023.
[5] From www.exampleslab.com/15-examples-of-contradictions/. Accessed June 19, 2023.
[6] From www.quora.com/What-are-examples-of-contradictory-sentences. Accessed June 19, 2023.
[7] From Socratic Q&A: https://socratic.org/questions/what-is-the-difference-between-a-contradiction-a-paradox-and-irony-can-someone-h. Accessed June 19, 2023.

Similarly, Zeno of Elea introduced the arrow paradox, suggesting that motion does not truly exist. Why? Because at each infinitesimally small-time interval, the arrow is motionless. This implies that it is motionless at any given moment in time (Aristotle, 2018; Clark, 2012).

Aristotle introduced another paradox of Zeno, known as the paradox of place, which questions the existence of place itself. If everything that exists has a place, then place itself must also have a place, and so on ad infinitum (Aristotle, 2018). This paradox is also reflected in contemporary literature, where the existence of place is considered essential (see, e.g., Relph, 2016; Rushing, 2009).

Eubulides of Miletus, a philosopher from the fourth century BC, is renowned for his liar paradox (Rescher, 2001, p. 78). In this paradox, a man declares, "What I am saying now is a lie." If this statement is true, then he has spoken the truth, contradicting his claim to be lying. Conversely, if it is a lie, then he has told the truth, again contradicting himself. Thus, if he is lying, he is telling the truth, and vice versa.

Plutarch (born in AD 46) presented the identity paradox: Theseus had to rebuild his ship by replacing all of the old parts with new ones. However, a question arises: When he finally arrives back home, is he still on the same ship he initially departed on? Undoubtedly, the ship has undergone changes, but the question remains: Is it still the same ship? (Plutarch, 2013). Interestingly, there are several variations of the Ship of Theseus paradox. For example, John Locke's sock: Would the sock remain the same after a patch is applied to a hole? What about after subsequent patches are applied, until all of the material of the original sock has been replaced with patches?[8] This paradox extends to human identity vis-à-vis its relation to physical (e.g., replacing body organs) and psychological changes over time, thereby raising the question of identity (Klein, 2014).

One version of the omnipotence paradox is the paradox of the stone: Can God create a stone so heavy that even He could not lift it? This question is paradoxical because if God could create something He could not do, then He would not be omnipotent. Similarly, if God were able to lift the stone, it would mean that He was unable to create something He cannot do, leading to the same outcome (Savage, 1967).

It is said that the philosopher Karl Popper wrote the following letter to his friend (Gardner, 1962, p. 71):

---

[8] See https://open.library.okstate.edu/introphilosophy/chapter/ship-of-theseus/. Accessed June 24, 2023.

Dear M. G.,

Kindly return this card to me but make sure to mark "Yes," or to put some other mark of your choice, in the black rectangle to the left of my signature if, and only if, you feel justified in predicting that, upon its return, I shall find this space empty.

Yours sincerely
K. R. Popper

If Popper's friend sends it back blank, then he should check it, as per the requirement to mark it if it arrives blank. However, if he checks it, it implies that he is certain that the spot will arrive blank, so it should not be marked. Conversely, if the friend were to send it back blank, it would mean that he is confident it will be marked.

This chapter, as well as in the Introduction, indicates the existence of a palette of various paradoxes. They differ from contradictions by adding an additional, higher-level meaning to the latter.

CHAPTER 2

Mind and Paradoxes

> One is fruitful only at the cost of being rich in contradictions.
> Friedrich Nietzsche (1997, p. 27).

Our minds, when confronted with paradoxes, react differently. In some cases, we are open and ready to connect and – as will be demonstrated – benefit from paradoxes. This specific trait is sometimes called *paradoxicality* (Hsiung, 2022). The remainder of this chapter provides a review of various delineations of this mind–paradox encounter.

Embracing Contradictions

While browsing the web, one can find statements such as "Acknowledging, owning, and embracing the paradoxical nature of our lives, the lives of others, and the world can lessen our resistance to change and increase our effectiveness."[1] Furthermore, it seems that embracing contradictions can enhance the creativity of individuals and teams. When seeking creative solutions, embracing contradictions proves considerably more productive than settling for a trade-off between them. Similarly, when resolving conflict situations, embracing contradictions – rather than just compromising – can serve as a stronger motivation to explore new paths (Ashkenas & Bodell, 2013; Markman, 2022).

This notion has been confirmed by research: it has been documented on an $N = 950$ sample that teams that embrace contradictions (paradoxical frames) and possess high epistemic motivation demonstrate greater

---

[1] See https://marclesser.net/contradiction-and-inconsistency/. Accessed June 19, 2023.

creativity. This is attributed to their increased engagement in exchanging, considering, and integrating diverse ideas and perspectives (Miron-Spektor et al., 2022).

Interestingly, embracing contradictions is perceived as deeply rooted in Chinese culture and also currently provides Chinese companies with a competitive advantage (Li-Hua, 2014; Peng & Nisbett, 1999).

Conceptual Blending

Conceptual blending is a method of generating new ideas by combining two concepts (Oakley, 1998). It involves cognitive processes that combine words, images, and ideas within a mental network to create meaning (Nordquist, 2019).

These elements may be distant or contradictory. The authors of this concept, Gilles Fauconnier and Mark Turner, hold that, in this process, elements from diverse fields and situations are blended in a conscious or subconscious manner. They posit that all learning and thinking involves blends of metaphors derived from simple bodily experiences. These blends are then merged and combined into mental functioning (Fauconnier & Turner, 2003). Thus, conceptual blending becomes a fundamental tool of the human mind, utilized in our basic construal of all aspects of reality, from the social to the scientific domains (Turner, 1998).

In a study focused on discourse participants, various functions of discussion were identified, including integration, conceptual change, metaphor projection to humor, literary invention, and the transfer of emotions and attitudes. It was observed that discourse participants construct mental spaces through conceptual blending to facilitate understanding and action. The conceptual blending perspective provides a suitable framework for understanding how participants construct new meanings (Oakley, 1998).

An example of its application is an AI model of creativity, whose premise is based on conceptual blending (Pereira, 2007).

Constructive Tension

The classical theory of tension caused by opposing ideas suggests a negative way of experiencing these contradictions. Leo Festinger's cognitive dissonance theory from the 1950s states that new information conflicting with one's beliefs induces discomfort. This discomfort motivates individuals to seek ways to reduce it by modifying their cognitive structures until they become consistent again (Festinger, 1957).

However, contemporary perspectives indicate that the tensions between opposing ideas can be constructive. We possess an inherent "opposable mind" that allows us to hold two conflicting ideas in constructive tension, leading to the generation of new and superior ideas regarding the conflicting elements (Martin, 2009).

Some authors have introduced the interesting concept of "aintegration," defined as the human ability to tolerate cognitive or emotional complexity and the aptitude to maintain incongruence and live with inconsistencies, discontinuities, contradictions, and paradoxes, while not experiencing stress or inconvenience (Lomranz & Benyamini, 2016). Interestingly, one of the findings from these authors' research is that individuals with a higher level of aintegration are more likely to report positive life events and to view negative events as not solely negative.

In the business context, embracing contradictions instead of rejecting them can generate positive tension that energizes employees, ultimately enhancing their performance and fostering innovation (Miron-Spektor et al., 2017). Business consultant and author Peter Senge also highlighted that in business this creative tension serves as a source of energy (Senge, 2006).

Overall, analysis of the literature confirms that creativity and innovation thrive, in part, through the presence of (constructive) tension. This tension can support individuals and teams when facing the pressure of searching for novel ideas (Potonik et al., 2022).

Nonlinear Thinking

Janusian Thinking

Opposites are around us. When we put opposites together in new arrangements, we arrive at the very wellspring of creativity (Barnett, 1997).

Janusian thinking, a term coined by the psychiatrist Albert Rothenberg (Rothenberg, 1971), draws inspiration from Janus, an ancient Roman god with two faces looking in opposite directions. Janusian thinking refers to the ability to simultaneously imagine or think about two contradictory concepts (Michalko, 2012), enabling an individual to think paradoxically. Interestingly, Janusian thinking has played a significant role in the inventions of exceptional scientists, who were found to have had the capacity to conceive multiple opposites simultaneously (Rothenberg, 1971, 2011).

An example of this is Niels Bohr's saying: How wonderful that we have met with a paradox. Now we have some hope of making progress.[2] This indicates that he believed that by holding opposites together, the mind can reach a new level where traditional convergent thinking is suspended,[3] allowing for intelligence beyond thought to act and create new forms. The interplay of opposites creates the conditions for a new point of view to emerge from the mind. This ability to hold two opposites together led Bohr to conceive his principle of complementarity, which inherently contains the inextricable self-contradiction that light is both a particle and a wave (Michalko, 2012).

There are several instances of renowned scientists applying Janusian thinking. For instance, Einstein's theory of relativity was developed, in part, by imagining a paradox involving a man falling from a roof – how could he be at rest and in motion at the same time?[4]

Paradoxical Thinking

The term "paradoxical thinking" was coined in the late 1990s, referring to an individual's internal contradictions. It posits that limitations arise from an individual's limited frame of reference, particularly when avoiding internal paradoxes. These limitations hinder the generation of creative solutions. Each person possesses a unique combination of contradictory and paradoxical qualities that have the potential to work together and produce optimal results. The process of identifying and accepting these contradictions is known as paradoxical thinking (Fletcher & Olwyler, 1997).

This book presents a different understanding of paradoxical thinking, aligning with the American Psychological Association's (APA) definition, which characterizes it as a cognitive process marked by contradictions. The APA acknowledges that, in extreme cases, paradoxical thinking may be associated with distorted thought processes, such as those observed in schizophrenia. However, paradoxical thinking is primarily embraced to foster creativity and facilitate personal, familial, and organizational change.[5]

---

[2] See Niels Bohr Archive: https://nbarchive.ku.dk/outreach/bohr-quotations/. Accessed June 16, 2024.
[3] For instance, A to B logic; see Chapter 13.
[4] See "What is the key idea that led Einstein to the general theory of relativity?" Quora. www.quora.com/What-is-the-key-idea-that-led-Einstein-to-the-general-theory-of-relativity. Accessed June 16, 2024.
[5] See https://dictionary.apa.org/paradoxical-thinking. Accessed June 22, 2023.

Following the APA's definition, paradoxical thinking is understood here as a cognitive process marked by contradictions. In one variation, paradoxical thinking can be used as a method to challenge societal beliefs and attitudes by conveying a message that aligns with the recipient's existing beliefs and attitudes, but in an exaggerated, amplified, or even absurd manner. This exaggeration of held societal beliefs leads individuals to perceive their current beliefs and attitudes as irrational and perhaps even senseless. This form of paradoxical thinking is employed in certain peace-building processes, particularly in the context of protracted conflicts (Bar-Tal et al., 2021; Hameiri et al., 2018). Interestingly, it seems to draw inspiration from the classic debating technique of *reductio ad absurdum*.[6]

Janusian and Paradoxical Thinking: Recapitulation

The significance of Janusian and paradoxical thinking is evident from research conducted on a population of twenty-two European and American scientists, including Nobel Prize laureates. Additionally, documentary investigations have targeted remarkable scientists from the past, such as Bohr, Darwin, Dirac, Einstein, and Planck.

The overall analysis revealed that actively engaging in the simultaneous conception of multiple opposites or antitheses (i.e., Janusian or paradoxical thinking) plays a significant role in the process of scientific creation (Rothenberg, 2011).

This role of constructive tension and Janusian or paradoxical thinking is further supported by a study involving 319 students in China. The findings documented that experiencing (constructive) tension has a positive effect on paradoxical thinking, thereby enhancing the creativity of college students. Likewise, experiencing constructive tension enhances creativity through paradoxical thinking. Conversely, a higher reliance on mentoring diminishes the positive effect of experiencing tension related to paradoxical thinking (Wang & Liu, 2023).

---

[6] See www.iep.utm.edu/reductio/. Accessed June 22, 2023.

CHAPTER 3

The Influence of Paradoxical Thinking and How to Evaluate It

This chapter reviews ideas and studies that confirm the positive consequences of paradoxical thinking. It also presents methods for measuring an individual's propensity to accept paradoxes and embrace contradictions.

Impact of Paradoxes

The title of this book may suggest that paradoxes are some kind of power-carrier. This claim deserves closer examination, especially since some authors argue that paradoxes must be accepted and managed in various domains such as life, work, communities, and among nations (Handy, 1995, pp. 11–12).

Some authors advocate for the establishment of a "science of contradictions" to explore the intricate psychological and social processes through which contradictions arise. The aim is to explain how and why such universal processes are employed (or not) within specific cultural and social contexts. It is argued that humans are inherently contradictory, living harmoniously, albeit occasionally painfully, with their oxymoronic selves (Berliner, 2017).

On the other hand, research demonstrates that a paradox mindset is associated with optimism and persistence, particularly in the face of failures. Individuals with a paradox mindset respond to a contradictory situation by cultivating optimism about their ability to navigate challenging situations. A paradox mindset is also associated with determination and persistence, even in the face of stagnation or failure (Sleesman, 2019).

A study involving 217 individuals randomly assigned to sixty-three culturally diverse teams documented that team members with a high multicultural paradox mindset are accepting of and energized by intercultural tensions, both emphasizing cultural differences and finding common ground. Moreover, teams comprising members with a high multicultural paradox mindset demonstrate higher levels of creativity (Mannucci & Shalley, 2022).

Another team-based study, which collected data at 2 points in time from 369 employees in 90 teams, revealed that an employee's paradox mindset positively influences their innovative behaviors and contributes to their thriving at work. Additionally, leaders' paradoxical thinking has a similar positive impact on employees (Liu et al., 2019).

Following these studies, various website articles claim that paradoxical thinking is key to success and fosters creativity (e.g., Berliner, 2016; Heracleous & Robson, 2020). Particularly noteworthy is a *Harvard Business Review* paper that investigated the root causes of Toyota's success. The conclusion was that Toyota prospers by creating contradictions and paradoxes in various aspects of organizational life (Takeuchi et al., 2008). The paper outlined several major contradictory dynamics that influence the company's strategy, such as:

- Toyota moves slowly, yet it takes big leaps;
- Toyota maintains a strict hierarchy, but it gives employees the freedom to push back;
- Toyota insists on simple internal communications, yet it builds complex social networks.

Interestingly, the latter was elaborated as follows:

> Toyota fosters a complex web of social networks because it wants "everybody to know everything." The company develops horizontal links between employees across functional and geographic boundaries, grouping them by specializations and year of entry; creates vertical relationships across hierarchies through teaching relationships and mentoring; and fosters informal ties by inviting employees to join clubs based on birthplaces, sports interests, hobbies, and so on. (Takeuchi et al., 2008)

Paradoxical Thinking: Evaluation

These reports revealed a need for measuring the propensity for embracing contradictions and engaging in paradoxical thinking. To address this gap, Professor Ella Miron-Spektor and her team developed a questionnaire aimed at assessing the paradox mindset (Miron-Spektor et al., 2017). Employees from the USA, the UK, Israel, and China were asked to rate their willingness to embrace contradictions, using statements such as:

1. When I consider conflicting perspectives, I gain a better understanding of an issue.
2. I am comfortable dealing with conflicting demands at the same time.

3. Accepting contradictions is essential for my success.
4. Tension between ideas energizes me.
5. I enjoy it when I manage to pursue contradictory goals.
6. I often experience myself as simultaneously embracing conflicting demands.
7. I am comfortable working on tasks that contradict each other.
8. I feel uplifted when I realize that two opposites can be true.
9. I feel energized when I manage to address contradictory issues.

The study also included a second factor related to experiencing tension, with statements such as:

1. I often have competing demands that need to be addressed at the same time.
2. I sometimes hold two ideas in mind that seem contradictory when appearing together.
3. I often have goals that contradict each other.
4. I often have to meet contradictory requirements.
5. Usually when I examine a problem, the possible solutions seem contradictory.
6. I often need to decide between opposing alternatives.
7. My work is filled with tensions and contradictions.

The psychometric qualities of the questionnaire were found to be good, based on reliability and factor analysis, leading to a split into two categories: embracing contradictions and coping with associated tension. The analysis of the sample revealed that employees who scored low on the paradox mindset scale struggled with constraints. On the contrary, those who embraced a paradox mindset – such as considering overcoming constraints as not only challenging but enjoyable – performed better, especially in terms of creativity and problem-solving. These results demonstrate that a paradox mindset is key to unlocking the potential of everyday tensions.

The major challenge with this questionnaire is that it consisted solely of positive statements, which could potentially influence respondents through the mechanism of the social desirability bias (SDB). To address this, and in order to investigate how individuals feel about holding conflicting concepts, the Influence of Contradictions Questionnaire (ICQ) was constructed, drawing inspiration from the original questionnaire and incorporating both positive and reversed statements (Praszkier et al., 2021).[1]

---

[1] With Prof. Miron-Spektor's permission, as of January 9, 2021.

Initially, a twelve-statement questionnaire was constructed and validated in an Anglophonic population ($N = 120$). Through statistical analysis, a ten-statement questionnaire with good reliability was identified, with reversed statements marked by an asterisk (*)

1. I am comfortable dealing with simultaneous conflicting ideas.
2. I avoid dealing with conflicting concepts.*
3. Tension between ideas mentally blocks me.*
4. Encountering conflicting perspectives makes me confused.*
5. Tension between ideas energizes me.
6. I feel disempowered when dealing with contradictory issues.*
7. When I consider conflicting perspectives, I gain a better understanding of an issue.
8. I feel dejected when I see opposites coexisting.*
9. I find dealing with conflicting ideas inconvenient.*
10. I feel energized when I consider addressing contradictory issues.

The validation process demonstrated that the ICQ is suitable for scientific purposes[2], such as making comparisons between segments of society or types of activities (Praszkier et al., 2021). However, it should be noted that the sample size was relatively small, highlighting the need to conduct validation studies with a larger population and including cross-segment analysis (e.g., examining how ICQ scores distribute across different age groups, genders, or educational backgrounds).

---

[2] Cronbach's alpha = 0.791.

Discussion and Summary

This section introduced the concepts of paradoxes and contradictions, reviewing ancient and classical examples (Chapter 1). It also covered the concepts of embracing contradictions, conceptual blending, paradoxical and Janusian thinking, and the associated constructive tension (Chapter 2). Finally, it presented methods for evaluating the impact of paradoxical thinking on individuals and their propensity for embracing contradictions (Chapter 3). The conclusion reached at the end of Chapter 3 highlights that there is still a need to expand the research to a larger, multicultural sample.

This book focuses on paradoxes: the variety of their occurrences and reflections on their definitions, especially regarding paradoxes being carriers of a higher-level meaning. Additionally, it explores the processes of embracing contradictions, conceptual blending, and paradoxical or Janusian thinking, showcasing various manifestations of these concepts (see the upcoming chapters).

Finally, this book does not contradict Aristotle's law of noncontradictions. Aristotle claimed that without this principle of LNC, we would be unable to know what we currently know.[3] Instead, this book explores how our minds react when confronted with contradictions or paradoxes and how these occurrences can potentially foster change.

---

[3] See https://plato.stanford.edu/entries/aristotle-noncontradiction/. Accessed June 26, 2023.

PART II

Sudden Unexpected Changes

Introduction

An example of a paradoxical situation is predicting the unpredictable— that is, significant, abrupt, and unpredictable events (so-called *singularities*) in the social arena, which is the focus of Part 2. Chapter 4 provides a review of the various delineations of such occurrences (e.g., black swan events, cusp catastrophe theory, and phase transition).

Following this general overview, Chapter 5 focuses on paradoxical singularities occurring in social movements. A series of five case studies is presented, epitomizing profound, peaceful, and successful social movements, highlighting their related singularity moments. Analyzing and drawing conclusions from these movements, Chapter 6 presents a model for the early indicators of similar movements to appear.

Lastly, conclusions are drawn from case studies, leading to the development of a predictive model.

CHAPTER 4

Abrupt Changes

Introducing the Singularities Concept

There is no doubt that we live in an ambience of change. Peter Drucker, a well-known business advisor and coach, encourages people to embrace change and consider it an opportunity, rather than a threat (Drucker, 2001; Rosenstein, 2022). He also authored the iconic message that to survive and succeed, every organization will have to turn itself into a change agent. The most effective way to manage change is to create it.

Some understand change as a gradual process. Others, however, claim that transformation implies radical change, because all elements of the structuring of the field are in flux (Fligstein, 2013).

There are some similarities between the social and the mathematics fields. For example, classical physics and mathematics, as well as classical sociology, used to be based on the notion that change is smooth and consistent with positive feedback, where the rate of change continuously modifies the existing state of any system, leading to exponential growth or decline (Batty, 2008). However, linear change is the least likely scenario in the contemporary world, where discontinuous jumps are predominant, with multiple causes working together, starting from the bottom up and generating tipping points, catastrophes, and bifurcations.

Markets represent a classic example. These are often governed by uncoordinated bottom-up actions that have the capability to generate abrupt change. Such change is unexpected, for it is the product of countless actions that cannot be managed and often cannot be tracked. In this sense, it is emergent and always surprising (Batty, 2008).

In mathematics, a point at which a given mathematical function is not defined or has strange properties (e.g., one that is – at this point – infinite) is called a *singularity*[1] (see the example shown in Figure 4.1).

---

[1] See https://en.wikipedia.org/wiki/Singularity. Accessed February 25, 2023.

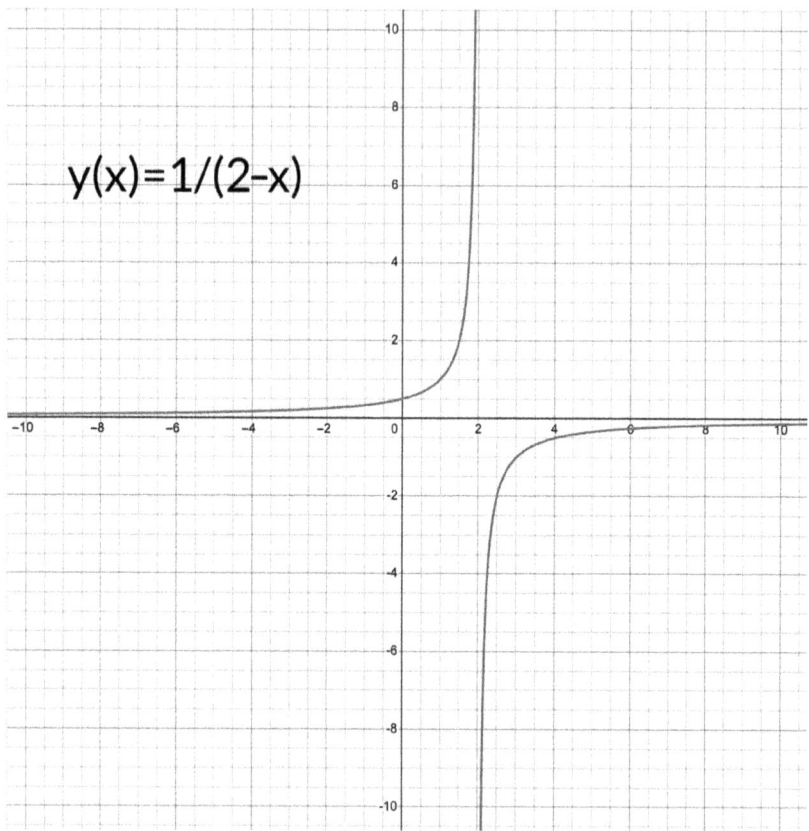

Figure 4.1 Function f(x) = 1/(2−x) and its singularity at point x = 2.
(Author's own sources)

James Clerk Maxwell, in the nineteenth century, used the term *singularity* beyond the scope of mathematics, holding that in dynamical systems theory (i.e., also within social systems) singularity refers to contexts in which arbitrarily small changes, which are commonly unpredictable, may lead to arbitrarily large effects.[2] In a social context, multiple currents of change converge to a point in time where the systems become radically different in their structure (Kurzweil, 2005), and – as for our contemporary world – these singularities will fundamentally change the way we live and work, ending the world as we know it (Kurzweil, 2005).

[2] See https://en.wikipedia.org/wiki/Singularity_(systems_theory)#cite_ref-1. Accessed July 18, 2024.

Singularities may manifest as disruptive for existing homeostasis upheavals, such as riots, peaceful protests, revolutions, or – in the case of families – acute conflicts (Praszkier, 2013). They may also constitute system-strengthening processes, such as commitment, propensity for cooperation, and trust (Pena-López et al., 2013; Zabłocka et al., 2016).

This chapter explores the singularity issue in a social context, demonstrating various ways in which it can be analyzed – for example, from the perspective of black swan events (Taleb, 2010), dynamical rare events (King & Zeng, 2001), cusp catastrophe theory (Flay, 1978), the butterfly effect (Érdi, 2008), bifurcations (Hazy & Ashley, 2011), and phase transition (Li et al., 2012). Several case studies (e.g., the civil rights movement, the peace process in the Basque Country, and the Polish underground "Solidarity" movement) are used to illustrate the ways in which singularities may manifest in the context of societal dynamics.

Moving beyond the state of the art, conclusions from the demonstrated case studies are drawn, showing early indicators of a possible forthcoming singularity. The conjectures related to the early indicators of singularity address the properties of networks, the role of a compelling vision, and the kinds of leadership.

Furthermore, various predictive methods are presented, such as computer and life simulations. Chapter 4 concludes with recommendations for social organizations and movements on how to prepare for potential forthcoming singularities and bifurcations.

Singularities in Different Variations

The growing contemporary interest in singularity phenomena is perhaps related to abrupt market changes. In 2010, Lucien Karpik introduced the concept of the economics of singularities, analyzing the goods and services that cannot be studied by standard methods because they are multidimensional, incommensurable, and of uncertain quality (Karpik, 2010). Karpik's conception has a particular application to studying the untypical phenomenon of the bitcoin market, which was initially predicted to be a short-term bubble and instead became a durable and significant segment of the market (Dallyn, 2017).

Beyond the market, singularities are also incorporated into various other disciplines, such as sociological analysis (Hamel, 1992), and, taking it a step further, the entire society may be delineated as "The Society of Singularities" (Reckwitz, 2020). Moreover, singularities enter the realm of culture (Leypoldt, 2014) and even the neuroscience of love (Solnyshko & Malpuech, 2022).

In the following sections, several paths for describing singularity phenomena are delineated. The first one – black swan events – comes from market studies, while the three that follow represent dynamical social psychology.

Black Swan Events

Nassim Taleb, who created the black swan event concept, proposed the following definition: A black swan event is a rare occurrence of enormous consequence that cannot be predicted or calculated (Taleb, 2010).

Upon closer inspection, Taleb holds that the notion of black swan events encompasses the following:

- **Unpredictability**: They exist outside the realms of possibility, mainly because nothing in the past suggests that they are coming, exceeding what is normally expected of a situation.
- Black swan events have an **extreme impact**.
- After the fact, people tend to fabricate an explanation that makes it appear more predictable than it really was (Taleb, 2010); in other words, people generate **hindsights**, devising explanations (after the event has happened) that make it seem plausible and predictable.

Market black swans are usually disruptive events, creating an extreme economic impact (Stodd & Reitz, 2017). A prime example is the global financial crisis caused by the stock market crash of 2007–2008, initially starting as a mortgage lending crisis and then expanding into a global banking crisis before resulting in the fall of Lehman Brothers, all leading to a global recession (Kenton, 2023).

Many drastic events, such as 9/11 (September 11, 2001), Hurricane Katrina (August 23–31, 2005), and the BP Deepwater Horizon oil spill and disaster (April 20, 2010), either did not register on anyone's radar as incoming or the indications were disregarded as implausible, resulting in various post-event explanations (Nafday, 2009).

People tend to underestimate black swan risks, likely because they overestimate one's knowledge and focus too narrowly on one's field of expertise (tunnel vision), ignoring other sources of uncertainty and mistaking concocted models for reality (Nafday, 2009).

The black swan event perspective is helpful for analyzing various occurrences – for example, the coronavirus (COVID-19) pandemic

(Antipova, 2021), which caused a global stock market crash in 2020 (in one month, S&P 500 lost more than 30 percent of its value). Consequently, investors had limited opportunities for investment, providing reasons for panic buying and selling (Ahmad et al., 2021).

Interestingly, this perspective may also be applied to the dynamics of animal populations: Researchers have found black swan events to occur mostly within bird, mammal, and insect species. Such events develop mostly as descending processes due to unexpected population collapses (Anderson et al., 2017).

Rare Events

Rare or extreme events are infrequent, high-severity occurrences that have far-reaching consequences and might destabilize entire systems. They are identified via stock market analysis (Sornette, 2017), ocean wave intensity (Dysthe et al., 2008), and society (King & Zeng, 2001). Moreover, rare events address natural phenomena (e.g., earthquakes, tsunamis, hurricanes, floods, asteroid impacts, and solar flares), as well as man-made dangers, such as violent conflicts, terrorism, industrial accidents, financial and commodity market crashes, and global warming effects (King & Zeng, 2001).

Rare events analysis is predominately based on statistical models and computer modeling of the processes (King & Zeng, 2001). It may relate to extreme situations, such as analyzing how statistical prognostic models estimate the probability of a single vote in a US election being decisive. For example, in the period 1900–1992, there were 20,597 US House elections, of which 6 were decided by fewer than 10 votes, 49 by fewer than 100 votes, 293 by fewer than 500 votes, and 585 by fewer than 1,000 votes (Gelman et al., 1998).

Cusp Catastrophe Theory

A cusp catastrophe represents a sudden destabilization of the equilibrium, causing a "jump" from one state to another. This concept is used for modeling several dynamical occurrences, such as sudden crowd traffic jams (Zheng et al., 2010). Additionally, cusp catastrophe models have been proposed for many psychological phenomena (Flay, 1978; Sussmann & Zahler, 1978; Zeeman, 1976). A key example is the riots in London in August 2011, where the control variable was the level of discontent and anger met by police brutality. The response to this brutality involved demonstrations, maintaining the stability of these dynamics. However, an isolated shooting acted as a catalyst for the rioting to occur; the threshold (singularity point) of behavior change had suddenly been met, and rather than seeing a gradual (smooth) change through an increase in the frequency and intensity of the protests, a sudden jump from a peaceful demonstration to rioting occurred (Flay, 1978).

Another example is a dog's response to stressful stimuli, called the fight-or-flight response (Cannon, 1963; Sussmann & Zahler, 1978). When a dog encounters a stranger, it experiences a mixture of fear and aggression. Driven by aggression, it moves toward that person, though fear makes him step back; there is a balanced fear–aggression distance taking place during this "dance." This equilibrium is maintained as long as that person walks far enough in front of the dog. However, if she or he moves closer, the singularity point may be crossed, in which case, the dog's aggressiveness will predominate, and he will jump at the approaching person. This "jump point" is called a "cusp catastrophe."

Butterfly Effect and Bifurcations

The butterfly effect is a metaphor reflecting the idea that small things can have a nonlinear impact on a complex system. The popular idea that the flap of a butterfly's wings in one place can have a major effect on weather conditions in a distant location illustrates how small changes at the outset lead to greatly different results or outcomes (Érdi, 2008).

The term "butterfly effect" was coined in the 1960s by Edward Lorenz, a meteorology professor at the Massachusetts Institute of Technology (MIT), while studying weather patterns. His insight was that some complex dynamical systems exhibit unpredictable behaviors such that small variances in the initial conditions could have profound and widely divergent effects on the system's outcomes (inspiring the so-called "chaos theory"). As for the weather forecast, when comparing two close starting points to indicate the current weather, they might drift apart and instead end up with completely different weather (Gleick, 2008).

In line with this finding, there should be a momentum of embranchment, when a slight change determines which direction dynamic processes tend toward. This embranchment is called bifurcation, as is visible in the dog's fight-or-flight response discussed in the previous section: There is a bifurcation point which separates "flight" from "flight."

As another example, one can imagine a bottle drifting in the current of the North Atlantic Drift encountering its bifurcation point.[3] At this point, a very slight breeze may determine whether the bottle ends up near the North American coast or closer to Norway (Praszkier & Nowak, 2012).

Phase Transition

The discontinuities and rapid jumps from one state to another (e.g., the previous example of London's nonrioting to rioting) are sometimes compared to the phenomenon of phase transitions in physics, such as when water transforms into gas at a temperature of 100 °C (212 °F) or into ice at a temperature of 0 °C (32 °F); see Figure 4.2.

While the water temperature grows, small nucleus bubbles appear, which connect, grow, and burst out of the surface; the bubbles in these dynamics are a metaphor for social clusters and groups growing and, finally, leading to a substantial transition (Nowak & Vallacher, 2005, 2018).

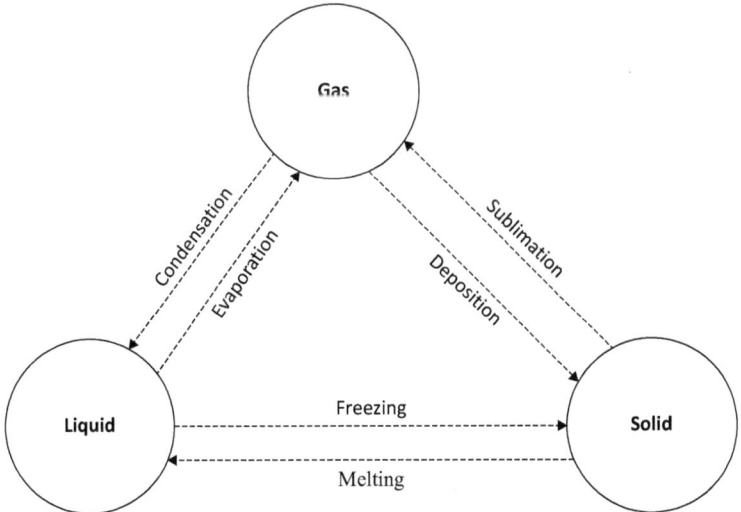

Figure 4.2 Liquid–gas–solid phase transitions.[4]
Source: Ryszard Praszkier.

---

[3] See https://en.wikipedia.org/wiki/Atlantic_meridional_overturning_circulation. Accessed April 22, 2023.
[4] Inspired by https://earthhow.com/states-of-water/. Accessed June 23, 2024.

The phase transition model allows analysis of several societal dynamics, such as how gossip spreads and influences public opinion, up to the point of a jump into radicalization (Li et al., 2012). Similarly, some cases of opinion formation may be seen as a phase transition in analogue to the jump from the "paramagnetic" to the "ferromagnetic" phase (Hołyst et al., 2000). Interestingly, analyzing the brain's reactions while moving from a state of liking to a state of love may be viewed as a naturally occurring phase transition (Solnyshkov & Malpuech, 2022).

Dynamical Approach: Introducing New Attractors

In some cases, no matter what one does, the system reverts to its initial state. Over time, the free-floating dynamics tend to drift back toward certain equilibrium. This often happens when external (exogenous) impulses are employed (e.g., to enliven a lethargic community). As long as the intervention exists, some change occurs; however, after the program expires, the community slowly reverts back to its initial equilibrium.

The set of forces maintaining the equilibrium is referred to as the *attractor*. In the community from this example, there may be several forces contributing to the "old" attractor (e.g., historically based distrust, misanthropy, or lack of cooperation), governing the natural homeostatic dynamics. It pulls the system back to the initial equilibrium, regardless of how impressive the exogeneous intervention might be (e.g., organizing a singing festival with celebrities) which could temporarily energize the community. However, in the long run, the festival may be forgotten, and the community may return to its initial lethargy.

Metaphorically, the old attractor may be symbolized as a hole pulling a ball down. When an external force is employed, the ball moves upward – as long as this force is present (Nowak & Vallacher, 1998). Once it is gone, the attractor pulls the ball back into the hole (see Figure 4.3).

There is an alternative to the "pulling-the-ball" approach: Instead of confronting the old attractor, an alternative and positive one may be

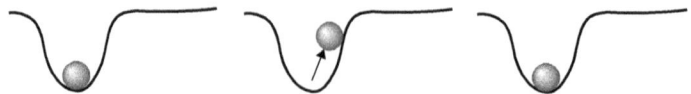

Figure 4.3 The system over time drifts back to the old attractor; the ball is pushed up by an external force and falls back after the force withdraws.
Source: T. Praszkier.

developed. Arif Khan (see Introduction) circumvented the conflict surrounding the traditional approach to the role of women in mountainous communities in Pakistan by focusing on economic development and drawing from the traditional handicrafts produced by women. By concentrating on upgrading this home-crafting to a marketable level, along with providing necessary training and education, he elevated – indirectly – the status of women. They began generating substantial resources for their families and the community, consequently improving the economic prospects of impoverished communities and enhancing women's positions.

From the dynamical perspective, instead of confronting the old attractor (e.g., promoting equality head-on, i.e., "pushing the ball up"), Arif Khan built an alternative attractor "elsewhere" (i.e., around the natural handcrafting, based on the community's endogenous potentials).

Metaphorically, this may be symbolized by building another hole, instead of focusing on the old one, as seen in Figure 4.4:

To recap: To achieve systemic and durable change requires much more than exerting force to keep the ball up. What is needed is a new attractor that shifts the natural societal balance point. It is not the external (exogenous) force that, in the long run, alters the dynamic; it is the new, endogenous societal balance point determined by new positive factors (e.g., trust, cooperativeness, and economic development) that leads to permanent systemic change (Vallacher et al., 2010; Vallacher & Nowak, 2007).

This dynamical perspective is visible in the case studies presented in this book (see, e.g., Chapter 14). It is demonstrated that the workable alternative attractors are based on the natural communities' potential and are significantly less expensive than confronting the existing attractors with the use of external interventions. It illustrates that the alternative attractors foster abrupt and unexpected change (singularities), introduced to systems previously remaining in a solid (seemingly unmovable) status quo, and as such, seen as paradoxical.

Figure 4.4 The new attractor (new hole), built outside the field of confrontation. It is initially shallow; however, over time, it grows and becomes dominant. The old and negative attractor decreases automatically.
Source: T. Praszkier.

Complexity and Emergence

Another view on singularities is offered by complexity theory, which mentions the unexpected appearance of new *emergent* entities. Complexity is considered in various branches of mathematics, physics, computer sciences, etc. In relation to the social and business fields, it is the study of phenomena that emerge from a collection of interacting objects or agents (Johnson, 2009). This process of emergence occurs in the "absence of any sort of 'invisible hand' or 'central controller'" (Johnson, 2009, p. 15). Emergence is also defined as the arising of novel and coherent structures, patterns, and properties during the process of self-organization in complex systems (Goldstein, 1999).

The emergence of new phenomena is due to the blend of upward, downward, and horizontal causations (Manz et al., 2009; Schilit & Locke, 1982), such as through five-level dynamics: The first is the individual level, which consists of individual intentions, memories, personalities, and cognitive processes. The second is the interaction level, which involves patterns of discourse, symbolic interaction, collaboration, and negotiation. The third is the emergence of some common topics, frames of interactions, structures for participation, and relative roles and statuses. The fourth is the stable-emergent level, at which there arise group structures, new language (group jargon), and conversational routines. The fifth is the social-structure level, where written texts (procedures, laws, and regulations), cultural and technological novelties, and systems of society emerge (Sawyer, 2007).

Emergence happens when diverse causations and feedback loops create an environment where, from unorganized interactions on the lower level, there emerge structural changes and new concepts on the higher level (Tourish, 2005; Tourish & Robson, 2003; Érdi, 2008). The appearance of the emergent phenomena is usually unpredictable, as they occur through unorganized interactions and feedback loops, seemingly resembling chaos.

The social movements mentioned in Chapter 5 are examples of emergence, all based on horizontal communication and cooperation, fueled by multiple feedback loops. This process generates an emergent phenomenon on a higher level: the movements' identity and self-reliance.

Singularities: Recapitulation

The abovementioned *singularities* may be visible in various dynamics (e.g., in the real estate market); sometimes, a *rare event* occurs when the price of a very low-value, unkept, underdeveloped, and underserved urban area suddenly starts skyrocketing. The mechanisms driving this change may start with a group of Scouts initiating street cleaning, someone else designating a space for a clean and safe kindergarten, and a group of residents planning a baseball square. Meanwhile, others might form a choir, while another group works on opening a gym.

All of those bottom-up initiatives are initially unrelated and isolated. The *bifurcation* point opens up two possible paths: Either these initiatives remain isolated (maintaining the low value of the community), or diverse connections between the groups appear and grow – for example, some Scout leaders meet with the kindergarten principal and the baseball coach; then, the choir director and fitness activists join the meeting. They deliberate on how to increase the safety and quality of their neighborhood, launching a "proud of our community" initiative. This network of ideas and connections, in a feedback loop, attracts other dwellers who are supportive of this new approach to community enhancement. People organize themselves, setting new safety and health paradigms. At some point, a sudden *phase transition* occurs, as the community turns into a neat, desirable location, and its market value breaks through the ceiling (Praszkier, 2018a). This rapid transformation may be perceived as a *cusp catastrophe*, initiated by the *butterfly effect* (i.e., by those few Scouts cleaning the streets). From the lens of the dynamical systems perspective, building alternative attractors may ignite a systemic and durable change process, as opposed to confronting the old attractors.

CHAPTER 5

Social Movements and Singularities

There are several examples of peaceful social movements having a significant, durable impact. This impact occurs after an initial development phase, when an inflection point (i.e., singularity) is reached.

Social movements are here understood, in accordance with New Social Movement (NSM) theory, as participating in pursuing a "big idea" that emphasizes social issues, accomplished through social relations, symbols, and identities based in the culture (Buechler, 1995, 2011; Scott, 1990). An important component is networks, generating a new kind of identity called a "project identity" (Castells, 2010). Jürgen Habermas added that critical for NSM theory is "communicative action," through which people communicate, interact, exercise trust, cooperate, and share information; people reach a consensus through public dialogue rather than an exercise of power (Habermas, 1985).

The following sections present examples of five social movements, diverse in terms of the time, location, and issues addressed. The subsequent analysis focuses on the associated singularities and, in line with the aforementioned NSM definition, on four dimensions:

- The big idea: a far-reaching, compelling vision;
- The properties of networks;
- The culture and identity;
- The kind of leadership enabling bottom-up initiatives.

The Civil Rights Movement, USA, in the 1950s and 1960s

> The civil rights movement in the USA was a nonviolent social movement of the 1950s and 1960s, aimed at abolishing legalized racial segregation and discrimination throughout the country. It was successful in the mid-1960s, causing the introduction of antiracist and antisegregation legal acts.

With millions of Black and White citizens participating in civic actions, marches, boycotts, sit-ins, and so forth, the civil rights movement finally succeeded through achieving judicial transformation, liquidating the legal grounds for segregation. The turning point (final singularity) was the implementation of two legal acts: The Civil Rights Act (1964), explicitly banning all discrimination based on race, including racial segregation in schools, businesses, and public accommodation, and the Voting Rights Act (1965), assuring voting rights in areas with a historic underrepresentation of minority voters.

The movement's inception (initial singularity) is attributed to Rosa Parks, who, on December 1, 1955, while riding a bus, refused to comply with the driver's order to leave her seat in the "colored" section for a White passenger once the "White" section was full. As a result, Rosa Parks was imprisoned.[1] After forty-four years, the US Congress honored her as "the first lady of civil rights" and "the mother of the freedom movement."[2]

Rosa Parks' struggle sparked public unrest and activity: the Montgomery Improvement Association (MIA) was formed in the days following her arrest, and played a leading role in fighting segregation in the city.[3] The association oversaw the civic bottom-up initiative of boycotting buses as a reaction to Rosa Parks' incarceration (Williams & Bond, 2002). During the bus boycott, MIA organized a carpooling system to provide transportation for the boycotters. White members of the Montgomery community also participated by offering rides. City officials and the police attempted, without success, to disrupt the carpooling service, which continued operating even after being declared illegal in June 1956 (Killian, 1984).[4] Martin Luther King commented that a miracle had taken place: Instead of riding buses, the boycotters had self-organized a system of carpools (King, 2001).

An example of a civic bottom-up initiative is the Club from Nowhere, founded by Georgia Gilmore, a midwife from Montgomery. The club raised money by selling food to beauty parlors, and designated the profits to support the antisegregation initiatives. The success of this venture led Gilmore and her friends to produce meals (including chicken dinners, cakes, and pies) to sell to the boycotters, involving White clients as well. Moreover, Club from Nowhere participants enjoyed their activities,

---

[1] See www.archives.gov/education/lessons/rosa-parks. Accessed March 22, 2023.
[2] See www.govinfo.gov/content/pkg/PLAW-106publ26/pdf/PLAW-106publ26.pdf. Accessed March 22, 2023.
[3] See http://encyclopediaofalabama.org/article/h-2567. Accessed March 22, 2023.
[4] See encyclopediaofalabama.org/article/m-5146. Accessed March 22, 2023.

singing songs such as the well-known "Keep Your Eyes on the Prize."[5] The money from these sales went toward helping to sustain the carpool system, and thus supported the bus boycott (Barnett, 1993; Nelson, 2020).

Another form of peaceful fighting for racial justice was "sit-ins," documented in Baltimore, Maryland (1955), Durham, North Carolina (1957), Wichita and Oklahoma City (1958), and Greensboro and Nashville (1960). Black protesters simply occupied places in "only for Whites" restaurants. These sit-ins drew public and media attention, especially when the police tried to remove the protesters (Wynn, 1991).

After the civil rights movement succeeded, Georgia Gilmore said "I was glad it was a success and nobody didn't get killed or injured or anything and uh, after the boycott we had a lot of white friends that we didn't realize that were really and truly interested."[6]

The Peace Process in the Basque Country, Spain, 2011

> The Basque terrorist organization Euskadi Ta Askatasuna (ETA) fought for full independence from 1959 to 2011, attacking Spanish representatives and terrorizing Basque citizens. Most of Basque society was peace- and nonviolence-oriented, regardless of their opinion on maintaining autonomy or achieving independence.

In 1959, ETA, an offshoot of the Basque culture preservation movements, started its insurgency against the Franco regime, the latter aiming at the eradication of Basque culture, language, and remaining autonomy. ETA strikes also continued after the Franco era, as the anti-Basque cultural pressure continued for decades (Astrain & Stephens, 2013; Llera, 1999; Llera et al., 1993).

ETA initially attacked the Spanish government's representatives, although they began to increasingly impact the Basque nation, both physically and mentally. For example, they targeted Basque independence groups such as the Basque Nationalist Party (PNV), whose leaders were attacked and often killed (Loyer, 1998). Moreover, a common target was private businesses (Miller & Smarick, 2011, p. 2). From 1959 to 2011, ETA

---

[5] See www.youtube.com/watch?v=xbq4vDG65_A. Accessed March 30, 2023.
[6] See "Interview with Georgia Gilmore, conducted by Blackside, Inc.," February 17, 1986, for Eyes on the Prize: America's Civil Rights Years (1954–1965), reply to question # 35. Washington University Libraries, Film and Media Archive, Henry Hampton Collection. http://digital.wustl.edu/cgi/t/text/text-idx?c=eop;cc=eop;rgn=main;view=text;idno=gil0015.0383.041. Accessed June 23, 2024.

was responsible for killing 829 people, injuring thousands more, and kidnapping dozens (Hammer, 2007); they were perceived as the most violent insurgent group on the European continent (Clark, 1984).

In response to the pressure of Basque civil society, ETA's tactics shifted, transitioning from ceasefires to violence and back (Miller & Smarick, 2011, p. 2). The aggression manifested in many different forms: killing, kidnapping, and blackmailing (Clark, 1984; Hammer, 2007; Loyer, 1998).

The violence was intensified by the Spanish government's terrorist attacks, especially in the 1980s, when GAL (Grupo Antiterrorista de Liberación), an illegal group secretly formed by police officials, began attacking ETA supporters. The group killed twenty-seven people, including women and children (Alonso, 2010; Diditwister, 2012; Woodworth, 2003).

As people were scared, the frequent outbreaks of violence were predominantly hidden through "the spiral of silence," understood as an attitude of intimidation, fear, and self-censorship that prevents an open conversation about terror, even after the abandonment of violence (Noelle-Neumann, 1974; Noelle-Neumann & Petersen, 2004; Spencer & Croucher, 2008).

The majority of Basque people did not support violent methods. A University of the Basque Country survey revealed that 64 percent of people completely rejected ETA; 13 percent identified as former ETA sympathizers (mainly during the Franco dictatorship); 10 percent agreed with ETA's ends, but not their means; 3 percent felt fear toward ETA; 3 percent expressed indifference; 3 percent were undecided or did not answer; and 3 percent were supportive of ETA, but still criticized some of their actions. Strikingly, only 1 percent totally supported ETA (Eusko Barómetro, 2009). Thus, over the years, a stark contrast between society's hope for peace (and repulsion against violence) and the violent methods used by ETA became apparent.

Despite ongoing acts of terror and forced silence, Basque society challenged and ultimately delegitimized political violence. Civil action was one of the engines for political transformation, helping to precipitate an end to the violence by undermining the support for ETA in Basque society (Argomaniz, 2019). One key example is Gesto por la Paz, a peaceful platform, which played an important role from its beginnings in the mid-1990s.[7]

---

[7] See www.gesto.org/es/que-fue-gesto-por-la-paz/mensaje/principios-fundamentales.html. Accessed April 22, 2023.

Additionally, the Basque nation had been intentionally transforming the environment through cultural, social, and economic development. The Basques achieved rapid economic growth (Markuartu, 2012; Porter et al., 2004; Uranga, 2002) through their specialty: A cooperative-based economic approach. In fact, in the Basque Country, workers owned and managed the world's largest successful cooperative, Mondragón (Herrera, 2004; Hollender, 2011; Whyte, 1991). Moreover, a significant line of innovation resulted (Arancegui et al., 2011; Espiau, 2011; Heras, 2014), while research has revealed a meaningful role of real-life networks in developing indirect pressure on peace (Praszkier & Bartoli, 2014). As a result, the violence became an impediment to the growing social, economic, and interconnected environment.

The terrorism suddenly and unexpectedly (singularity) stopped on September 5, 2011, when ETA announced the definitive cessation of its armed activity.[8] There were no particular actions or incidents that could have predicted this ceasefire. The black swan effect seemed to be a cumulative result of the multiple ways in which civil society was striving for peace.

Polish Underground Peaceful Solidarity Movement, 1980s

> Polish citizens under the Soviet regime had, since the end of the Second World War, been renewing their uprisings for liberation. In August 1980, multiple strikes covered most of Poland, forcing the communist regime to acknowledge the free and independent trade union "Solidarity." Afraid of the power of the new movement, a regime was enforced in December 1981, termed "martial law," which delegalized "Solidarity." However, "Solidarity" continued its clandestine profreedom initiatives, involving most of the Poles. After a decade of underground peaceful operations, "Solidarity" won and, through roundtable talks, this led to free elections in 1989, subsequently resulting in freedom and independence.

The nationwide strikes put pressure on the communist government to legalize "Solidarity" in 1980 – the first independent trade union in the Soviet zone. Under the hardliner Brezhnev rules, while Soviet tanks and missiles were being prepared on the Polish border, this was an

---

[8] Basque ceasefire statement: Full text. *The Guardian*, October 2010. www.theguardian.com/world/2011/oct/20/basque-ceasefire-statement-full-text. Accessed March 23, 2023.

extraordinary, unexpected singularity-type event. Operating legally for over a year, it was delegalized during the martial law imposed in December 1981. From then on, it operated illegally for a decade as a peaceful civic resistance movement, carrying out multiple clandestine and bottom-up activities (Kenney, 2001, 2002).

Examples include supporting illegal education (classes or lectures at home); publishing and distributing illegal books, brochures, and newsletters; running self-help groups; supporting the families of arrested activists; boycotting governmental TV (the only available source of media). The TV boycott was carried out by both celebrities and recipients, with actors performing sub-rosa at homes and supporting themselves as taxi drivers (Kenney, 2001).

An example of an unpredictable and seemingly impossible black swan event is the horizontal peer-to-peer nationwide communication that occurred during a time when government authorities had cut telephone and telex lines, jammed radio broadcasts, and shut down post offices (Osa, 2003), with multiple checkpoints on the roads, and train travel available only with special permission.

One example is the evening candles in windows that were lit in unison, all throughout Poland, in small and big cities alike, to commemorate special events. Another example is that of people effectively boycotting government-sponsored TV news. Each evening, at exactly 7:30 p.m., when the propaganda broadcast began, people left their homes to take walks around their neighborhoods, socializing with other families along the way, until 8:00 p.m. sharp, when the nightly news ended and everybody returned home for dinner. The police were helpless to stop the "protest," given that no one was verbally or physically confronting the regime. However, the collective action taking place at a specific time was exceptionally bonding for the participating communities, having a powerful impact on the society and sending a strong message.

Instead of directly confronting the regime, tanks on the streets, house raids, and arrests instigated innovative clandestine methods. Many initiatives appeared ad hoc, using personal and professional networks (Friszke, 2006). One example of this comes from Gdańsk: An activist was asked to organize an illegal broadcast, called Radio Solidarity, without any detailed instructions on how to do it. He developed his own plan and assembled a team; he authored the news and asked a friend who was uninvolved in the movement to read and record the news. He recorded this on several separate tapes, keeping them in his pocket as he boarded a crowded local train. Here, another person (whom he barely knew) took the tapes out of his pocket and placed them in three portable tape recorders, each of which was stored in a suitcase, together with homemade broadcasting equipment. Finally, these suitcases were placed on three roofs and set to play sharply at the time of the official TV news, in effect replacing said news with their own broadcast that drowned out the regime's propaganda. After the broadcast, a different team observed whether the police detected the suitcases. If not, then they collected the equipment for further use (Praszkier, 2018b).

In the face of the prevailing lack of goods on the market, the movement developed covert groups to experiment with whatever was available. For example, the technical section found a way to make printing ink by mixing cleaning agents with boot polish; another group developed a method for portable DIY printing equipment that could fit into a backpack. Manuals on how to fabricate the equipment were disseminated, and, consequently, thousands of small publishing units became engaged in printing and disseminating illegal newsletters, magazines, and banned books.

Important to mention is that this civic engagement was not treated as an overwhelming burden; on the contrary, it was a source of joy for the participants, particularly because of its use as a tool to ridicule (instead of confronting) the regime. One example is the Orange Alternative, a loosely organized group of antigovernment individuals who arranged street theater and happenings, mocking the communist system. For example, before Christmas, somebody dressed as Santa Claus was giving out free toilet paper in one of Wrocław's main squares. This was a reaction to the proverbial lack of toilet paper under martial law. People laughed and waved toilet paper around. The police were disarmed: Should they publicly arrest Santa Claus? If so, what for, as nothing had been said against the regime? Finally, they arrested Santa Claus. People laughed and chanted "Free Santa Claus!" For months afterward, the city's walls were covered with symbolic drawings of Santa's hat (Kenney, 2002).

In the essentially leaderless underground movement (leaderless in the sense that the original Solidarity leaders were either in prison or in hiding), 10 million of the total population (which was 40 million, including children and senior citizens) participated (Brown, 2003). By initiating multiple decentralized, flourishing, bottom-up, covert initiatives, Poles prepared to take over and adapt easily to a democratic civil society (Brown, 2003; Misztal, 1992; Tyszka, 2009).

This movement created a constant though nonconfrontational pressure on the government through a self-organizing civil society. This finally led to a phase transition (singularity): In 1989, the regime was forced to agree to roundtable transition talks, leading to "phase transition" – namely, the first free elections in the communist zone.

In this way, the Solidarity movement contributed to the transformation of Central and Eastern Europe and to the fall of the Berlin Wall (Ash, 2002; Kenney, 2001, 2002; Kubik, 1994).

Arab Spring

> The Arab Spring was a series of unexpected antigovernment protests that spread across much of the Arab world in the 2010s. It began in Tunisia in response to corruption and economic stagnation and spread to other countries, including Libya and Egypt. The protests in Tunisia and Egypt were peaceful, organized ad hoc through social media. Protesters demonstrated solidarity and mutual support, such as Christians protecting Muslim prayers at Cairo Tahrir Square and vice versa. Authoritarian rulers were ousted.

The Arab Spring started abruptly in 2010 (singularity) with demonstrations in Tunisia (after a young street merchant set himself on fire). The movement, called the "Jasmine Revolution," spread through the country. The government tried to deter demonstrations through violence and incentives such as economic concessions. However, protests soon spread and forced the authoritarian president Ben Ali to flee the country and change the system, allowing Tunisians to participate in a free election. Tunisia became the first country of the Arab Spring in which protests caused a peaceful transformation to truly democratic elections (black swan event).[9]

In Egypt, the revolution began in 2011 and spread across the country. It consisted of demonstrations, marches, occupations of plazas, nonviolent civil resistance, acts of civil disobedience, and strikes. Millions of protesters from various socioeconomic and religious backgrounds demanded the overthrow of the authoritarian president Ben Ali.[10]

One of the essential communalities of the Arab Spring in many countries was the centrality of dignity and respect, understood as being associated with the idea of citizenship. Additionally, there was a feeling of cross-religious and cross-social-strata solidarity in pursuing common civic ideas (Khosrokhavar, 2015).

---

[9] See www.britannica.com/event/Jasmine-Revolution. Accessed March 2, 2023.
[10] See www.aljazeera.com/features/2021/1/25/remembering-tahrir-square-10-years-on. Accessed March 2, 2023.

This solidarity was manifested, for example, through the mutual protection of prayers between Christians and Muslims: Christian protesters stood together and joined hands, facing outwards, surrounding hundreds of Muslim protesters that would otherwise have been left vulnerable as they knelt in prayer.[11] Meanwhile, Muslims formed human shields to protect praying Copts from the police (Saleh, 2011). One of the important days (Martyrs' Sunday) was celebrated by Egyptians of both religions as an affirmation of national unity in struggle.

There was also music, singing, and dancing involved; for example, a group formed a circle and, accompanied by a guitar, sang the song "Arise O Egypt, arise. Arise Egyptians: Muslims, Christians, and Jews" (Alexander, 2011). Dancing and joy occurred in diverse Arab Spring locations, such as in improvised site-specific dance moments or sardonic joking in Tahrir Square in Cairo (Abaza, 2011; Martin, 2016). Musicians, especially rappers, performed in the protesting areas (Kimball, 2014). To sum up, old and young of various backgrounds found and discovered themselves and enjoyed being both patriotic and rebellious (creating a phase transition) (Allagui & Kuebler, 2011).

The Arab Spring also revealed the significance of ICT and electronic connectivity, which was embedded in its organization by networks and played an important informational and organizational role. Communication technologies in the Arab Spring empowered citizens and brought them together (Allagui & Kuebler, 2011; Wilson & Corey, 2012), creating a cumulative transformational singularity effect that was previously unexpected.

Euromaidan

> Euromaidan (also known as the Revolution of Dignity) comprised a wave of demonstrations and civil unrest in Ukraine, which began on November 21, 2013, with large protests in Maidan Independence Square in Kyiv, and then spread across the country. In a bottom-up, citizen-driven movement, people opposed the pro-Russian orientation of president Yanukovych and supported parliament's decision to sign a cooperation treaty with the European Union. The protesters also opposed governmental corruption, abuses of power, and human rights violations. The determination and scope of the resistance caused an unexpected phase transition, forcing the president to flee to Russia, thus sparking democratic changes.

---

[11] See www.dailymail.co.uk/news/article-1353330/Egypt-protests-Christians-join-hands-protect-Muslims-pray-Cairo-protests.html. Accessed March 2, 2023.

Euromaidan was perceived as a "critical case of mass protests" (Onuch, 2015a), spreading across the country and uniting various previously conflicting groups, such as the deep regional splits that manifested linguistically, culturally, and economically (predominately between the Russian-speaking east and the Ukrainian-speaking west). The Euromaidan rebellion was also beyond the divisions of the political system, embodied in rivalry between the two main groups of influence (Shevsky, 2022). The directly triggering factor was pro-Russian President Yanukovich's sudden refusal to sign an agreement for European association (passed by parliament). Other provoking factors were also protesting against the ineffective public budget management that weakened the State, and against the destructive influence of oligarchs (Onuch, 2015; Shevsky, 2022).

The singularity black swan event was, first of all, the unity of the previously divided nation: Euromaidan protests took place not only in the western part of the country (naturally leaning toward the EU and Western culture), but also in the eastern part, e.g., in Donetsk and Kharkiv (previously prevailingly under Russian influence) (Zubar & Ovcharenko, 2017).

The emergence of unexpected and unpredicted singularity-type protests in Ukraine in 2013–2014 is also attributed to the "social" component of social networks and media, both on and offline (Onuch, 2014). Social media and the Internet played an important role in diffusing information and framing protest claims, as well as engendering and facilitating pre-existing social network ties, which were especially influential in the mobilization process (Onuch, 2015b).

The Euromaidan participants shared values of love, friendship, mutual help, freedom, and dignity (Trach, 2016). There was also the feeling of joy; for example, BBC News featured protesters playing piano and singing in front of armed police, under the falling snow, and Euromaidan guitar playing; one of the songs was "Your land is waiting: Do we go East or West?"[12] Funny banners created by young Ukrainians were mushrooming: "Ukraine, WTF?!"; "No Putin No Cry"; "Europe, dear, we are coming back home"; and "Putin, if you love us – let us go!", as well as graphics such as a drawing of the regime police beating someone up, signed "Welcome Ukraine."[13]

---

[12] See Ukraine protests: Singing in the cold, *BBC News*, December 20, 2013. www.bbc.com/news/world-europe-25468055. Accessed April 4, 2023.

[13] See Smart and funny Euromaidan posters, *Kyiv Post*, December 25, 2013. https://archive.kyivpost.com/article/content/euromaidan/smart-and-funny-euromaidan-posters-334231.html. Accessed April 4, 2023.

CHAPTER 6

Early Indicators of Possible Singularities
The Lessons Drawn from NSMs

Basic Characteristics of Social Movements

Singularities

The five examples of peaceful and successful social movements detailed in Chapter 5 indicate that their indispensable attribute was reaching one or more singularity turning points, which were unpredictable in advance (i.e., black swan events). The civil rights movement's decisive moment was Rosa Parks' refusal to give up her seat on the bus to a White passenger. Through a *butterfly effect*, this triggered further processes, such as the bus boycott and the resultant (and initially illegal) carpooling system set up to provide transportation to boycotters. This broad societal self-organization unleashed more bottom-up initiatives (e.g., the Club from Nowhere), spreading in a cusp catastrophe-like manner. Such developments led to the eradication of segregation and discrimination (the Civil and Voting Rights Acts): a total *phase transition* in American history.

In the Basque Country, the black swan event was ETA's totally unexpected permanent renouncement of violence. The decade-long Polish underground Solidarity civic peaceful movement of the 1980s (as a response to martial law) was an unpredicted *rare event* in the Soviet bloc; as a result, the 1989 peaceful transformation to freedom and democracy occurred as a *phase transition*. The appearance of the self-organizing Arab Spring in Tunisia was an unpredicted *black swan event*; so too was the cross-segment solidarity and support of the protesters (e.g., mutual prayer protection by Muslims and Christians). The Ukrainian Euromaidan, a successful civic pan-national protest (against pro-Russian policy), was a totally unexpected black swan event in the post-Soviet zone, especially given that it was self-organized, occurred in many cities, and, in the end, led to pro-Western Ukrainian orientation.

Chapter 6 Early Indicators of Possible Singularities 53

The Big Idea

In all five cases, the attracting and mobilizing factor was a compelling, far-reaching, big idea, sounding at first like a utopia. Equal rights and desegregation in the USA were the dream of many generations, though they seemed impossible to achieve against millennia-long traditions. Similarly, peace in the Basque Country, freedom and democracy in Poland, liberal laws and eliminating corruption in Arab countries, and Ukrainian pro-Western-oriented democracy sounded, at the onset, unrealizable. However, in all of these cases, addressing people's dreams became a compelling magnet.

The Properties of Networks

In all cases, connections between participants developed; for example, during the civil rights movement, people organized themselves around the bus boycott and carpooling, as well as in clubs such as the Club from Nowhere. They weaved new connections that involved both Black and White people. The Polish underground Solidarity movement was predominately based on horizontal people-to-people communication; despite the threat of the secret police, there was an increase in trust, cooperation, and solidarity even between unknown underground activists. During the Arab Spring, despite being unfamiliar to one another, people cooperated, and protected other believers' prayers. Most of the Euromaidan activists were people from diverse walks of life, meeting for the first time at a demonstration, and supporting and relying on one another.

The exceptional trust, cooperation, and solidarity that was formed between unknown individuals during these movements indicates the formation of social capital – an important lever for growth (Praszkier, 2013; Putnam, 1993; Zabłocka et al., 2016). Moreover, two kinds of social capital were manifested: bonding (connectivity within homogenous groups), and bridging (linking across diverse social groups) (Putnam, 2000). Connecting with people from outside one's close-knit circle means establishing weak ties, which provides connectivity with the outer world, as opposed to strong ties, which create links within "small worlds." The significance of weak ties is that they are far more likely than strong ones to bridge the gap between groups – even between distant network participants or groups (Granovetter, 1973, 1983).

Important to mention is that a network effect of NSMs may also be generated due to the multiple nonlinear interaction effects between individuals and the interplay and feedback loops between individual behavior and social dynamics (Squazzoni et al., 2013).

Social Movements' Culture, Identity, and Joy

The civil rights movement's bottom-up culture was constitutive, producing and solidifying trust, contacts, solidarity, rituals, and meaningful systems (Andrews, 2004). Moreover, this culture spread through networks, mobilizing and bringing "structural proximity" to the movement (McAdam, 1999).

In general, in contemporary social movements, communication and social media play an eminent role, becoming part of their culture (Bennett & Segerberg, 2012). This was especially visible during the Arab Spring (Comunello & Anzera, 2012; Wolsfeld et al., 2013), Euromaidan (Bohdanova, 2014; Onuch, 2015b), and the recent Occupy movements, blurring the internal and external boundaries of the movement, and bridging and opening space for inclusiveness and direct participation (Kavada, 2015); for example, women played an exceptional role in building connectivity and networking (Boler et al., 2014).

Interestingly, high-level horizontal communication was also a societal fulcrum during the pre-Internet era. For example, the underground Solidarity movement operated in an environment where telephone connections were initially cut, and, when restored, were heavily bugged, so information could only be spread by word of mouth. This proved efficient, such as when the idea of lighting candles in windows at a certain time, as a symbolic protest, spread instantly throughout all of Poland.[1] Another example is the well-orchestrated national demonstrations of civil disobedience that spread through word of mouth regarding the boycotting of the government-sponsored TV news, whereby people left their homes when the broadcast began to take walks around their neighborhoods, socializing with other families along the way (Praszkier, 2018b).

As mentioned earlier, singing, dancing, cultural interests, and joy have accompanied several movements. Associated with NSMs is a specific culture, which is also supportive of the project identity and subsequent social transformation (Kendall, 2005; Langman, 2013); the specific emotions involved (e.g., loyalty to the movement, pride, and calmed fears) support the NSM identity (Goodwyn et al., 2004). Recently, this was clearly visible

---

[1] Author's recollection.

during the Occupy protests in the USA and the UK (Kavada, 2015; Langman, 2013).

During the Polish underground Solidarity movement, artists and actors boycotted official institutions, though the interest in art did not fade away, so art exhibitions and theater performances were carried on in homes, each time changing the location. Dancing also accompanied the Occupy movement (Steinhelfer, 2011). It is important to mention that joy is seen as an inevitable component of social movements, accompanying the feeling of participating in the fight for serious goals (Hynes & Sharpe, 2009; Shepherd, 2005).

The Kind of Leadership Enabling Bottom-Up Initiatives

Some of the movements were basically leaderless: In the case of the Polish underground Solidarity movement, the leaders were either arrested or stayed in hide-outs, so people took the initiative into their own hands. However, there was still an inspirational influence from the leaders, even if they had been arrested: for example, the iconic Lech Walesa or the Pope of Polish origin (JPII). Similarly, Martin Luther King and other civil rights leaders were frequently arrested, yet people self-generated bottom-up initiatives, aggregating over time into a powerful, common opus. In the Basque Country, the pro-peace trend was leaderless, with responsibility instead distributed among many individuals; similarly, during the Arab Spring and at Euromaidan, people were self-motivated to assemble, thus harnassing the power of civic movement.

The inspirational role of social movement leaders seems important (see Gusfield, 1966), as does a distributed kind of leadership (Brown & Hosking, 1986). This distributed leadership is characterized as an emergent property of a group or network of interacting individuals open to shifting the boundaries of leadership and possessing varieties of expertise distributed across many individuals, instead of a few (Bennett et al., 2003; Bolden, 2011).

An example of distributed leadership is the position of one of the Solidarity leaders, who said that he sees his role as limited to making sure that the movement remained peaceful and that any violent concepts were knocked down – the rest being in the people's hands (Praszkier, 2018b).

The conjecture is that a distributed kind of leadership is the best fit for NSMs, where initiatives are usually dispersed over multiple distant individuals and groups.

The Prognostic Model

The foregoing analysis indicates a "gluing" role of the big idea, seen as a source of durable energy and a driving force for social change (Sztompka, 1993). A specific kind of network, supporting trust, cooperation, and solidarity, serves as a scaffolding structure, fostering identity and being a reference point empowering participants. A distributed kind of leadership leaves space for participants' initiatives, leading to a bottom-up process of coordination (see Figure 6.1).

The conjecture is that the cumulative effect of these four factors over time increases the likelihood of a singularity occurrence, similar to the processes outlined here. This would lead to the conclusion that identifying the four factors within newly emerging movements could pave the way for predicting forthcoming singularities.

Along these lines, one may discuss other NSMs – for example, considering why the Occupy movement did not reach a singularity point. The conjecture may be that although there were strong networking and cultural/identification components, a positive big idea was missing, as participants united around negative ideas (i.e., opposition to social and economic inequality and against large corporations and the global financial system). Moreover, there was no specific leadership, especially of the indicated distributed kind.

However, for additional confirmation, it would be beneficial to complement these conclusions with other predictive methods.

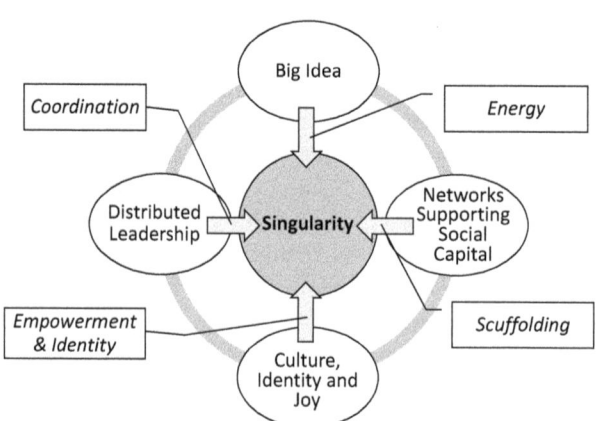

Figure 6.1 Prognostic indications drawn from analysis of New Social Movements.
Source: Ryszard Praszkier.

CHAPTER 7

Predicting the Unpredictable

In Chapter 6, the first paradoxical step in predicting unpredictable societal dynamics was taken by presenting a prognostic model based on New Social Movements analysis (Chapter 5) and concluding that it would be beneficial to complement these suggestions with other predictive methods. This chapter elaborates on this indication, presenting both digital and real-life methods, leading to expanding the understanding of future occurrences.

Digital Methods of Predicting Singularities in Social Dynamics

Predicting black swan events may sound like an oxymoron, as the black swan definition indicates unpredictability. However, even if problematic, attempts at predicting singularities may be beneficial for teams and organizations, so as to develop a deeper knowledge of the dynamical approach to (possible) changes, as well as to evolve the predictive way of thinking. For example, rare events modeling (REM) encompasses efforts to forecast the occurrence of similar events over a future time horizon, which may be of interest for both scholarly and applied purposes (Goodwin & Wright, 2010).

In business and in life, one small and seemingly meaningless individual decision or action can cause significant consequences for large groups. This was compellingly illustrated by Thomas C. Schelling's computer modeling project (Schelling, 2006).[1] One of his well-known examples deals with segregation/integration. Schelling showed that slight (though far from malicious) preferences for neighbors of the same race eventually leads, over time, to a completely segregated population. This discovery prompted the introduction of formal prediction methods in the social sciences and the design of the well-known Schelling simulation. This computerized simulation program[2] adjusts pixels on a grid using preset rules.

---

[1] See also Avetisov et al. (2018).
[2] For example, NetLogo: see: https://ccl.northwestern.edu/netlogo/. Accessed October 21, 2023.

In Schelling's example, each pixel (red or green) represents the race of a community member and was programmed to have, for example, a relatively small desire to have neighbors of a similar race (e.g., 30 percent) on a scale of 0 percent (meaning that race makes no difference) to 100 percent (absolutely no neighbors of another race). To each pixel was then assigned a rule that, in each step of the computing, it would attract (e.g., with 30 percent strength) pixels of similar colors and repel pixels of different colors (Wilensky, 1999). Each computer tick may represent a period of time (e.g., one month). In the case of 30 percent similar race, the prediction is that for over one year (or thirteen computer ticks), community dwellers will finally reach the desired state of semi-isolated islands of red and similar islands of green.

The next stage could be setting the rate of desire for a similar race to a higher level (e.g., 70 percent). Clear segregated bubbles maintain the homogeneousness of neighborhoods, reached in over six years (80 computer ticks).

A threshold can be set, assuming that after a certain degree of isolation the singularity phenomenon appears, making both sides alien and malevolent. Similarly, beyond a certain degree of integration, a singularity point may be defined, creating unity and a harmonious community.

Computer simulations can create a multitude of scenarios. They can model the transmission and perpetuation of a virus in a certain human population to show how many people might get infected and how many might remain immune. Simulations can forecast the dynamics of social networks, as well as the flow of traffic on a highway, and weather that is unique at its level of complexity. Especially critical are simulations of human behavior in a disaster situation (not possible to simulate in real life). Some see sophisticated predictive computer systems as essential, outperforming both the imperfect market and the best of the experts (Chen et al., 2003).

One of the practical applications of computer modeling is predicting road catastrophes. An example is a model applied in Athens: After an increasing number of car accidents, traffic data were assembled (on flow, occupancy, mean time speed, and percentage of trucks).[3] For the first time, a novel approach to REM was applied in the field of safety evaluation of motorways. Computer modeling revealed some insights into traffic dynamics – for example, a negative relationship between accident occurrence and the natural logarithm of speed in the accident

---

[3] In the 2008–2011 period, pursued by Athens Attica Tollway.

location, allowing the restructuring of real-life roadway communication (Theofilatos et al., 2016).

Computer modeling has become an important resource in many fields, such as predicting market financial bubbles and shocks (Oya et al., 2014; Smug et al., 2018) and modeling complex health dynamics in medicine (Darabi & Hosseinichimeh, 2020; Davahli et al., 2020).

Real-Life Predictive Methods

Instead of computer modeling, some processes can be roleplayed in real-life. Roleplaying is an active explorational and learning method, in which individuals (e.g., employees) act out situations under the guidance of a trainer. Participants enact the scenes as though they were real.

Red Teaming

Red teaming is a kind of roleplay, providing a methodology to explore the uncertainties and challenge of situations associated with cusp catastrophe etiology. Some participants take on the role of the enemy or the competitor. Similarly, another variety is scenario planning, which involves imagining and playing with various possible future scenarios. As such, it requires flexibility and imagination to envision and roleplay simulations of one's own and one's competitor's far-future behavior and the related dynamics (Fuller, 2018; Masys, 2012; Yang et al., 2006). Red teaming represents a competitive or conflict situation, also used for the analysis of military operations (Gold & Herman, 2003; Longbine, 2012).

Green Teaming

On the contrary, green teaming represents open situations, also encompassing cooperative and noncompetitive behaviors. It is pursued through real-life roleplaying games, where participants imagine future situations. This way of playing with the future enables combining individual cognition with social interactions (Squazzoni et al., 2013) and, as a result, leads to potential aggregated outcomes.

Green teaming may provide a more open space to explore than red teaming, for example by setting a scenario to explore the future market trends related to a team's specific interests. These scenarios can be located far in the future, such as in the game "We after 10 years" (Praszkier, 2019). As a side-effect, projecting the imagination of participants far into the future helps to augment their creativity, as it has been documented that temporal distance increases creative thinking (Förster et al., 2004).

Green teaming may be applied to forecasting singularities. In particular, roleplaying in the far future may help to circumvent Taleb's black swan event definition's impediment of unpredictability, as black swan events are specified as generate hindsight explanations (after the event has happened). Setting the time of roleplay in the far future opens a justified avenue for such "hindsights," because the team analyzes hypothetical black swan events from a future perspective.

As an example of an instruction in a green-teaming-based roleplaying game, focused on predicting future singularities, imagine that you are meeting as the same team, but ten years older. During those years, you gained multiple experiences worth analyzing. Start the roleplaying game by imagining that the meeting (ten years from now) is set for analyzing the lessons learned from the past ten years of dynamics in your market's segment. Discuss the past leverage and inflection points, as well as market growths and declines; in particular, focus on any rapid, abrupt changes that happened over those ten years, and discuss how your team reacted, and so on.

The ten-year temporal distance perspective allows us to look at the dynamics from outside the box and, in this way, to detach from current pressing occurrences. Moreover, from a more general and distant perspective, one may discover unexpected solutions embedded somewhere in the fringes of the issue (e.g., in the back of one's mind). Finally, as said before, it augments creative thinking, opening new cognitive avenues. It is important to mention that, with the assistance of a family therapist, the green teaming concept may be applied to family games (e.g., exploring "our family after ten years").

Using roleplaying to explore opportunities, or for training, also has its disadvantages: It may make some participants feel uncomfortable or may be perceived as "not serious" (Fuller, 2018). This should be an important and sensitive matter to consider when planning a red teaming program.

Discussion and Summary

It is trivial to simply say that analyzing societal dynamics is important for understanding the flow and its consequences. The focus of this section was on a specific manifestation (i.e., singularities) – such as paradoxical occurrences – creating unpredicted, abrupt system changes. It should be considered only as the first step in studying this phenomenon, as there are numerous related issues to explore, such as the educative role of NSMs for their participants, who experience the benefits of being part of a long-term cooperative and trustful environment, together achieving a system-changing transformation. Other open issues may be related to cross-movement communication and cooperation: Do NSMs influence, directly or indirectly, external societies or groups, and, if so, how successfully?

Important to mention is that there are limits to the presented approach. First, this section challenged an oxymoron, aiming at predicting something that is, by definition, unpredictable (see the definition of black swan events in Chapter 4). In this vein, there will always remain space for unanticipated occurrences. Second, the implication of choosing criteria for selecting the abovementioned five cases could be considered a limitation, as profound, peaceful, and system-changing movements fall under the definition of NSMs. It is important to mention that, along these lines, the selected movements were perpetuated by endogenous dynamics, whereas there are also examples of movements close to reaching a singularity point, though impeded, and derailed by exogenous forces (e.g., the close-to-success civil society opposing the totalitarian regime in Venezuela, devastated by the invited Russian troops). Such movements are worth studying as well.

The paradox of predicting the unpredictable is associated with simulations of future scenarios, be them digital or real-life – especially given that the dependence of existing processes on present and future dynamics is a common intuition both in biology and the societal arena (Longo, 2018) – becoming a call for using imagination to construct a "time machine."

Such simulations have the potential to allow the study of cognitive and social processes together and to help bridge the gap between the individualistic and social approaches (Squazzoni et al., 2013). Simulations connect knowledge on human cognition and social networks, and as such may be more holistic than traditional approaches (e.g., Sutcliffe & Wang, 2012; Sutcliffe, Wang, & Dunbar, 2012). Finally, social simulations have the potential to retain some of the "messiness" of possible future scenarios and, in this vein, are able to harness "chaos-into-order" processes (Edmonds, 2010) (for chaos-into-order, see the elaboration in Chapter 16).

PART III
Challenging the Impossible

Introduction

Are there limits to thoughts? And, consequently, are there limits to intended actions?

Addressing the first question leads to the most striking paradoxes, embedded in the concept of limits of thoughts – that is, boundaries that cannot be crossed, yet are crossed (Priest, 2003). This paradox accompanies philosophers such as Erich Fromm, who encourages us to explore the impossible and transcend limits through philosophy; Fromm believed that, by transcending the impossible, individuals attempt to surpass the boundaries of chaos (Fromm, 1990). Before Erich Fromm, the limits of thoughts were a concern for French philosophers of the 1960s attempting to grasp the unthinkable (Gutting, 2013). Jacques Derrida's passion for "impossibility" in particular is seen as essential (Collins, 2000; Derrida, 1991, 1995; Mason, 2007). More recently, Professor Vlad Glăveanu has opened conceptual avenues for "the possible," positing that it is a human phenomenon and capacity, exploring the limits of the possible, and going beyond what is present, visible, or given in our existence (Glăveanu, 2020).

Thinking may lead to intended actions, where the next paradox is embedded if one purposefully intends to act beyond the boundaries of the possible. Several philosophers support the concept that it is possible to act with intentions beyond the limits of the possible (Hedman, 1970; Thalberg, 2006). This conviction is also supported by experiments documenting that the subjects confirmed that it is conceptually possible to intend to do something they believe is impossible (Buckwalter et al., 2018).

The next step after thinking beyond the boundaries of impossibility and after intending the "impossible" action is perceiving oneself as ready to pursue this impossibility. Of course, beginners who do not realize the scope and complexity of their undertakings may overestimate their aptitudes – a syndrome called the Dunning–Kruger effect (Kruger & Dunning, 1999). However, we are considering individuals who engage in rigorous thinking prior to contemplating the intended action and before diving into the

Part III Introduction

action itself. In this vein, the third paradox is related to surpassing oneself, a subject being addressed in transgression studies (Madsen, 2014; Sokal, 1996). The three steps into possibility, and the associated paradoxes are illustrated in Figure 8.1.

For some individuals, these three steps into the impossible are not only a unique cognitive experience, but also a permanent personality trait. Chapter 8 introduces this characteristic, while Chapter 9 presents some examples of people addressing insurmountable challenges.

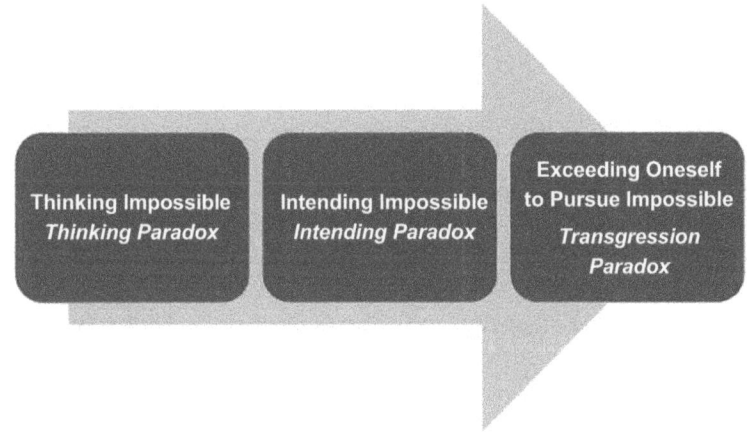

Figure 8.1 The three steps into the impossible.
Source: Ryszard Praszkier.

CHAPTER 8

Possibilitivity
Perceiving Insurmountable Challenges as Doable

Prior to introducing this new "crossing the line" concept, it is helpful to provide an overview of the related personality traits.

Relevant Personality Traits

Some individuals believe in their capacity to execute behaviors necessary to achieving specific goals. This trait, known as *self-efficacy*, was proposed by the Canadian American psychologist Albert Bandura, and reflects confidence in one's ability to exert control over assumed achievements (Akhtar, 2008; Bandura, 1977, 1982). According to this theory, self-efficacy not only pertains to achieving planned goals, but also plays an essential role in psychological well-being, physical health, and flexibility in altering strategies for change (Maddux, 2011).

Another related characteristic pertains to the degree to which people believe that they have control over the outcomes of the events in their lives. Grasping this issue, American psychologist Julian Rotter introduced the concept of the *locus of control*. An internal locus of control leads to perceiving the environment as responsive to one's deliberate actions, while an external locus of control (i.e., the belief that life is controlled by external factors beyond one's influence) diminishes one's sense of control over their life (Rotter, 1966).

A similar concept was developed by the American professor Carol Dweck. She proposed an implicit theory[1] that suggests that people differ in their *perception of the malleability and plasticity of other people and the world*. Belief in the adaptability of others and the surrounding world is amenable to change, accounting for persistence, tenacity, and commitment in pursuing one's goals (Chiu et al., 1997; Dweck, 2000, 2006). However, some individuals do not believe in this malleability and are convinced that things are predetermined. Professor Dweck's research

---

[1] Implicit theories are a priori beliefs about the features and properties of people and objects.

Chapter 8 Possibilitivity

team documented that these individuals have a significantly higher tendency to stereotype others and are more inclined to seek acceptance while avoiding the risk of rejection (Levy et al., 1998). On the contrary, those who believe in the plasticity of the world tend to learn from failure instead of focusing on avoiding rejection (Dweck, 2000).

Need for achievement (n-Ach) is another related feature, initially proposed by Henry Alexander Murray and further developed through research by the American psychologist David McClelland. This trait signifies a strong desire to accomplish goals and attain a high standard of performance and personal fulfillment. Individuals with a high n-Ach often take on tasks with a high probability of success and tend to avoid tasks that are either too easy, due to a lack of challenge, or too difficult, due to fear of failure (McClelland, 1967).

Optimism is a cognitive construct whereby people hold generalized favorable expectations for their future. Higher levels of optimism are prospectively linked to better subjective well-being in times of adversity or difficulty. Optimism is also associated with proactive behavior and has implications

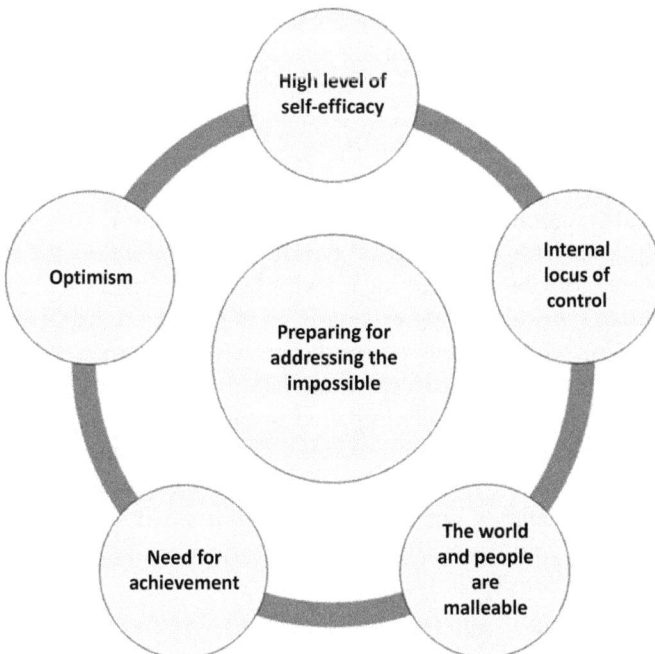

Figure 8.2 Laying the ground for addressing the impossible.
Source: Ryszard Praszkier.

for one's own health (Carver et al., 2010). Conversely, there is pessimism. Research has shown that optimistic individuals tend to embrace effort, whereas pessimistic individuals shy away from it. Moreover, optimists tend to have stronger social connections as they recognize the value of investing in social relationships (Carver & Scheier, 2014).

Metaphorically speaking, these five classical characteristics lay the groundwork for the potential next step, a kind of leap of faith: addressing seemingly impossible challenges (see Figure 8.2).

Impossible Yet Possible Paradox

To take this step into the impossible, one must be convinced that even the most insurmountable challenges are achievable. Let us consider the following example: It is crucial to detect early signs of breast cancer. The most common detection method is palpation, which involves using the fingers to feel for the potential presence of a tumor during a physical examination. The earlier a tumor is detected, the greater the chances of a healthy survival. However, there exists a certain size of tumor that can be detected with palpation, below which even the most skilled professionals are unable to assist. However, early detection significantly enhances the prospects of a positive outcome. How can we identify these seemingly unattainable smaller growths? This sounds like a paradox: reaching the unreachable. This presented a challenge for the German gynecologist Dr. Frank Hoffmann, who firmly believed that a concealed method existed to enable the very-early-stage detection of cancer through palpation. His conviction faced skepticism from those who believed it was a futile endeavor if the best experts were incapable of detecting growths below a certain size. However, Dr. Hoffman's unwavering determination and persistence led to an "aha!" moment: blind women! They possess far greater sensitivity in their tactile abilities, as this compensates for their lack of eyesight. Dr. Hoffman established a school for visually impaired women, harnessing their unique tactile abilities to conduct examinations capable of detecting even the smallest abnormalities. To promote and disseminate this idea, he founded the Discovering Hands organization,[2] which trained blind women to become experts, ultimately aiding in the early identification of cancer indications and, consequently, saving lives.

---

[2] See www.discovering-hands.de/international/page-international. Accessed May 29, 2023.

Defining Possibilitivity

Dr. Hoffman and his skeptical critics suggest that people tend to assess challenges along a spectrum ranging from "It is obviously undoable" to "it is obviously doable." In light of this, it appears that a certain quality influences the degree of conviction that even insurmountable challenges are achievable. This characteristic of mind is proposed to be called *possibilitivity*, a portmanteau of "possible" and "creativity," echoing the pronunciation of "realizability" (Praszkier, 2019, 2021; Praszkier & Zabłocka, 2021). Dr. Hoffman, along with many others who share a similar mindset, appears to master the paradox of addressing the impossible and transforming it into the possible.

It is important to distinguish possibilitivity from the tendency of uninformed novices to overestimate their own abilities – a phenomenon known as Dunning–Kruger syndrome (Kruger & Dunning, 1999; Stone, 2002). Possibilitivity relies on a combination of self-assessment, such as evaluating one's own capabilities (e.g., self-efficacy), and a cognitive analysis of the target. In some cases, it is supported by academic knowledge of problem-solving (e.g., Taylor et al., 1994) or mapping of the challenge (e.g., Harry et al., 2005). In other instances, it draws from practical skills and intuition stemming from praxis. Dr. Hoffman, despite being an expert in his field, was resolute in pushing boundaries generally considered impossible.

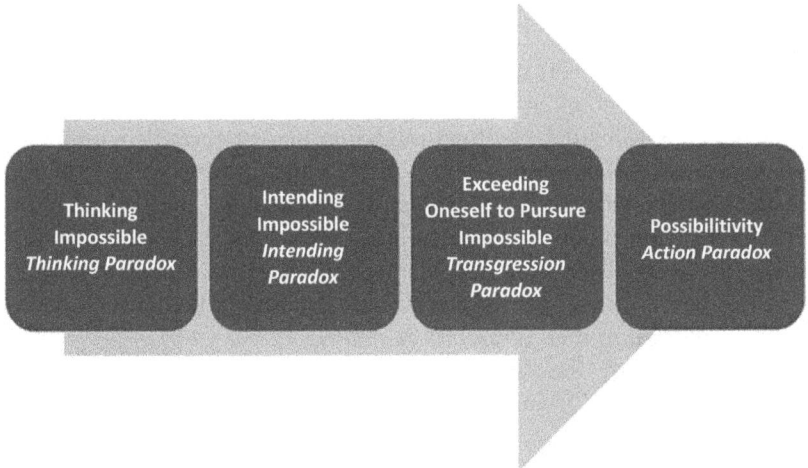

Figure 8.3 Possibilitivity: Action paradox.
Source: Ryszard Praszkier.

A high level of possibilitivity represents the ultimate stage, following the phases of thinking the impossible, intending the impossible, and exceeding oneself, leading to the execution of paradoxical actions aimed at turning the impossible into the possible (see Figure 8.3).

Measuring Possibilitivity

The foundational concept behind the development of a measurement tool for assessing the level of possibilitivity was the aim of capturing how individuals evaluate challenges. Diverse challenges were depicted through several stories to ascertain a generalized perspective not contingent on specific situations. The questionnaire requested respondents to assess the "doability" of various challenging scenarios faced by different individuals. The assumption was that the respondents would identify with the presented characters and evaluate their challenges based on their own approach, employing the Projective Life Stories method.[3]

Following several pilot rounds, three stories (out of twelve) were selected,[4] featuring protagonists from different cultures and genders (including a male from Kenya and two females from Nepal and Columbia). These narratives reflected moments when these individuals had devised innovative and ambitious solutions to seemingly insurmountable and previously intractable problems.

Subsequent to the pilot phase, six statements that met psychometric criteria were identified. The respondents were asked to evaluate these statements using a Likert scale, including expressions such as "X seems to be on a roll and she/he can do it," "I doubt if X will succeed," and "It's too challenging, X will fail." The final validation phase targeted a representative sample of Polish society (N_2 = 1117), which positively verified the questionnaire's psychometric properties. Moreover, the sample size allowed for the creation of a societal index measuring the level of possibilitivity. Additionally, a cross-segment analysis was conducted, revealing, among other findings, that women scored significantly higher on possibilitivity compared to men (Praszkier & Zabłocka, 2021).

In this context, the final version of the Perception of Doability Questionnaire (PoDQ) questionnaire is presented as follows.

---

[3] This method was a combination of a projective test (Piotrowski et al., 1993) and the Psychology of Life Stories approach (McAdams, 2001).
[4] By independent raters.

Chapter 8 Possibilitivity 71

Table 8.1 *The Perception of Doability Questionnaire (PoDQ).*

1	This challenge is too big, Collins (Lucky, Olga) will not make it *	1 2 3 4 5
2	This can be done	1 2 3 4 5
3	What X is planning to do does not look realistic*	1 2 3 4 5
4	X's intention is difficult but feasible	1 2 3 4 5
5	It looks like he is on a roll, and he can do it	1 2 3 4 5
6	I believe X will achieve his goal	1 2 3 4 5
7	X's vision is convincing	1 2 3 4 5
8	I have doubts about whether X will succeed *	1 2 3 4 5

* Reversed.

The Three Stories: Projective Life Stories Approach

The following stories served as the basis for the Projective Life Stories approach. All three were followed by the same set of eight questions (see Table 8.1).

1. Collins, Kenya

As a high school student in Kenya, Collins showed a keen interest in technical lessons. He noticed that various assignments (e.g., making figurines) were often completed sloppily and were thrown away after students receive their grades. He came up with an idea to not only improve the quality of the work, but also to make money from it. After graduating, Collins decided to establish a business that would involve purchasing, for a small fee, student products that had already received a passing grade and then selling them online. To achieve this, he needed to set very high standards for the "production" of items in technical lessons.

His vision is not solely about making money from buying and reselling handcrafted products; Collins aims to foster a culture of higher (market) standards among students while ensuring that teachers are satisfied with the outcomes of their instruction.

Collins is also planning an acquisition network spanning the whole of Kenya and online selling abroad.

Collins' goals encompass building a network for the redistribution of handcrafted products across Kenya, while elevating the technical skills of young people and providing them with a modest income.

2. Lucky, Nepal

In Nepal, high in the Himalayas, villages are cut off from the rest of the world and the journey for essential supplies such as bread takes several days.

Usually, it is just the women who stay in the villages because the men find work in Kathmandu valley or join British or UN military missions as mountain operations specialists.

The major issue in these remote areas is the neglect of education, especially for girls. One can imagine the challenges faced by teachers attempting to reach the next high-mountain Himalayan village. Compounding the issue are parents who fail to see the value in educating girls as they believe their daughters are destined for household work.

Lucky, who hails from one of these villages, has always been passionate about education and desired to provide girls from similar villages with access to learning. She began to contemplate a different approach: Could she find a profession related to the mountains, one universally accepted, and "secretly" incorporate regular education into the training for this profession?

Lucky believed that a profession such as guiding through high-altitude mountainous regions could serve this purpose, and she considered establishing a female Himalayan guide school. After all, these were "their" mountains, and she counted on parents' support. During the training, she planned to teach the girls English (necessary for client communication), geography (for field orientation), and biology (about the mountains' flora and fauna), amongst other topics.

She envisioned that her planned school would likely be more popular than traditional men's schools, given the tendency toward empathy and the lower levels of competitiveness of women. Additionally, during the off-season, she expected her guide school students to share their new-found knowledge with other children and women in their home villages. This would not only provide girls with an income, but would also make them esteemed educators. Furthermore, the success of the female guide school would transform the perception of women in Nepalese society.

Ultimately, Lucky's goal is to educate girls in hard-to-reach Himalayan settlements and, at the same time, change the image of women in Nepal.[5]

3. Olga, Columbia

Olga grew up in extreme poverty in the Colombian slums. Having cleaned rich homes since she was a child, Olga saw a wealth of food and dreamed of children from poor backgrounds also having access to nutritious meals and dietary supplements (such as vitamins and minerals).

---

[5] Lucky's case study is elaborated in Chapter 14.

Despite being self-taught and learning by reading books from the shelves of the houses where she worked, Olga's life took a turn one day when she came across a book about banking. This book made a profound impression on her, sparking an innovative idea: What if she created a bank, in the poorest area, that traded in waste instead of money? This bank would function like a typical bank – running accounts, counters, payment cards, and loans – but instead of dealing with money, clients would bring in collected waste, earning points in return. These points could then be used with the bank's payment card to purchase food and dietary supplements from the bank's shop.

In addition to this, Olga envisioned the bank offering educational programs in economics, marketing, and banking for children and young people.

Furthermore, Olga believed that the bank's customers should have the option to obtain insurance based on the surplus they deposited. In the event of illness, this insurance would cover the necessary food provisions. She also considered the possibility of food loans in emergencies, which could be repaid later using collected waste.

The bank would sell the collected waste to factories for recycling, and the resulting profits would be reinvested in establishing similar banks in other impoverished regions of Colombia and Latin America.

Olga's ultimate goal is to provide food for children and families from the poorest regions of Colombia and Latin America.

The Questionnaire
It may be important to research how possibilitivity relates to other characteristics, such as empathy, adversity quotient, and creativity. Moreover, the PoDQ has only been tested in Polish society thus far; therefore, it is important to adapt it to other cultures as well.

CHAPTER 9

Possibilitivity Heroes

How does this theory apply to real-life personal visions and their implementation? This chapter presents three examples, diverse in terms of walk of life, gender, location, and field.

Verónica Abud Cabrera: Public Libraries in Chile

Thinking the Impossible (Thinking Paradox)

Verónica dreamed of something unthinkable: instigating a love for reading, especially among the young generation in Chile. She envisioned libraries as hubs for reading, recitation, theater, painting, movies ... no limits.[1]

Intending the Impossible (Intending Paradox)

When thinking about implementation, a pivotal question popped up in her mind: How to do it? How to make libraries visible and a magnet for all? This seemed impossible at first glance, but then the solution appeared as an "aha!" moment: libraries located in shopping malls!

Exceeding Oneself (Transgression Paradox)

Being a primary school teacher, Verónica felt that the challenge required her to adopt a different role – that of someone who sparks and seeds novel concepts, far beyond one school, one location, or one city.

---

[1] Based on www.fundacionlafuente.cl/ and The Schwab Foundation for Social Entrepreneurship resources; see www.schwabfound.org/awardees/veronica-abud-cabrera. Accessed June 2, 2023.

Chapter 9 Possibilitivity Heroes

Possibilitivity (Action Paradox)

Believing that her dream was realizable, Verónica finally took a leap of faith: Stepping out of her comfort zone as a primary school teacher, she launched a non-profit organization – Fundación La Fuente – and developed the first public libraries in shopping centers throughout Chile, all of which included multiple additional resources such as theaters, art facilities, and movies. As a result, these libraries became popular and were recognized as "Biblioteca Viva," with a program called "Creando los Lectores del Mañana" (Creating Tomorrow's Readers). The focus is to introduce the community, particularly children and youth, to the pleasures of reading, as well as to include training for school teachers and librarians in reading promotion activities and cultural development.

Ani Choying Drolma: The Singing Nun in Nepal

Thinking the Impossible (Thinking Paradox)

Ani Choying Drolma was born to Tibetan exiles in Kathmandu, Nepal. She faced a difficult life, with her father being both mentally and physically abusive. When she was thirteen years of age, she escaped, entering a Buddhist nunnery.[2]

Ani experienced the hardships of the Buddhist nuns' lives, but all the while an idea was forming in her mind: How to improve the lives of Buddhist nuns, who have traditionally received less support and education than the monks.

However, to empower nuns, it was essential to educate them and provide exposure to formal education, which was much broader than the usual religious studies within the monasteries and nunneries. Holding these thoughts in the back of her mind, she envisioned the nuns performing their roles as much-needed social change agents, raising the awareness, status, and living standards of women in poor rural Himalayan communities through access to education and health services.

This seemed impossible, especially due to the distant and impoverished environments in which the monasteries are located and the influence of centuries-long traditions.

---

[2] Based on https://en.wikipedia.org/wiki/Ani_Choying_Drolma (accessed June 2, 2023), and on the author's own resources (i.e., an interview in Katmandu, conducted on June 28, 2004).

Intending the Impossible (Intending Paradox)

Finally, Ani decided that she wanted to address this problem and that something must be done. These thoughts were somewhat daunting, as establishing a school for nuns that provided multifaceted education had never been done before. What is more, perhaps the second layer of education could empower nuns to become teachers and health educators?

Exceeding Oneself (Transgression Paradox)

This idea would require funding and complex management. Ani imagined herself – a formerly uneducated girl from an abusive family and now a member of the nuns' community living in poverty – as a person who could bring it all to life. How could she do that?

Then came an idea: She is a gifted Tibetan spiritual music chanter. What about developing the nuns' school through her own musical endeavors? This would mean changing her role from that of a modest nun to that of a performer and, in this way, raising funds for her idea. She became the founding leader of this new endeavor.

Possibilitivity (Action Paradox)

Ani Choying Drolma became famous as a "singing nun," and delivered international concerts; many of her artistic performances are available on CD and on YouTube.[3] The funds raised were all invested in her educational project: The Arya Tara School was the first school to offer free education to nuns from remote villages in Nepal, Tibet, and India. There, students learn Tibetan, Nepali, English, mathematics, history, science, and art. After basic education, the nuns are trained to be either teachers or health workers. Equipped with these skills, they return to their communities (i.e., remote mountain villages) and transfer their knowledge to others. Additionally, Ani launched a scholarship program and the Aarya Tara Pre-School.[4]

---

[3] See, for example: www.youtube.com/watch?v=FjJTu0F7MS8, www.youtube.com/watch?v=AAdSUAJ7ngQ&list=RDEMi7m-WU1pmYdt7BwzDK2dGQ&start_radio=1, www.youtube.com/watch?v=AAdSUAJ7ngQ, www.youtube.com/watch?v=yP3YurOfqDY. Accessed June 2, 2023.

[4] See https://choying.com/category/projects/. Accessed June 2, 2023.

Andrew Kassoy, Bart Houlahan, and Jay Coen Gilbert, USA: B Corps

Thinking the Impossible (Thinking Paradox)

In 2006, three colleagues – all Stanford alumni – quit their well-paid jobs, sharing hopes for a better way to do business; as they put it: "Better for workers, better for communities, better for the planet." They did this because they realized the extent to which business is responsible for many of the social and environmental problems that plague our world. They envisioned business as offering a unique opportunity to address these same challenges. At the time, for many, their visions seemed naïve and utopian. [5]

Intending the Impossible (Intending Paradox)

Their thoughts turned to creating a community of entrepreneurs who care about making a difference. Moreover, they aimed to build companies that address pressing social problems. They believed that it was important to clearly define the model for such companies, as they would serve as role models for others, sparking a global movement.

Exceeding Oneself (Transgression Paradox)

Before the transition, Andrew Kassoy spent sixteen years in the private equity industry. He was a principal at MSD Capital, the $12 billion investment vehicle for Michael Dell, and also served as managing director in Credit Suisse First Boston's private equity department. Additionally, he was a founding partner of DLJ Real Estate Capital Partners.

Bart Houlahan was CFO, COO, and president of AND 1, a $250 million basketball footwear and entertainment company. As the principal operator of the business, Bart scaled up the AND 1 business from $4 million to $250 million in brand revenue, with distribution in eighty-five countries worldwide. Before AND 1, Bart was an investment banker.

Jay Cohen Gilbert was CEO of the Imperative 21 network, overseeing organizations such as B Lab and B Team. He was also CEO of Corporate Purpose, Common Future, Conscious Capitalism Inc., and the Global Impact Investing Network, among others.

---

[5] Based on https://som.yale.edu/blog/discussion-with-andrew-kassoy-from-b-lab and www.bcorporation.net/en-us/. Accessed October 10, 2023.

All three partners had significant business experience and had achieved success as business leaders. At some point, they decided to take a leap of faith by putting their successful careers on hold to launch a business-for-good idea. This required them to redefine themselves as changemakers working for the benefit of the people and the planet.

Possibilitivity (Action Paradox)

In 2006, they established B Lab with the aim of driving systemic change through certified B Corporations (B Corps). These are corporate certifications for sustainable businesses and social enterprises that meet higher standards of social and environmental performance and legal accountability. They also introduced a new legally recognized kind of corporate form known as "Benefit Companies," which allows companies to create shareholder and social value.

Certified B Corps are companies that meet rigorous standards for overall social and environmental performance, public transparency, and legal accountability while balancing profit and purpose.

B Corps are at the forefront of the broader movement for responsible business practices. They have inspired more than 220,000 companies to use the B Impact Assessment to measure, manage, and improve their impact. Many have also adopted the benefit corporation legal framework, aligning their business interests with the interests of society. As they put it: "The B Corp movement must continue to lead, to take risks, to demand an economic system that works for all people and the planet. That is why we exist."[6]

---

[6] From www.bcorporation.net/en-us/news/blog/passing-the-torch-note-b-lab-co-founders/. Accessed June 4, 2023.

Discussion and Summary

This section analyzed paradoxes related to planning and carrying out actions addressing seemingly impossible goals (i.e., the thinking, intending, exceeding oneself, and action paradoxes). The personality traits that may be involved in perceiving difficult challenges as realizable were introduced: namely, self-efficacy, locus of control, perceiving people and the world as changeable, need for achievement, and optimism. This laid the foundation for introducing the personality trait of "possibilitivity" (i.e., that people perceive insurmountable challenges on an undoable–doable continuum). The theory of this trait was followed by presenting the process of constructing and validating the PoDQ scale, including with the presentation of three diverse possibilitivity cases.

Given the significance of possibilitivity in solving human problems, it is valuable to explore methods for training future leaders and the younger generation to enhance their propensity for perceiving challenges as doable.

Finally, this concept may prove especially critical in conflict areas for innovating peacemaking methods (see Part 4) and in high-poverty areas for creating novel solutions to combat hunger and impoverishment. Further studies may identify methods to increase the level of doability conviction so that previously intractable yet pressing problems can be successfully addressed.

PART IV
Peace and Its Challenges

Introduction

The paradox of peacemaking lies in the fragility of peace, which, according to the dynamical systems theory of change, despite being highly desired, can easily revert to conflict (Nowak & Vallacher, 1998; Vallacher & Nowak, 2007). One of its dynamic manifestations is the formation of two distinct and relatively independent dimensions: constructive and destructive conflict processes. These dimensions have different dynamics and correlates (Deutsch, 1973) and are often viewed as orthogonal to one another (Samson & Nowak, 2010).

One reason for this lies in the tendency of protracted conflicts to lead to the development of a specific sociopsychological infrastructure that includes elements such as collective memory, narratives about "what others have done to us," an ethos of conflict, and collective emotional orientations. Additionally, there is also a conflict-centered economy that provides jobs and income. Over time, this "around-the-conflict" environment becomes a key factor in reinforcing the core conflict (Bar-Tal, 2007). Therefore, it becomes a strong dimension, adjacent to the tendency for peace. In light of this, peacebuilding should be aware of, and focused on, the conflict environment, paradoxically circumventing its origins and core.

In line with this concept, Chapter 10 elaborates on the dynamics and psychology of conflict's milieu and discusses the relevant personality characteristics that can aid in peacebuilding. It also introduces the concept of the peace-oriented mindset (POM) and details the process of constructing and validating a measurement tool for it. Finally, Chapter 11 provides diverse examples of peacemaking through a milieu-centered approach, illustrating the POM concept.

CHAPTER 10

Peace-Oriented Mindset (POM)

Conflict Transformation

It often happens that various top-down office-based solutions or conflict resolution attempts led by external experts are short lived. After a limited period, the suppressed conflict starts to resurface or even explode once again. Dr. Yehudah Paz, from the highly conflicted Negev area in Israel, pointed out that people become accustomed to living in a conflict-ridden environment. They adapt mentally and economically to the presence of conflict. When peace is suddenly "imposed" from the outside, people feel lost and disempowered in the new, unfamiliar, conflict-free environment. Consequently, they tend to revert to the familiar conflictual situation. Paradoxically, one should refrain from pursuing peace until the environment is prepared to support it. This highlights the importance of focusing on environmental transformation so that the ambience can actively sustain and support peace instead of risking a relapse (Praszkier et al., 2010).[1]

In this context, the fundamental challenge lies in transforming the sociopsychological environment into one that promotes peace (Lederach, 2003). The related paradox is that, counterintuitively, peacebuilding efforts should refrain from directly confronting the core conflict and instead focus on circumventing it by transforming the surrounding environment (Miall, 2004; Praszkier et al., 2010). The milieu-based approach is likely to be more effective in the longer-term perspective than directly addressing the history of conflict escalation, which can lead to setbacks and reverse the prevailing dynamics (Kelman, 1990). This approach aligns with the concept of "conflict transformation" rather than "conflict resolution," encompassing the social, economic, and cultural contexts (Lederach, 1996, 2003).

Moreover, the destructive patterns of conflict may be perceived as attractors, becoming a kernel for self-organization of multiple elements

---

[1] From an interview with Dr. Yehudah Paz led by the author on August 29, 2009.

of conflict systems (Coleman, 2003; Coleman et al., 2007; see also section on "Complexity and Emergence" in Chapter 4 of this book). The complex systems approach appeared useful in intermitting and preventing protracted conflicts, such as those in Mozambique (Bartoli et al., 2010) and South Sudan (Bartoli, 2021).

Furthermore, paradoxical thinking is also employed in the resolution of protracted conflict, serving as a method for altering societal beliefs by presenting messages that align with the recipient's existing beliefs but in an amplified, exaggerated, or even absurd manner. The goal of paradoxical thinking messages is to prompt individuals to perceive their own societal beliefs and attitudes as irrational and possibly even senseless (Hameiri et al., 2014; Hameiri et al., 2018; Swann et al., 1988).

For the conflict transformation to be effective as a long-term process, a specific psychological context is required (Halperin, 2016; MacNair, 2012). Additionally, the conflict parties must be psychologically prepared to engage in a peace process (Rifkind & Yawanarajah, 2019).

Personality Characteristics of Peacemakers

Along these lines, a fundamental question arises: What are the necessary characteristics of individuals engaged in the conflict transformation process? This pertains to professionals who serve communities in conflict, as well as individuals on the ground who are willing to build bridges.

Indeed, a specific approach driven by a particular *mindset* is required to establish the psychological context needed for peacemaking. As for the term "mindset," among its various definitions it is understood herein as a set of beliefs that shape how one comprehends the world and oneself, influencing one's thoughts, emotions, and behavior in any given situation (Cherry, 2021; French, 2016). This definition aligns with the idea of mindset as a set of beliefs that guide how we approach situations, such as determining how we interpret events and decide on appropriate actions (Klein, 2016).

Consistent with these definitions, a peace-oriented mindset encompasses a cognitive dimension (how one comprehends and orients oneself in the process) and a performative dimension (how one behaves and determines appropriate actions). Additionally, given the substantial challenges of peacebuilding (i.e., addressing often seemingly intractable and insurmountable conflicts), there is a need for yet another dimension: a belief that difficult challenges are achievable, a category defined in Part 3 as *possibilitivity* (Praszkier, 2019, 2021; Praszkier & Zabłocka, 2021).

Constructing the POM Questionnaire

In light of this, a three-dimensional construct appears to reflect the characteristics of a milieu-oriented peacemaker:

- Cognitive dimension: Recognizing the role of the sociopsychological context, the ability to listen, and an understanding of the significance of teamwork.
- Performative dimension: Proactively preventing dormant or looming conflicts and often pre-emptively building bridges between conflicted parties.
- Doability conviction (possibilitivity) dimension: The capacity to anticipate and mitigate conflicts, along with a strong belief that peace is possible, even in seemingly intractable situations.

In the next step, some subdimensions were identified:

- Cognitive dimension:
  - Finding neutral common ground;
  - Listening to others while maintaining own values;
  - Understanding the importance of teamworking.

- Performative dimension:
  - Preventing conflict;
  - Building trust.

- Possibilitivity dimension:
  - The ability to contain conflicts;
  - A sense of being able to anticipate conflicts.

In the subsequent phase, 18 statements were assigned to these subcategories, randomized, and validated on an $N = 1,074$ sample. Some statements were reversed (items 4, 5, 12, 13, and 14 in Table 10.1) to avoid potential SDB (Nederhof, 1985). The statistical analysis identified fourteen statements with strong psychometric qualities, resulting in the final Peace-Oriented Mindset (POM) Questionnaire (see Table 10.1).

This final version of the questionnaire demonstrated good reliability (Cronbach's alpha = 0.81). Factor analysis confirmed the three-dimensional model (cognitive, performative, and doability dimensions). As the $N = 1,074$ sample was representative of the Polish society, societal norms could be identified. Moreover, cross-segment analysis revealed that women achieved significantly higher POM scores than

Table 10.1 *Final statements identified for the POM questionnaire.*

	Categories		Items
1	Cognitive	Finding neutral common ground	Opposing groups should find some neutral fields of cooperation.
2		Listening to others while maintaining own values	Debating with others helps me see the world from a different perspective.
3			Listening to others' viewpoints without losing sight of one's own convictions is important for creating peace.
4			I can maintain my own convictions, even when they differ to the majority.
5		Teamwork	I think that the power of peacemaking lies within teamwork.
6			It is best to join a peacemaking organization instead of acting singlehandedly.
7	Performative	Preventing conflict	I try to keep peaceful any situation in which conflict could arise.
8			I can design an appropriate reconciliation process for a conflict situation.
9			Indications that a conflict is looming make me think of how to prevent its outbreak.
10		Building trust	I often think about how to foster trust between conflicted groups.
11			I can think of innovative ways to build trust between individual parties of a conflict.
12	Doability conviction	The ability to contain conflicts	It's possible for me to find an appropriate solution to a conflict situation.
13			I feel capable when I see groups in conflict.
14		A sense of being able to anticipate conflicts	I think that one can predict a conflict before it breaks out.

men. Furthermore, people involved in social activities achieved higher POM scores than those not involved; those who consider themselves an innovator also achieved higher scores than those who do not (Praszkier & Munnik, 2022; Praszkier et al., 2023).

Other Attempts to Measure Peace Attitudes

One of the earliest attempts to measure attitudes toward peace was the Ironemeter scale (Bardis, 1983). However, the issue with the Ironemeter scale is that all ten statements seem to illicit the same response from all respondents. For example, everybody would respond "Definitely yes" to "Human society does not need an occasional war," "Peace leads to much greater progress than war does," and "Historians should never glorify war." Consequently, these questions fail to differentiate respondents, since everyone would answer them in the same manner. Another concern is its exclusively positive wording and lack of reverse statements, which might influence respondents through the aforementioned SDB mechanism.

The more advanced Peace Attitude Scale (PAS; 22 statements) was proven to have good psychometric properties on an $N = 499$ sample (Broccoli et al., 2021). Factor analysis showed that 5 domains appear to be relevant: sociopolitical, personal well-being, ease with diversity, environmental attitude, and caring. Further analysis of the PAS has provided additional insights, such as individuals motivated to seek out new experiences tending to exhibit stronger peace attitudes (Cavarra et al., 2020).

CHAPTER II

POM Heroes

The following examples were selected to represent diverse (in terms of gender and location) peacebuilding projects, all intentionally avoiding the core conflicting issues and instead circumventing the conflict through various bottom-up civic initiatives, creating a milieu of empowering, peace-oriented dynamics.

Fatuma Abdulkadir Adan, Kenya

Fatuma Adan was born to parents from two warring tribes in northern Kenya. She always dreamed of peace in her homeland. With this idea in mind, she pursued her legal education – as the only woman from her area to become a lawyer, returning next to her hometown to promote peace between the conflicting Borana Oromo, Gabra, and Rendille peoples.[1]

Observing how traditional conflict resolution methods had failed, she understood the need to pave the way to peace by empowering the communities. She initiated the Horn of Africa Development Initiative (HODI), which believes that peace is possible only by involving and empowering the most vulnerable citizens among them: women, children, youth, and the elderly.

In this vein, Fatuma Adan launched the Traditional Elders for Peace program, which involved and empowered elders to resolve conflicts peacefully. It evolved into a rapid-response body, instantly addressing looming and emerging conflicts. Similarly, she initiated Women for Peace groups in rural areas to address pressing and sensitive issues.

However, her core concern was children and youth. She thought about how to nurture a new, peace-oriented generation and came up with the

---

[1] Schwab Foundation Fellow: www.schwabfound.org/awardees/fatuma-abdulkadir-adan. Additionally: www.peace-counts.org/kenya-shoot-to-score-not-to-kill/; https://en.wikipedia.org/wiki/Fatuma_Abdulkadir_Adan. Accessed June 10, 2023.

novel idea of promoting soccer, instead of violence, through a program called "Shoot to Score, Not Kill," which was also supported by FIFA. This program has prevented more than 10,000 school-aged children from being drawn into ethnic rivalry and conflict by teaching them a culture of nonviolence through football.

Girls were also addressed through Fatuma's "Breaking the Silence" program, which created a peer network that provides a safe space to discuss sensitive topics. Additionally, a program for the most vulnerable children was initiated to provide access to free primary education.

Fatuma's initiatives created a peace-enforcing environment, as participants experienced the benefits opened up by the peaceful milieu, and, as a result, they became ambassadors for peaceful cross-boundary cooperation.

Due to the success of her programs, Fatuma was invited to speak about her work with the HODI at the UN Geneva Peace Talks in 2013. She also won a Commonwealth Points of Light Award in 2018 for building bridges between previously conflicted communities and for championing the rights of women and girls.

Referring back to the classification in Chapter 7, Fatuma demonstrated the intending paradox (willing to change mortal conflicts into peace), the transgression paradox (as a result, becoming the only woman from her region to obtain a legal education), and the action paradox (building a cooperating, peaceful community).

The following POM Hero, Hahrie Han, is a clear example of the thinking paradox, merging ancient Athenian democracy with contemporary cross-segment dialogue.

Hahrie Han, USA

Hahrie Han, the daughter of Korean immigrants, is the inaugural director of the SNF Agora Institute, inspired by the ancient Athenian agora, which served as the heart of democratic governance and provided a forum for debate, disagreement, and deliberation. The Agora Institute aims to follow the ancient forum, in which Athenians learned both the rights and responsibilities of democracy, and where they developed the capacity for participation in public life. Hahrie believes that civic engagement is the cornerstone of global democracy.[2]

---

[2] Schwab Foundation Fellow: www.schwabfound.org/awardees/hahrie-han. Accessed June 11, 2023.

She has published numerous related articles and books. In her pursuit of civic engagement, she analyzes various ways of instigating and enhancing civic participation and has identified three management styles that organizations use to motivate people: lone wolves, mobilizers, and organizers (Han, 2014, p. 9).

In her most recent book, Hahrie and her coauthors analyzed the differences between winning movements and those that fail, as well as the factors that make collective action powerful (Han et al., 2021).

Through the Agora Institute, Hahrie has created an academic and public forum that integrates research, teaching, and practice to study and augment civic engagement through dialogue, which is seen as the core of democracy. The institute enables scholarly insights to be transformed into knowledge for civic and political actors to bring about real-world change.

As a professor, lecturer, advisor serving at various public institutions, and consultant for social movements, Hahrie is spreading the concept of agora-based dialogue in various regions of the world, thereby preventing conflicts by building a peace-enforcing environment.

The agora idea is also pursued on the ground by Krzysztof Czyżewski, representing the action paradox.

Krzysztof Czyżewski, Poland

A region located in north-eastern Poland and situated between the borders of Poland, Lithuania, and Belarus had been economically disadvantaged due to the crossethnic, crossreligious, and crosscultural conflicts that hindered its economic development. Krzysztof Czyżewski, a social entrepreneur from Poland,[3] coined, and put into practice, the term "xenopolis" (meaning a meeting point for aliens), similar to Han's agora. He stated: "Encountering the Other means overcoming oneself" (Czyżewski, 2020, p. 1), appealing to the transgression paradox (Chapter 9). Krzysztof believes, and has demonstrated, that attempting to overcome deeply ingrained crossborder and crossreligious prejudices can be far more effective when addressed through a variety of small, community-based initiatives rather than confronting and tackling the issues head on. To pursue his ideas, he founded and serves as the CEO of the Borderline Foundation,[4]

---

[3] Ashoka Fellow, elected 2003; see www.ashoka.org/en-us/fellow/krzysztof-czyzewski; founder of the Borderland Foundation, see www.pogranicze.sejny.pl/en/?s=flash&lang=eng. Accessed October 10, 2023.

[4] See: www.pogranicze.sejny.pl/en/. Accessed June 11, 2023.

which promotes a range of bottom-up citizen, youth, and children's initiatives (Czyżewski, 2006).

The Borderline Foundation encourages children to publish a local chronicle, publicizing youth efforts in searching for (e.g., in family attics), collecting, and exhibiting old postcards and photos, as well as tracing the multiethnic history of the area. This rescues the historic Catholic, Jewish, Orthodox, and Protestant roots in the region from oblivion and disseminates them throughout the community. Other initiatives involve mutual learning of multitraditional crafts and crosscultural music. Furthermore, local youth, who, in the past, had suffered from a sense of hopelessness and depression, are now involved in reviving Indigenous Jewish folk music, having founded a Klezmer orchestra that performs locally and abroad.

There are also vital borderline Ukrainian–Polish and Belarussian–Polish cultural programs, as well as a Beyond Borders Academy that nurtures an active community of young people from Ukraine, Belarus, and Poland to build relationships and create new opportunities for cooperation in Central and Eastern Europe.

These civic initiatives together provide hope and a new vision for the future. They accumulate and foster a shift in the collective mindset of a community, engendering social and economic development. The community benefits from cooperation and, in this way, strongly supports peace as an essential condition for growth.

Discussion and Summary

In Chapter 10, the concept of peacemaking through transforming the conflict environment, rather than addressing the conflicting issues head on, was introduced. Protracted conflicts are typically reinforced, in a feedback loop, by the environment, which has adapted to the conflict (e.g., generating multiple narratives that justify hate and revenge). This milieu-based approach, also known as conflict transformation, requires specific characteristics in those engaged in peacemaking.

Following this concept, the peace-oriented mindset (POM) was introduced, along with a method for constructing a POM assessment tool and its validation process.

Since the POM questionnaire was validated in Polish society, it would be beneficial to verify this tool in other cultures.

Meanwhile, Chapter 11 presented three diverse examples of building peace through transforming the milieu.

PART V

Paradoxes and Creativity

Creativity is seeing what others see and thinking what no one else ever thought.
Albert Einstein (Madan, 2024).

Introduction

This section introduces and delves into the concept of paradoxical thinking involved in the process of generating novel ideas. First, the concept of creativity and its specific kind of thinking, divergent thinking, are analyzed through the perspective of paradoxes in Chapter 12. Next, the essential foundation for generating new ideas (brain plasticity) is reviewed in Chapter 13. Finally, some methods for augmenting neuroplasticity are demonstrated in Chapter 14.

CHAPTER 12

Generating New and Useful Ideas

This chapter focuses on creativity and divergent/convergent thinking, as they are related to paradoxes and paradoxical thinking.

The Paradoxes of Creativity

Creativity

Creativity is the ability to produce work that is both novel and appropriate (Sternberg & Lubart, 2004), or novel and useful (Csikszentmihályi, 1997a; Mumford, 2003; Perkins, 1988). This definition reflects the cultural relativity (as things that are creative at some time or some location may not be creative temporarily or elsewhere) (Flaherty, 2005). In this way, creativity is a *specific process* resulting in a novel work that is accepted as tenable, useful, or satisfying by a group at some point in time (Stein, 1953, 1974; Amabile, 1996; Sternberg & Lubart, 2004).

Creativity may also be viewed as a *capacity of the human mind* – that is, an ability to generate ideas that are novel, unexpected, and valuable (Boden, 2004, 2013; Simonton, 2017) (note the inclusion of unexpectedness, as relates to Chapter 4, and its singularities and unexpected occurrences).

Following the personality path, creativity indicates *a constellation of traits* (Findlay & Lumsden, 1988). Creative persons are self-confident, independent, and unopposed to risk-taking. They have good intuition and display flexible, original thinking; moreover, they dare to differ, challenge routines, and – if necessary – bend a few rules (Davis, 1993 Guilford, 1950; Fink & Benedek, 2013).

The Paradox of Creativity

The paradox of creativity relates to the double and contradictory immersion of the creators: On the one hand, they are engaged, often with passion and commitment, in their environment and field of interest; on the other hand, as indicated by Professsor Vlad Glăveanu, they simultaneously gain some distance to look at their engagement from outside the box (Glăveanu, 2018a). In this way, creative action bridges the actual and the possible, as well as the "existing" and the "non-existing" (Glăveanu, 2018b).

Professor Robert Sternberg, an expert in the field of creativity, mentions on his website that creative people generate ideas that, at the time, are viewed as novel and perhaps ridiculous,[1] as well as "unreasonable" (see Elkington & Hartigan, 2008). These individuals often have to violate social norms to promote change, sometimes with negative consequences for themselves, such as social exclusion or ostracism (Bonetto et al., 2021); however, against all odds, they persistently pursue their innovative ideas.

Some authors perceive the origins of creativity as a "wonder," happening in both historical and mundane contexts, from big breakthroughs in science to the everyday discoveries of children at play (Glăveanu, 2018b; Praszkier, 2019).

Examples of Creativity

The best examples of creativity come from children, as they are free from the pressures of achievement or competition. Children simply play, addressing challenges and innovating.

For example, one child created a home theater, operating in a lying-on-his-back position. He cut a hole on the side of a paper box to put his head inside and a smaller hole on the top of the box for placing his smartphone face down. When laying with his head inside the box, he could view videos in darkness, even in daylight. Another child adjusted his junior bicycle to cut the grass, replacing the front wheel with a small rolling trimmer. He had fun driving around the lawn while cutting the grass. These innovations are simple but useful, such as an iPad holder built from Lego block.[2]

There are multiple examples of adult creativity. One of the most compelling seems to be the path to acquiring human organs for transplantation, especially considering that the need far surpasses availability. One such innovation was preparing animal organs instead of human organs; the pivotal challenge, however, was overcoming the human body's natural tendency to reject the transplant. To overcome this barrier, a novel project

---

[1] See www.robertjsternberg.com/investment-theory-of-creativity. Accessed July 6, 2023.
[2] Examples from www.boredpanda.com/share-your-kids-most-awesome-inventions/?utm_source=Facebook&utm_medium=Branded+Content&utm_campaign=ScienceDump. Accessed July 7, 2023.

for editing animal's genes was implemented, modifying their organs to be compatible with human bodies. The next creative step was 3D-printing of human organs (e.g., lungs) using patients' own cells.[3]

The Paradoxes of Divergent Thinking

Creativity is a complex phenomenon. Various tracks of creative thinking can be identified, such as *psychological* creativity, where the discovered idea is new to the individual, and *historical* creativity, where the idea is also new to the world (a contribution to global development) (Boden, 2004). Another approach distinguishes three types of creativity: *Combinational*, which involves generating unfamiliar combinations of familiar ideas; *exploratory*, which occurs when existing rules or conventions are used to generate novel ideas; and *transformational*, which generates ideas that are not only new, but also even strange and seemingly impossible. The latter involves breaking or ignoring culturally sanctioned rules (Boden, 2013).

However, the most essential distinction seems to be between convergent and divergent kinds of creativity.

Divergent and Convergent Thinking

Creativity can be characterized as the mutual reinforcement of two distinct mental models: namely, divergent and convergent thinking (Basadur & Hausdorf, 1996). Convergent thinking follows a particular set of logical steps to arrive at one solution, viewed as "correct," whereas divergent thinking is the ability to generate novel ideas by exploring many possible solutions. The latter is usually a spontaneous, free-flowing process, whereby thoughts appear in a "non-logical" manner (Guilford, 1957; Runco, 2007).

Divergent thinking means generating ideas, imagination, and nonlinear thoughts (Chen et al., 2015). Importantly, it may be perceived as the process of connecting concepts, even if they are disparate and seemingly unrelated, into an unexpectedly functional idea (Guilford, 1957; Runco, 2007). Some authors metaphorically refer to the creative act (i.e., divergent thinking) as "quantum leap thinking," analogous to an electron changing its orbit while generating a quantum of energy (Mapes, 2003).

---

[3] From www.technologyreview.com/2023/01/09/1064867/engineered-organs-10-breakthrough-technologies-2023/. Accessed July 9, 2023.

Convergent thinking is the ability to identify appropriate solutions to standard questions; this sort of "from A to B" thinking does not seem to require significant creativity – for instance, when solving most tasks in school (Guilford, 1957). It may seem that convergent thinking hampers creativity but is also necessary for it (Cropley & Cropley, 2007). Indeed, the ideas generated by divergent thinking need to be arranged in an orderly manner to reach the functionality level (this definition of creativity includes usefulness). In this way, divergent and convergent thinking complement one another and are like *yin* and *yang*, becoming a virtuous cycle (Bertagnoli, 2022).

However, these two ways of thinking seem to be different phenomena. Research involving N = 118 elementary school children dealing with mixed tasks showed that divergent and convergent thinking are only weakly related to one another, indicating that they are two relatively distinct processes (de Vries & Lubart, 2018).

Returning to the previously mentioned types of creativity – combinational, exploratory, and transformational (Boden, 2013) – divergent thinking seems to lie somewhat between combinational (juxtaposing distant, unrelated concepts) and transformational (resulting in the generation of new, seemingly impossible though functional ideas).

Divergent thinking may also manifest as *serendipity*, defined as the art of making unsought findings (Van Andel, 1994); in this way, it may be perceived as a singularity (see Chapter 4). Serendipity is undoubtedly a desirable phenomenon that indicates the generation of new ideas, playing an essential role in making interdisciplinary discoveries (Darbellay et al., 2014; Lindsay, 2014).

Divergent thinking may also mean joining distant elements into meaningful entireties (Gestalts) (Duncker, 1945; Wertheimer, 1959). This ability to blend distant elements is sometimes referred to as *remote association* (Backman & Tuckman, 1972; Marko et al., 2018; Mednick, 1962). A related remote associates test (RAT) was introduced by Sarnoff A. Mednick (1962), and was followed by a later, advanced version: the associative chain test (ACT) (see Marko et al., 2018).

Generating ideas that are outside the prevailing status quo is paradoxical, as it is comparable to the magic of creating the unpredictable. Along these lines, there is no doubt that divergent thinking is seen as something "magical"; see the aforementioned referral to generating ideas as magic (Glăveanu, 2018b) or making wonders (Praszkier, 2019).

Chapter 12 Generating New and Useful Ideas

Examples of Divergent Thinking

As mentioned, divergent thinking may be perceived as the process of connecting completely disparate and unrelated concepts into an (unexpectedly) functional entity (Guilford, 1957; Runco, 2007). The best illustration may be the story heard by the author in Africa:

> A physics teacher complained that students were not interested in his favorite subject, physics. At the same time, being passionate about the environment, he campaigned against the streets being polluted by empty soda cans. He also noticed that in most family compounds there was no electricity and no way to heat water for cooking or washing.
>
> The serendipitous solution merged all of these three unrelated tracks into one: He organized an annual competition for youth to collect cans from the streets and fashion concave mirrors out of them. As concave mirrors focus the sun's rays, the competition was on the most efficient heating device, evaluated during a public and media event (e.g., comparing the times for heating a can of water).
>
> This colorful festival was disseminated by the media, instigating student and public interest in physics (e.g., curiosity about how the sun rays flow so that they focus in one point). Second, it contributed to cleaning up the cans polluting the streets. Finally, after the competition day, the students brought their devices home, proudly handing them over to their parents as a cost-free device for heating water. In this way, three completely unrelated and distant things were merged into one functional concept: triggering interest in physics, cleaning the streets, and providing families with devices to heat water.

The exemplary concepts mentioned in Chapter 8 are good illustrations of divergent thinking.

The challenge to detect the earliest possible manifestation of breast cancer through palpation (i.e., feeling the cells of a tumor with his fingers during a physical examination) resulted in Dr. Frank Hoffman from Germany discovering that the most sensitive sense of touch is developed by blind women, who could detect the smallest cancer nuclei. Looking through divergent thinking lenses, Dr. Hoffman juxtaposed two completely unrelated phenomena – breast cancer and visionary disability – in one functional process.

Olga Bocarejo from Colombia merged two entirely isolated realms: malnourished children from an underserved community and affluent banks. She did so by establishing a bank in the slum area, which is as business-like as "normal" banks but operates with waste instead of money. Young people collect and deliver waste to the bank, receiving points in return. Through a credit card loaded with these points, they can purchase food and health supplements from the bank's food market. The bank generates revenue by selling the waste to factories for further recycling.

Collins Apuyo blended school technical lessons with a prosperous business: By purchasing students' products (after they had been rated by the teachers), he developed a sales system, offering these products to the public.

This kind of creativity, which is divergent thinking, requires specific mind processing, as the brain should be able to jump through distant and unrelated issues, connecting them in the creation of something useful. This suggests the brain's agility and flexibility. This trait is called *brain plasticity* or *neuroplasticity*. Neuroplasticity plays a key role in creativity by facilitating connections among disparate brain regions (Kennedy, 2023), and is discussed further in Chapter 13.

CHAPTER 13

Brain Plasticity

Opening the brain to novel, unexpected solutions, especially when merging completely unrelated phenomena into a functional concept, indeed requires flexibility and openness of the mind. This resembles the definition of a paradox: a juxtaposition of contradictory concepts, often opposed to common sense, yet conveying a higher-level meaning (see Chapter 1). It sounds like the brain transcends itself, requiring changeability and malleability.

However, does the brain change? Fifty years ago, the predominant conviction was that the adult brain is fixed and unchangeable. In contrast, the new concept of recent decades is that the brain can adjust and modify itself (Costandi, 2016; Pascual-Leone et al., 2005). This property is called neuroplasticity, understood as the ability of neural networks to change through growth and reorganization; in other words, it is the brain's ability to rewire itself to function in new ways (Costandi, 2016). This newly discovered property allows the (young, but also the adult) brain to adapt to environmental changes, to learn, to repair itself after injury or disease, and to slow down aging effects (La Rosa et al., 2020).

In other words, experience can shape brain anatomy (neurogenesis plasticity) and brain physiology (synaptic plasticity) (Jäncke, 2009). Although plasticity is highest during childhood, current science acknowledges that the adult brain retains the capacity for functional and structural reorganization (Johansson, 2004). As such, neuroplasticity is an intrinsic property of the brain across the lifespan (Pascual-Leone et al., 2011) and represents "evolution's invention," enabling adaptation to environmental pressures, physiological changes, and life experiences (Pascual-Leone et al., 2005). Moreover, neuroplasticity is not only a theoretical concept, it also opens avenues for treating brain damage or neuropsychological disorders (Sasmita et al., 2018). This is because neuroplasticity can be manipulated in both healthy and diseased brains. Harnessing the brain's ability to create and open new neuronal pathways often plays a key role in rehabilitation and improvement of life quality (Voss et al., 2017). Moreover, healthy brain neuroplasticity may be augmented, such as through training in music or rhythmical movements (Abraham, 2018; Schlaug, 2006, 2015). Anna Abraham, in her book *The Neuroscience of Creativity*, provides an example of a man born in the seventeenth century without hands or feet, who developed several artistic dexterities through a self-invented stump overlay, and concludes that this is an example of "extreme neural plasticity" (Abraham, 2018, pp. 221–222). It is worth mentioning that there are multiple examples of disabled people using their mouths for painting (e.g., Roberts, 2012; Simpson, 2019).[1] In all of these cases, neuroplasticity enabled a shift from hand- to mouth-operated painting. Interestingly, some authors claim that practicing a new skill may change "hundreds of millions and possibly billions of connections between the nerve cells in our brain maps" (Doidge, 2007, p. 47; Merzenich et al., 1999).

As mentioned, the brain can modify itself in different ways, in both physical structure (anatomy) and functional organization (physiology) (Chaney, 2007). This leads to the identification of three basic kinds of plasticity:

- Synaptic plasticity: forming new neural paths and connections.
- Neurogenesis: stem cells can reproduce fully functioning brain cells, especially critical in the case of catastrophic events.
- Functional compensatory plasticity: important after brain injury or stroke. The irreversibly damaged cells in certain locations are replaced by different cells in different locations, with a modified neural network; also, some older adults' brains, instead of synaptic plasticity, apply functional compensatory plasticity, involving, as a replacement, new parts of the brain (Shelton, 2013).

The latter, involving rehabilitation, is well known and widespread and, as such, needs no further elaboration. The focus is hence on the first two, lesser-known kinds of neuroplasticity.

Synaptic Brain Plasticity

Synaptic brain plasticity refers to changes in neural pathways and synapses that are due to alternations in behavior, environment, and neural processes

---

[1] See also the following press reports: https://disabilityhorizons.com/2019/04/finding-a-voice-and-an-outlet-through-mouth-painting/; www.globaltimes.cn/page/202109/1233044.shtml; www.aapd.com/the-mouth-painter/. Accessed August 14, 2023.

(Kolb & Whishaw, 1998; Pascual-Leone et al., 2011). Moreover, synaptic plasticity is one of the important neurochemical foundations of learning and memory (Hughes, 1958). It is a major mechanism by which the neural activity generated by experience modifies brain synaptic transmissions (Citri & Malenka, 2007). Synaptic neuroplasticity is the ability of neurons to modify the strength of their connections and is an important neurophysiological process involved in memory, sensory adaptation, development, and recovery from injury (Fox & Stryker, 2017).

Synaptic neuroplasticity is a dynamic process balancing short-term Hebbian plasticity – that is, a mechanism detecting and amplifying coactivity between neurons (Abbott & Nelson, 2000; Zenke et al., 2017), with longer-term homeostatic kinds of plasticity – that is, stabilization by additional compensatory processes (Zenke et al., 2017).

Hebbian plasticity is considered a key ingredient underlying learning and memory in the brain. However, Hebbian plasticity alone is unstable, leading to runaway neuronal activity, and it therefore requires stabilization by additional compensatory processes. Scientists are still studying how to integrate both forms of plasticity into a synchronized whole (Fox & Stryker, 2017; Zenke et al., 2017).

One of the underlying mechanisms leads to changes in the quantity of neurotransmitters released into a synapse and in how effectively cells respond to those neurotransmitters (Gaiarsa et al., 2002). As plastic change often results from the alteration of the number of neurotransmitter receptors located on a synapse (Gerrow & Triller, 2010), the role of neurotransmitters is worth a closer look.

Neurotransmitters

Neurotransmitters convey a message from one neuron to another. More precisely, they are chemical messengers that allow electrical signals from neurons to be transmitted to synapses of other neurons – and, subsequently, to postsynaptic neurons. A substance is generally considered a neurotransmitter if it is synthesized in the neuron, transmitted to the presynaptic location, and later released to have an effect in the postsynaptic cell (Cuevas, 2019). Both short- and long-term neuroplasticity depends on the presynaptic neurotransmitter release, and its disruption may participate in several neuropsychiatric disorders (Monday et al., 2018).

Some neurotransmitters are as simple as protons, regulating synaptic plasticity in the lateral amygdala (Du et al., 2014). These neurotransmitters exert their effects within a small area near to where they are released.

However, some neurotransmitters are more complex, such as neurohormones, which have a wide range of actions related to many targets, possibly extending far from their site of synthesis (Burrows, 1996).

The multifunctionality of these neurotransmitters, which are also neurohormones, is of special interest, as some of them may also contribute to altering mood or emotions, influencing the brain's reward and pleasure centers, as well as human creativity (Beversdorf, 2013; Chermahini & Hommel, 2010; Flaherty, 2005). Examples include dopamine, whose role as a neurotransmitter was discovered in the mid-twentieth century (Conrad, 2018; Evans, 2024), and endorphin, an endogenous opioid peptide that provides pleasure and euphoria (Hawkes, 1992; Stoppler, 2014). Dopamine rather influences a long-term state of mind, whereas the impact of endorphin, compared to the dopaminergic system, is short-lived (Rusu, 2013).

In the following sections, three neurotransmitters belonging to the class of so-called "happy neurohormones" are discussed.

Dopamine

One role of dopamine is to control the brain's reward and pleasure centers; through dopamine, the brain transmits "rewards" to the dopaminergic system, initiating further motivated behavior (Ballard et al., 2011). In this way, it mediates reward-seeking activity, ranging from gambling and cocaine addiction to the appreciation of beautiful faces and music (Aharon et al., 2001; Breiter et al., 2001; Flaherty, 2005).

Dopamine also influences novelty seeking and creative drive (Flaherty, 2005), as it is associated with pleasure (Sprouse-Blum et al., 2010), and therefore contributes to a divergent mindset (Kaufman, 2010). Achieving a proper balance in the level of dopamine helps increase creativity, such as in the treatment of Parkinson's disease in artistic patients (Kulisevsky et al., 2009).

Conversely, a deficiency in dopamine influences various diseases (e.g., Parkinson's disease) (Klein et al., 2018). In such cases, dopamine therapy is prescribed: for example, in the form of antidepressants with dopaminergic effects in the treatment of depression (Brown & Gershon, 1993).

Endorphins

Endorphins (a compound term for "endogenous morphine") serve as a brain-controlled painkiller (MacLean Jr. et al., 1985; Scheve 2014;

Sprouse-Blum et al., 2010; Stoppler, 2014); they also deliver feelings of pleasure and euphoria (Stoppler, 2014).

The effects are similar to codeine or morphine, but without addiction. Several human activities are rewarded by the pleasure stemming from the endorphinergic system in the brain, especially sex and some intense and prolonged sports, where endorphins decrease muscle pain (Hawkes, 1992; Stoppler, 2014). As such, endorphins play a role in the reward system, causing, in some instances, an addiction to exercise (Boecker et al., 2008; Hockenbury & Hockenbury, 2011). Moreover, endorphins contribute to analgesia, temperature regulation, appetite and thirst control, sexual behavior, and blood pressure regulation (Hawkes, 1992).

However, the effect of endorphin lasts for only a short time compared to dopamine (Rusu, 2013).

Serotonin

Serotonin, besides being a neurotransmitter, is probably best known for its role as a neurohormone in conveying a sense of contentedness, often called the body's natural "feel good." When serotonin is at normal levels, one feels focused, emotionally stable, happier, and calmer. It also plays a critical role in the maintenance of mood and the treatment of depression. Carriers of multiple serotonin-mimetics and modulators of adult neurogenesis (AN) are used clinically (Alenina & Klempin, 2015). For example, an increase in serotonin levels in the brain enhances AN in the hippocampus (Jacobs et al., 2000), indicating its potential for treating depression.

The difference between dopamine and serotonin is that the former is associated with emotions, whereas the latter regulates mood (Baixauli, 2017) and cognition (Merens et al., 2007).

Neurogenesis and Brain Plasticity

Neurogenesis is the process by which neurons are produced by the brain's stem cells. It is most active during embryonic development and is responsible for producing all of the various types of neurons in an organism, but it continues throughout adult life as well (Kandel et al., 2021). Adult neurogenesis is a stem-cell-driven process of modifications in the genetically determined structure of nervous tissue, including neuronal replacement (La Rosa et al., 2020; Song et al., 2002; van Praag et al., 2002). It is worth mentioning that stem cells were discovered in parts of the adult brain as late as the mid-1990s, and, since then, AN has been accepted as a normal process that occurs in the healthy brain over the entire lifespan.

Neurogenesis is changeable; its level may be reduced by sleep deprivation or fragmentation (Guzman-Marin et al., 2007) and increased by physical exercise such as running (van Praag et al., 1999; Yau et al., 2014) or by environmental enrichment (Olson et al., 2006). Interestingly, instigating positive emotions (e.g., by simple tickling) increases the neurogenesis plasticity in a rat's hippocampus (Yanpallewar et al., 2010).

Enhancing neuroplasticity seems an intriguing path, and this is elaborated in Chapter 14.

CHAPTER 14

Avenues for Enhancing Neuroplasticity

As mentioned, opening the mind to paradoxes and paradoxical thinking requires a malleable and plastic brain. The question is whether it is possible to plasticize the brain – in other words, to boost its neuroplasticity.

The answer is yes, and there are several ways to achieve this. The predominant approach relates to treating neurological and psychiatric disorders, such as through the neurohormone dopamine (see Kuo et al., 2008). Another example is increasing experience-dependent plasticity (a property critical for the everyday function of the brain, impaired in a range of neurological and psychiatric disorders) through specific medication (Forsyth et al., 2015).

A more natural approach is noninvasive transcranial brain stimulation (NIBS), based on transcranial magnetic incitement, which is helpful in various instances (such as in stroke patients) to facilitate the effects of subsequent physiotherapy (Aaron et al., 2018; Devanne & Allart, 2019).

The focus of this chapter is on nonmedical, natural methods of enhancing neuroplasticity, such as through physical exercise, metaphors, joy, and dance.

Physical Exercise Boosts Neuroplasticity

The brain, and especially motor cortex plasticity, can be influenced by various factors, such as rehabilitation, physical exercise, or NIBS, and combining these interventions can have a synergistic impact on inducing neuroplasticity (Devanne & Allart, 2019). Combining approaches such as physical and cognitive activity enhances brain plasticity and the capacity to respond to new demands with behavioral adaptations (Hötting & Röder, 2013). Augmenting neuroplasticity through physical exercise is applied in the rehabilitation of disorders such as Parkinson's disease (Petzinger et al., 2013) and Alzheimer's disease (Tzu-Wei et al., 2018).

The important question is whether and how neuroplasticity can be boosted as a way to enhance divergent thinking and embrace paradoxes. One promising method is the Feldenkrais approach.

The Feldenkrais Approach to Augmenting Neuroplasticity

The Feldenkrais approach uses atypical yet gentle and mindful sets of movements to expand the range of motion in a balanced way. It focuses on seeking overall bodily harmony rather than concrete goals, as is common in regular physical training or rehabilitation. The premise of this method is that the brain, rather than the muscles, controls the style and range of motion. The focus is on enhancing movement possibilities (expanding the range of mobility) and alleviating the pain caused by bad movement habits (Praszkier, 2019).

The method is based on a gentle combination of different types of movements that are atypical for the brain. The brain must accommodate these new sets, thereby opening new paths of neuronal connections and enhancing synaptic plasticity.

By learning new ways to move and practicing these movements, the body's ability to function improves, promoting positive change. The Feldenkrais approach works as a neuromodulator, where the new, slow, and precise movements aid in "rewiring" the brain. An important caveat is that slower movement leads to more subtle observation, allowing for more significant change (Doidge, 2016).

Dr. Moshé Feldenkrais was an engineer and physicist at Sorbonne, as well as a passionate soccer player. He badly injured his knee during a game, and the doctor's verdict was that he would never be able to play sports again. Against all odds, Feldenkrais applied his knowledge of physics and engineering, along with human anatomy, to find a way to alter his own movement habits and patterns. He was convinced that his limits were embedded in the psychoneurological motor patterns "stored" in his brain, and that he should address these patterns through atypical yet gentle sets of movements. This approach proved successful, and Feldenkrais was able to return to practicing sports. This experience led him to develop his techniques, which he called "Functional Integration," and which are documented in his books (Feldenkrais 2002,[1] 2005).

Importantly, this approach highlights the harmonious unity of mind and body (Feldenkrais, 1980; Plonka, 2021). The conjecture is that an

---

[1] Originally published in 1985.

atypical combination of different kinds of movements, carried out in a gentle and slow way, stimulates synaptic connectivity and plasticity. The brain needs to develop new paths of neuronal connections to accommodate the new circumstances. Practiced frequently, this may influence the overall propensity for creating new connections and, hence, may also influence the mind's generalized openness and creativity (see also Bach-y-Rita, 1980; Doidge, 2016).

Along these lines, the Feldenkrais approach is used for enhancing the neuroplasticity and, consequently, the creativity of an individual's mind. It is also applied to alleviate and remove pain in various circumstances. One example involves treating patients with scoliosis: The application of neuroplasticity theory with the Feldenkrais approach to a 42-year-old female runner with a history of adolescent idiopathic scoliosis, and who suffered hip and lumbar pain, demonstrated clinically meaningful improvements in pain intensity. This enabled the resumption of pain-free running and other physical activities (Myers, 2016). Additionally, when applied to a multiple sclerosis patient with severe instability and spasticity, the Feldenkrais approach led to a significant balance improvement and spasticity reduction. In this case, the level of neuroplasticity was measured using the Neuroplasticity Scale, revealing changes in sensory-motor and cognitive processes during the period of interventions (Reziti, 2023). There are also reports on the positive impact of the Feldenkrais approach to patients with Parkinson's disease: An N = 30 group of patients with Parkinson's disease who underwent a fifty-session program based on the Feldenkrais approach significantly improved, as measured by the Parkinson's Disease Quality of Life questionnaire and the Beck Depression Inventory, compared to the control group (Teixeira-Machado et al., 2015). Interestingly, dance interventions based on the Feldenkrais approach, applied for six months to a group of twelve subjects with Parkinson's disease, led to significant improvements in motor and nonmotor symptoms, quality of life, and objective parameters of gait. These improvements were confirmed even three, six, and twelve months after treatment (Kang et al., 2022). Indeed, dance promotes neuroplasticity (Teixeira-Machado et al., 2019) and engages various brain networks related to perception, action, and emotions (Elst et al., 2023).

The Feldenkrais approach also significantly alleviates back pain, both among athletes, simultaneously expanding their range of motion (ROM) (Krešimir et al., 2017), and among adults with chronic back pain (Pugh & Williams, 2014).

One concept of the Feldenkrais approach may sound like a paradox: Sensory awareness (imagining), without any real-life movements, leads to improvements in ROM. An experiment involving imaging a soft bristle brush passing over one-half of the body was given to twelve subjects. A significant majority reported that this mere imagination changed their proprioception of the "brushed" side of the body, perceiving it as longer and lighter than the other side; moreover, there was also a significant increase in ROM on that side (Dunn & Rogers, 2000). Following Feldenkrais concept of the role of sensory awareness, it is also worth mentioning that pure imagination, without movement, can influence dancing abilities (Franklin, 1996; Perica, 2010; Short et al., 2001). The paradox is that real movement abilities may be significantly influenced by mere imagination.

Metaphors

Not only physical operations instigate neuroplasticity; so do some specific mental activities. In a neuroscience experiment where subjects were asked to complete sentences using either synonyms or metaphors, it was found that creating metaphors activates parts of the brain that involve flexible imagination and, as a result, the construction of novel figures of speech, facilitating creativity (Benedek et al., 2014). Metaphors were used to spark divergent thinking – that is, the combination of two existing elements into something different and novel functionalities (Runco, 1991; Wurth, 2018).

Joy

In some studies, joy seems pivotal for creativity, such as in Professor Mihaly Csikszentmihályi's[2] analysis of ninety-one videotaped interviews with the world's most creative people of various professions. Three criteria were used for selecting the subjects: (1) the person had to have made a difference to one of the domains of science, the arts, business, government, or human well-being; (2) during the study, they should still be actively involved in their domain; (3) they should be at least sixty years old. These interviews indicated that the subjects, above all, enjoyed discovering and innovating. When asked to choose from a list of which life

---

[2] A Hungarian–American psychologist, head of the department of psychology at the University of Chicago.

experience delivers the most pleasure, the answer most frequently chosen was "designing or discovering something new" (Csikszentmihályi, 1997a). The study demonstrated that creative individuals are motivated not so much by the hope of achieving fame or making money, but rather by the opportunity to do the work that they enjoy. They simply "enjoy discovering and creating above all else" (1997a, p. 108). This may indicate that, for some people, joy comes from creating new things and making discoveries. In this vein, enhancing one's creativity may therefore also enhance joy and well-being (Csikszentmihályi, 1997b). Some authors even explicitly state that creativity engenders happiness (Barron & Barron, 2013; Gruber, 1988).

As mentioned in Chapter 13, innovating means opening new neural pathways. These neuronal connections are facilitated by neurotransmitters, some of which are also neurohormones, such as dopamine, endorphin, and serotonin – that is, "happy hormones." The conjecture is that the positive feelings associated with innovating are facilitated by an increased secretion of happy hormones.

Does it also work the other way round? Does boosting the level of happy hormones activate innovativeness? Some authors have replied to this question positively, indicating that the level of happy hormones can be augmented in natural ways. For example, joy in the workplace may contribute to boosting the level of happy hormones (Ghosh, 2018) and, in this way, create an enabling ambience for divergent thinking and embracing paradoxes. Popular media also mention exercising, listening to music, meditating, and dancing.[3] Some physical activities (such as soccer) may also be interrelated with happy hormones (Islam, 2021).

Dancing

The influence of dancing on enhancing the brain's structural and functional capacities has been documented in several studies. Analyzing the existing literature on the impact of dancing on the brain demonstrates a positive change at the structural level (increased hippocampal volume). Additionally, at the functional level, there appeared to be a significant improvement in memory, attention, body balance, psychosocial parameters, and an altered peripheral neurotrophic factor. Based on the evidence, dance practice integrates brain areas to improve neuroplasticity (Teixeira-Machado et al., 2019).

---

[3] See www.henryford.com/blog/2021/05/how-to-boost-feel-good-hormones-naturally; www.health line.com/nutrition/how-to-increase-dopamine#fa-qs; https://neurosciencenews.com/fitness-neuro science-23228/; https://the-hummingbird-life.com/blog/4-ways-a-secret-sunrise-experience-will-im prove-your-brain-the-neuroplasticity-of-unleashing-joy. Accessed September 2, 2023.

Another analysis of the related literature confirmed that dance is associated with an improvement in functional connectivity and cognitive performance (Nascimento, 2021).

Senior citizens' brain functions in particular benefit from dancing. In a research study, seniors ($N = 22$) were randomly assigned to either a dance group or a sports group. The longitudinal study revealed that participating in a long-term dance program significantly induces neuroplasticity compared to engagement in physical exercise (Müller et al., 2017). The positive influence of dancing on brain health is also mentioned in some popular media (e.g., Powers, 2010; Bläsing, 2020).[4]

More methods for boosting neuroplasticity are discussed in Chapters 15 and 16.

---

[4] See https://socialdance.stanford.edu/syllabi/smarter.htm; www.theguardian.com/technology/2011/jul/31/peter-lovatt-dance-problem-solving. Accessed September 4, 2023.

Discussion and Summary

Paradoxical thinking requires a higher level of creativity and divergent thinking, as analyzed in this part. Divergent thinking operates like paradoxical thinking – that is, merging unexpectedly completely unrelated ideas into one functional concept. This "thinking paradox" requires specific brain properties – namely, flexibility and malleability – called "neuroplasticity." In this process, synapses are generated and dissolved in a continuous process that occurs during wakefulness and consciousness (Askenasy & Lehmann, 2013).

Neuroplasticity is, above all, the propensity for creating new neuronal connections, called "synaptic plasticity." An important function in augmenting neuronal connectivity is performed by neurotransmitters. Some neurotransmitters are also neurohormones, and their role is twofold: neurohormones influence emotions, and some generate pleasure and joy. In this way, augmented neuroplasticity may be correlated with joy.

Studies related to synaptic and neurogenesis plasticity indicate that:

- Neuroplasticity, most intensive at a younger age, exists up to adulthood, and indeed over the entire lifespan.
- The level of neuroplasticity can be modified.
- Positive emotions correlate with the level of neuroplasticity, either through neurohormones or neurotransmitters (dopamine, endorphins, and serotonin); moreover, positive emotions may influence the level of neuroplasticity.

Interestingly, some researchers hold that it is not only the case that certain neurohormones trigger positive feelings, such as joy; joy may also create an environment conducive to enhancing neuroplasticity. The augmentation of neuroplasticity may also happen through metaphors and dancing. Some studies indicate that joy is one of the factors that contributes to the augmentation of divergent, paradox-like thinking.

PART VI

Paradoxes in Action

Start by doing what's necessary; then do what's possible; and suddenly you are doing the impossible.
St. Francis of Assisi

Never depend upon institutions or government to solve any problem. All social movements are founded by, guided by, motivated and seen through by the passion of individuals.
Margaret Mead (Khuzaima, 2014)

Introduction

This section refers to and elaborates on the concept of the three-stage paradox of action, previously presented in Part 3. First, there is the thinking impossible paradox; second, the intending impossible paradox; and, finally, the transgression and action paradoxes (exceeding oneself to pursue the impossible) – see Figure 8.3. It is important to mention that addressing insurmountable social issues is sometimes seen as a continuous paradoxical dilemma (Cooper, 2018; Harmon & Pava, 1981).

Along these lines, Chapter 15 illustrates the pursuit of the seemingly impossible through literature analysis and case studies of changers-for-good, especially those called "social entrepreneurs." Chapter 16 provides the context of psychotherapy, where paradoxes often help solve critical problems. Finally, Chapter 17 reviews several paradoxical situations in everyday life, demonstrating how they can be harnessed positively.

CHAPTER 15

Turning the Impossible into the Possible

An overview of the concepts of changemaking-for good (C4G) and social entrepreneurship is provided herein, followed by examples from the past and the present day. Paradoxes related to addressing "impossible" challenges are mentioned, as well as ways to make change possible, systemic, and durable.

Changers-for-Good

There are individuals who want to change dysfunctional social situations, acting for the good of others (individuals, groups, and communities) to improve the conditions of the addressees (Carriere, 2018; Wright et al., 1990). This requires a specific identity, empathy with the issues needing action, and a belief that the problem may be resolved (Van Zomeren et al., 2008). Some call them "changers-for-good" (C4G) (Praszkier, 2023a).

C4G are not only empathetic with their target population, but also compassionate. Empathy is commonly seen as a prosocial and morally positive factor; however, it may also serve as a tool for pursuing negative acts, e.g., through narcissistic or manipulative use of the deepened knowledge of another (Breithaupt, 2018; Konrath et al., 2014). This indicates that empathy is not enough to assure caring relationships. The complementary parameter should hence relate to sympathizing with others (i.e., having a high level of compassion).

However, compassion may be blind without understanding the real needs of another, and may even turn out to be dangerous (Wel, 2020). In this vein, there emerges a need for a blended phenomenon: *Empassion*. Recent neuroscience research posits that merging compassion with empathy may be considered a predictor of an individual's prosocial behavior (Chierchia & Singer, 2017; Stevens & Taber, 2021). Along these lines, the Empassion Scale (ES) was developed, demonstrating good reliability and validity. ES also correlates significantly with empathy and compassion scales (Praszkier, 2023b).

Example: Elizabeth Fry

One example of a C4G is of the British Victorian era. There were many rules for and expectations of women in Victorian times, such as: "Be not too often seen in public," "Never be afraid of blushing," and "Form no friendship with men,"[1] especially when you were, as Elizabeth Fry (1780–1845) was, from a high-society Quaker banker family. Furthermore, The *Lady's Guide to Perfect Gentility* of 1859 stated that a lady should "always seek to converse with gentlemen into whose society you may be introduced, with a dignified modesty and simplicity . . . ; but never say or do anything that may lead them to suppose you are soliciting their notice."[2] The paradox is that Elizabeth Fry broke all these rules and spoke in public bluntly to men, gaining their attention and making them follow her ideas. Breaking the rules made her and her ideas successful, so much so that, 200 years later, Elizabeth Fry was featured on the Bank of England £5 note (from 2002 to 2016).

Elizabeth Fry's mission started when she visited a prison (not at all a suitable place for a woman from a Victorian family to visit), where she was horrified by the living conditions. The women's section was overcrowded with hundreds of women and children, some of whom had been held for years without trial. Serious criminals were mixed with those incarcerated for minor offenses. Children lived in the prison with their mothers, in rags, filth, and idleness.

Elizabeth Fry returned the next day, despite her family's fears, bringing food and clothes. She stayed overnight in the cells, despite the atrocious sanitary conditions, to experience and understand firsthand the conditions of female prisons. She was driven by compassion and empathy for incarcerated women, relentlessly devoting her time to this mission in the future as well.

Her dream was to change life in prisons by raising public awareness of the dreadful conditions and initiate legislation to humanize the treatment of female prisoners and their incarcerated children. When ready, she

---

[1] See Weeks, L. (2015). 18 Rules of Behavior for Young Ladies In 1831. *NPR*. www.npr.org/sections/npr-history-dept/2015/11/20/456224571/18-rules-of-behavior-for-young-ladies-in-1831. Accessed September 12, 2023.

[2] See https://dp.la/primary-source-sets/victorian-era/sources/1849. Accessed September 12, 2023.

decided to disseminate this knowledge and started talking to influential people, inviting them to see for themselves the conditions in women's jails.

In 1817, Elizabeth Fry cofounded the Association for the Reformation of Female Prisoners, which led to the creation of the British Ladies' Society for Promoting the Reformation of Female Prisoners, believed to be the first national women's organization in Britain (Cooper, 1981; Rose, 1980).

She also started a prison school for children who were incarcerated with their mothers; moreover, she initiated an education system, which included teaching women to sew and to read the Bible. In 1827, she published a short book based on her experience (Fry, 2018).

Elizabeth Fry followed the scheme mentioned in Chapter 8: starting with thinking and intending impossible paradoxes, and, in doing so, transgressing oneself as to take action paradoxes.

Social Entrepreneurship

In recent years, the most representative kind of changemaking-for-good has been social entrepreneurship, defined as a multidimensional construct involving entrepreneurial behavior to achieve a social mission, the ability to recognize social value-creating opportunities, applying innovativeness, and risk-taking (Mort et al., 2006; Praszkier & Nowak, 2012). Social entrepreneurs differ from entrepreneurs and social activists in that the former create opportunities and new values, whereas the latter discover existing opportunities and capture existing values (Betts et al., 2018).

The term "social entrepreneurship" was coined in 1980 by William Drayton, the founding CEO of the global organization Ashoka: Everyone a Changemaker[3] (Sen, 2007), who identified individuals that are, on the one hand, committed to solving social problems and, on the other hand, pursuing their ideas with an entrepreneurial aptitude (Drayton, 2002, 2005; Praszkier & Nowak, 2012).

Among the large number of definitions that are currently in use (Mair et al., 2006; Mair & Martí, 2006), the definition used by Ashoka is seen as the most comprehensive (Bornstein, 2004). In this vein, social entrepreneurs are characterized as:

- Having a new idea for solving a critical social problem;
- Being creative;
- Having an entrepreneurial personality;

---

[3] See www.ashoka.org/en-us. Accessed September 11, 2023.

- Envisioning the broad social impact of the idea;
- Possessing an unquestionable ethical fiber (Drayton, 2002, 2005; Hammonds, 2005).

Additionally, they also:

- Open new possibilities by introducing innovative ideas;
- Combine visions with down-to-earth realism;
- Are creative and highly ethical problem-solvers;
- Exhibit a total commitment to their ideas of social change (Bornstein, 1998).

Martin and Osberg (2007) proposed a shorter definition: Social entrepreneurs as those who:

- Target underserved, neglected, or highly disadvantaged populations;
- Aim for large-scale, transformational benefits that accrue either to a significant segment of society or to society at large.

To recap, social entrepreneurs – educated or illiterate, regardless of their age or gender, independently from the cultural context – address pressing, often intractable, social problems and introduce novel, systemic, and durable solutions (Praszkier & Munnik, 2021). Social entrepreneurship means creating social value and pursuing it through recognizing and exploiting untapped opportunities, accepting higher risk, overcoming limitations, and generating and engaging innovations (Mort et al., 2006; Peredo & McLean, 2006).

Along these lines, there seem to be several paradoxes embedded in social entrepreneurs' approach: First, they merge up-in-the-air dreaming with down-to-earth ways of implementation. Second, they successfully address protracted, insurmountable problems, predominantly perceived as unrealizable. Third, they find innovative methods to make things happen.

Examples of Doing the Impossible

David Kuria, Architect from Kenya

In Nairobi's Kibera slums, there were prejudices against sanitation, leading to environmental pollution and outbreaks of disease. Various governmental and international efforts attempted to change the situation, such as building new toilets or organizing educational campaigns; however, these

Chapter 15 Turning the Impossible into the Possible

top-down attempts failed, as the prejudice against dealing with human waste was ingrained in historically established practices.

David Kuria,[4] a recently graduated architect, spent all of his time in the Kibera slums, exploring ways to change the disastrous and dangerous sanitary situation. His loved ones were against his engagement with the slums, which were perceived as unsafe and filthy. Instead, family and friends persuaded him to take advantage of his architectural specialty and build nice, well-funded houses, instead of fixing "dirty" areas. However, against all opposition, David remained persistent in his endeavors to help the Kibera dwellers.

After talking to them and learning by trial and error, David[5] understood that combating the threat of an epidemic can be achieved only through making sanitation a bottom-up agenda. He learned that it is critical to engage dwellers as early as the planning phase, and that hygiene and sanitation must come bottom-up from the people; it was clear that otherwise, all of the top-down, costly projects would be opposed and derailed.

To do so, he initiated several group activities wherein community members could design their ideal toilets. After several meetings, the participants identified with their own sketches. David collected all of these drawings and, based on them, prepared a professional architecture blueprint. At a community gathering, he showed his charts and asked if they wanted to build a toilet based on their drawings. The response was positive. Using community resources, they built the "toilet of their dreams" and continued to care for, protect, and maintain it.

From a dynamical perspective (see Chapter 4), David understood that costly head-on external interventions confronting the homeostatic status quo (old attractor) would all fail, and the only chance was to build a new attractor based on the dwellers' identification.

The new toilet, being a nice, clean spot, became a focal point for community meetings (e.g., for women coming to cook on the bio-gas derived from human waste). The success of the "toilet of their dreams" led the dwellers to think in a more entrepreneurial way about other undertakings as well.

After the success in Kibera, David's goal became to provide high-quality sanitation facilities accessible to other urban poor by connecting sanitation with the dignity of the people living in these communities. He is doing so by including and involving the community in the design, construction,

---

[4] Interviewed by the author of this book in Kampala on March 25, 2007.
[5] See www.ashoka.org/en-us/fellow/david-kuria#accordion. Accessed September 14, 2023.

and management of the facilities. He founded EcoTact, a global organization based in Nairobi and operating globally (Mohaupt & Ziegler, 2014).[6]

Lucky Chhetri, High Mountain Guide from Nepal

High in the Himalayas, villages are cut off from the world, and the journey for bread or other goods takes several days. Usually, the women stay in the villages while the men find work in the Kathmandu valley or in British or UN military missions as specialists in mountain operations.

In these high mountain villages, education is neglected as parents do not see any sense in educating girls due to a belief that they are destined to work solely in the household. Accessibility is also a challenge: Teachers sent by the government face difficulties in reaching these locations, especially considering the overall context of male occupational dominance in Nepal.

Lucky Chhetri,[7] who is from one of these villages, always had a drive for her own education, and wanted education to be available for girls from similar villages. However, she was not well accepted when talking to villagers. Learning from her failures, she understood that the educational offer should be shaped in a way that parents could see as natural and beneficial. Along these lines, she thought about founding a new profession for girls related to the mountains.

Such a profession could be as guides of high-altitude mountainous areas – a role traditionally performed only by men. She thought about establishing a female Himalayan guide school. This was about "their" mountains, after all, so she counted on parents' support; also, after the season, the girls would bring back some financial resources. Moreover, Lucky thought that, during the off-season, the students at her guiding school should be required to pass on their new-found knowledge to other children and women in their villages. Thanks to this, the girls would not only bring in an income, but also become valued educators.

During the training, she planned to teach the girls English (needed to communicate with clients), geography (for orientation in the field), biology (about the species found in the mountains), and so forth, effectively matching the regular school curriculum.

She thought that the planned school could be quite popular – and more so than traditional men's schools, given the empathy and lower

---

[6] See also www.circleofblue.org/2010/world/david-kuria-sanitation-and-toilet-entrepreneur/. Accessed September 14, 2023.
[7] Interviewed by the author of this book in Katmandu on June 27, 2004.

competitiveness of women. Indeed, her female guides soon outperformed the traditional men's guide schools and became famous in Nepal. This set a precedent for positive perceptions of the role and importance of women and contributed to a related mindset shift. Lucky, whose ideas were initially rejected, finally reached her goal to educate girls in hard-to-reach Himalayan settlements and, at the same time, changed the image of women in Nepal.[8]

Through dynamical lenses, Lucky, instead of pushing for education in high-mountain villages – difficult to access by teachers, expensive, and against traditional beliefs – built an alternative attractor: The girls' guide school, leading to a new equilibrium, bringing education to remote regions in a roundabout way and, in the long run, changing the previously dominant patterns of thinking about the role of women.

Lorenzo Lewis, Solving Mental Health Disparities in Communities of Color, USA

Lorenzo Lewis was born in prison, while his mother was serving a jail sentence. Raised by his aunt and uncle, he struggled with depression throughout his childhood, making him familiar with mental health services. As a teen, he joined street gangs and narrowly avoided being incarcerated. Luckily, he encountered positive mentors and became motivated to begin a journey toward wellness.

Delving into the mental problems of young African Americans, Lorenzo[9] learned – from his life experiences and from external literature – that significantly more young Black Americans commit suicide than White ones, yet, African Americans are 20 percent less likely to receive mental health treatment than the general population.

Against the prevailing public opinion that nothing could be done about this, he became committed to the idea of building a culture of mental health support for Black men. He understood that part of the problem is related to a reluctance to show "weakness," as well as the culture of stigma surrounding mental health. He kept thinking about and exploring how to change this pattern, and finally had an Aha! moment: Where do Black men and boys meet, sit, and chat? At the barbershop!

---

[8] See www.ashoka.org/en-us/fellow/lucky-chhetri#accordion; www.3sistersadventuretrek.com/blogs/3-sisters-mission-to-transform-nepals-mountain-guide-industry. Accessed September 14, 2023.
[9] Interviewed by the author of this book virtually in April 2022 and in person in Washington DC in June 2022.

Lorenzo Lewis became the founding CEO of his Confess Project,[10] which trains barbers in Black barbershops across the USA how to listen, understand, and talk to men and boys who may show depression symptoms. Barbers share various narratives that enable emotional opening up, and guide individuals toward professional support. Additionally, Lorenzo prepares therapists in the neighborhood of these shops to understand the context and specifics of communities of color.

His Confess Project has (as of September 2023) trained 3,236 barbers and beauty professionals across the country in fifty-three cities and thirty states, reaching more than 2.4 million people per year. A Harvard study concluded that barbers equipped with a mental health lens have a significant impact on the mental health challenges in their communities and are critical agents for public health. Lorenzo Lewis has created a win–win situation for everyone, including barbers, who are happy to make a positive difference. He has achieved this through creating an alternative attractor: the involvement and empowerment of barbers.

Dr. Cindy Blackstock, Academic Researcher from Canada

Cindy Blackstock[11] from Canada was born to a First Nation father, spending her early years in the shadow of the repercussions of residential schools (which aimed to eradicate the Aboriginal language and culture), in which her father and many others had to participate. None of her family members were educated, and she was not aware of any First Nation person at that time who had graduated from high school. Her mother passed on to Cindy her spiritual heritage, embedded in nature. She remembered her mother asking, during walks, questions such as "What is below the ground?"

However, Dr. Blackstock was motivated by education and, against all odds, graduated and obtained a PhD in social work; she chose social work because she wanted to help the First Nation communities regain their child protection power, based on their traditional culture. Dr. Blackstock became the first Executive Director of the Caring for First Nation Children Society. She started with a six-month field study to understand the expectations of First Nation communities regarding the health of their families. With this research, and complemented by tradition, Dr. Blackstock developed a curriculum for Aboriginal and non-Aboriginal social workers, which is

---

[10] See www.theconfessprojectofamerica.org and www.ashoka.org/en-us/fellow/lorenzo-lewis. Accessed September 15, 2023.
[11] Interviewed by the author of this book in Toronto on May 5, 2010.

now part of the official program for any social worker dedicated to child protection in the province of British Columbia. She intentionally merges Western science with Indigenous knowledge and traditions, showing that these two can mesh well if perceived as complementing one another.

Dr. Blackstock[12] created the Touchstones of Hope for Indigenous Children, Youth and Families program.[13] One of the pillars of this organization is the reconciliation movement, which encourages grassroots approaches to caring for Indigenous children, engages in respectful collaboration, and works with Indigenous people participating in reconciliation initiatives. Moreover, the movement allows for respectful and meaningful relationships between Indigenous and non-Indigenous peoples to occur.

Community gatherings are held to create a vision of a healthy child and family, involving people who have traditionally been outside of the childcare system, to ensure that the resultant outcome is inclusive of all and open to new ideas. Symbolism is invoked throughout this process. For example, participants bring chosen stones or other objects appropriate to the culture, which they first touch with spiritual intention, then pile them all up to build a symbolic community committed to shared well-being. This is why Dr. Blackstock's approach is called Touchstones for Hope. The core idea is that, through several meetings, each community comes up with its own ideas and is then prompted to take responsibility for the realization of their dream vision for children, taken into its own hands. At the end of this process, each of the participants takes a stone from the pile, symbolizing their further identification with the gatherings' decisions and serving as a reminder of their personal responsibility for action. In this way, instead of implementing the Western social care system head-on, Cindy Blackstock created an alternative attractor referring to tradition.

As an academician, university professor, and researcher, she has published many articles in refereed journals and has implemented several systemic innovations – all merging the traditional culture with a modern Western approach.

Munir Hasan, Mathematician from Bangladesh

Munir Hasan,[14] as a student and graduate, made his living through statistical analysis jobs for businesses, which is what was expected of him

---

[12] See www.ashoka.org/en-us/fellow/cindy-blackstock. Accessed September 19, 2023.
[13] See https://fncaringsociety.com/touchstones-hope. Accessed September 19, 2023.
[14] Interviewed by the author of this book in Dhaka on November 23, 2007.

by those around him. Simultaneously, he was active in restoring a fading sports and cultural organization for students, which he later chaired. He was also a student movement leader at a time when student organizations were officially banned.

However, he postponed any profitable business opportunities for full-time involvement in pursuing his idea of transforming education into high-level mathematical teaching, hoping to encourage his country to be more "mathematical." He always dreamed of turning Bangladesh – a place where mathematics is taught at a dramatically low level – into a nation of world-class, advanced mathematicians, with strong representation at the International Mathematical Olympiads.

Exploring new ground, he talked to teachers and parents and discovered that all were satisfied with the existing low-level mathematical education (e.g., some parents said that children needed to know how to milk cows, not making complex calculations). Moreover, when Munir presented his idea to prepare students for the mathematical Olympiads, the predominant reaction was fear and anxiety.

Munir[15] found a way to circumvent resistance and introduce high-level mathematical education through joy: by introducing enjoyable festivals. Instead of "Olympiads," he proposed holding Mathematical Festivals. He organized pilot sessions in a few local schools. The first day involved singing, dancing, and jumping over a bonfire. Next, there was a public event, with students asking questions and teachers replying, to break the authoritarian tradition of students sitting quietly and not asking questions. Finally, there was the Olympiad itself. These events attracted public attention, with businesses, school authorities, and the local government participating, as well as the media broadcasting the colorful event, thus creating growth opportunities for schools. Simultaneously, Munir placed funny mathematical riddles in national newspapers, thereby gaining more attention, supported by TV footage from the Mathematical Festivals.

These festivals have spread over Bangladesh through a snowball effect, as other schools also wanted to attract the attention of the media and the authorities. All of these events have aggregated into a "mathematical fashion," with people wanting more mathematical riddles in newspapers and parents supporting their children in advancing their mathematical skills.

As a result, Bangladesh has been accepted into the International Mathematical Olympiads movement. To sustain this trend, Munir

---

[15] See www.ashoka.org/en-us/fellow/munir-hasan. Accessed September 14, 2023.

established a mathematical teachers association, which cares for high-level educational standards; moreover, he helped with an organization for university students willing to volunteer for arranging festivals and Olympiads all over the country.

All of the previous exogenous, expensive, and top-down attempts to improve the teaching level of mathematics failed, as the old attractor maintained the status quo. Munir created an alternative endogenous attractor, based on the bottom-up dynamics of people's involvement and identification. This alternative attractor led to the acceptance of a new system.

As mentioned, Bangladesh was accepted into the International Mathematical Olympiads movement, achieving several successes in global competitions. The increased interest in mathematics has resulted in more students enrolling in mathematical and technical studies.

C4G: Commonalities

All of the aforementioned C4Gs – Elizabeth Fry, David Kuria, Lucky Chhetri, Lorenzo Lewis, Cindy Blackstock, and Munir Hasan – went through the thinking, intending, transgression, and action paradox phases (see Chapter 8). They were contemplating and intending something that, at the time, was deemed unthinkable: to revolutionize and humanize the conditions in female prisons; to bring sanitation to the slums where all costly top-down attempts had failed; to provide education to girls from the high-mountain Himalayas; to create a novel model for First Nation childcare, blending traditional Aboriginal culture with a modern Western approach, based on rigorous studies; and to elevate mathematical education to a significantly higher level in Bangladesh. They were all motivated to transform themselves into C4Gs and take bold actions to pursue their ideas.

Moreover, all of these individuals demonstrated a high level of divergent thinking, having novel, breakthrough ideas related to their far-reaching vision and the strategies needed to achieve it. Elizabeth Fry had the novel idea of humanizing female prisons and found innovative ways to attract key actors in that field, as well as public opinion. She also founded the first national women's organization in Great Britain, opening up an avenue for women's social activity. David Kuria's innovation was to instigate a bottom-up movement for sanitation by enabling dwellers to experiment with drawing sketches of their dream toilets. Lucky Chhetri brought education to high-Himalayan girls by engaging them in the guiding profession and, through their success, changed perceptions of the role of women in Nepal. Lorenzo Lewis discovered a way to reach depressed Black men at risk of suicide by engaging barbers as those who create an open and encouraging environment for them to open up and, eventually, seek specialist support. Cindy Blackstock merged theory (rigorous academic research) with traditional Aboriginal culture and rituals, bringing a high-level childcare system to First Nation communities. Munir Hasan innovated a way to attract teachers, parents, and public opinion through organizing Mathematical Festivals, bringing colorful joy and becoming attractive to the media.

Looking at these cases from a dynamical perspective, these individuals at first encountered a certain homeostatic equilibrium (low-level mathematical engagement in Bangladesh, antisanitation tendencies in Kibera slums, etc.), that created a negative attractor that resulted in head-on change attempts failing in the long run. Instead of confronting this negative attractor directly, they each invented a novel and positive alternative attractor outside the direct confrontation area, making this new attractor grow and, with time, become dominant (see Chapter 4), thereby reversing the current system dynamics. Moreover, they all passed the singularity point, turning the impossible into the possible, and next paradoxically, out of this "impossible," achieving large-scale systemic change.

CHAPTER 16

Paradoxes in Psychotherapy

In Chapter 13, some exemplary ways of enhancing brain plasticity were presented. There are additional methods, such as medical approaches like transcranial magnetic stimulation (TMS), which are being used experimentally to enhance brain plasticity and recover function (Johnston, 2009). However, it is also possible to boost neuroplasticity through "just talking" (i.e., through psychotherapeutic interventions) (Gingell, 2020). This chapter focuses on modifying brain plasticity through psychotherapy.

Psychotherapy and Neuroplasticity

From a general perspective, psychotherapy can be seen as a specific and intensive learning context, and, as such, it is related to neuroplasticity. Psychological techniques stimulate new growth (neurogenesis) and increased connectivity of neurons (synaptic plasticity) (Cozolino, 2017). Appropriate psychological interventions open "windows of plasticity" (McEwen, 2016). Research demonstrates that successful psychotherapy is indeed correlated with changes in brain activity and connectivity (Gingell, 2020).

Interestingly, there are indications that Sigmund Freud, the founder of psychoanalysis, initially developed the concept of the "contact barrier" – that is, the synapse between neurons – and, hence, neuroplasticity (Doidge, 2007; Frank, 2008). In this way, psychoanalysis may be perceived as "neuroplastic therapy" (Frank, 2008).

Psychotherapy can instigate modifications in the neural mechanisms contributing to durable effects, thereby documenting a convergence between neuroscience and psychotherapy. The science of neurogenesis and synaptic neuroplasticity opens avenues for psychological interventions (Malhotra & Sahoo, 2017) aimed at *The Brain that Changes Itself* (the title of Norman Doidges' book, Doidges 2007).

Cognitive behavioral therapy (CBT) and other kinds of psychotherapies alter consciousness in important and lasting ways. Specifically, consciousness changes as a result of plasticity in the linked systems of the frontal, cingulate, and limbic cortices (Collerton, 2013).

Additionally, various forms of group psychotherapy influence the central nervous system through feedback loops from other participants; a secure attachment with others provides stable neurophysiological homeostasis. Group psychotherapy may be seen as regulatory attachment relationships aimed at revising implicit emotional memory of attachment patterns; along these lines, various forms of group psychotherapy may enhance growth in relevant neurocircuitry (Flores, 2014).

Measuring the effects of CBT for psychotic patients (N = 22, measured immediately and again after eight years) indicated that the rearrangement occurring at the neural level following psychotherapy may be a predictor for the subsequent recovery path of people with psychosis (Mason et al., 2017). Moreover, PTSD patients receiving trauma-focused CBT (N = 14) and eye movement desensitization and reprocessing (EMDR) showed statistically significant changes in clinical scores. Neuroimaging data suggested a neurophysiological base for clinical improvement (Santarnecchi et al., 2019). Similarly, patients with panic disorder either received four weekly CBT sessions or were allocated to a waiting group (N = 14 in both cases). Four sessions of CBT led to reductions in symptoms: 71 percent of the patients from the first group reached recovery status, compared to 7 percent in the waiting group. The brain hyperactivation, previously seen in panic disorder, was significantly normalized. Neural markers of anxiety changed very early during CBT, highlighting potential neural mechanisms that might drive clinical recovery (Reinecke et al., 2018).

These findings may indicate that neuroplasticity is an important variable involved in the changes appearing as a result of psychotherapy. Synaptic and neurogenesis plasticity, as indicated in Part 5, may – as a side effect – augment the brain's openness to paradoxes and contradictions – and, presumably, vice versa: Paradoxes may instigate neuroplasticity and contribute to improvement in patients in psychotherapy. This way of thinking led some psychotherapists to develop a paradoxical interventions (PDXI) method, using paradoxes as therapeutic techniques.

Also, this may occur conversely: an impairment of neuroplasticity may be a critical part of the development of neuropsychiatric disorders. In that case, interventions that augment neuroplasticity may reduce symptoms (e.g., depressive) when applied as stand-alone treatments (Wilkinson et al., 2019).

Paradox Psychology

> The curious paradox is that when I accept myself just as I am, then I can change.
>
> (Rogers, 1995)

The concept of paradox psychology (PDXI) was likely developed by the well-known psychotherapists of the 1960s and 1970s, including Milton Erickson, Viktor Frankl, Jay Haley, Virginia Satir, Salvador Minuchin, and Fritz Perls. However, the first to use this kind of intervention was Alfred Adler – Sigmund Freud's student and an Austrian psychotherapist – in the 1920s (Mozdzierz et al., 1976; Sheras et al., 1978). Dr. Eliot Kaplan, one of the current representatives of this approach, is known as "The World's Most Paradoxical Therapist"[1] (Kaplan, 2020). According to Kaplan, PDXI's innovative premise is that instead of trying to change separate aspects of behavior, emotions, or thoughts, it offers an overall shift in perspective called "existential reorientation." The process is counterintuitive, incorporating absurdity and humor; interventions simultaneously address the client on many levels and motivate the initially unmotivated (Kaplan, 2020).

Paradox psychology may be applied in various ways, such as paradoxical interventions, Gestalt paradoxical practice, and paradoxical intensions (Seltzer, 1986; Weeks & L'Abate, 1982).

Paradoxical Interventions

The paradoxical approach is used with various kinds of addressees. One example is working with alcoholic patients; for instance, some Alcoholic Anonymous (AA) steps may be analyzed from a paradoxical perspective. Step one states "We admit we were powerless over alcohol, that our lives had become unmanageable." In this way, one must acknowledge powerlessness to experience power in the recovery process; moreover, by admitting powerlessness, one regains power over one's life.

Humor is also important, as the humorous aspects of one's problems often help a client detach from the everyday pressures, feel more human, and experience enhanced self-esteem. Some exemplary therapist's paradoxical phrases may deny what is intended – for example, "I don't think you'll do this" or "This may sound strange to you." Other interventions may,

---

[1] See www.paradoxpsychology.com/dr-kaplan. Accessed July 3, 2024.

paradoxically, prescribe what is unwanted and destructive; for example, the continuation of maladaptive behavior (this time under the therapist's control) or the recommendation that a highly resistant client becomes even more resistant (Shore, 1981).

Milton H. Erickson's[2] session with an alcoholic war hero may serve as an illustration: he came to the therapist's office with an album of photographs of himself and press clippings highlighting his previous achievements. He showed this album to the therapist, who threw it into a trashcan, saying "It's nothing to do with you currently. Tell me how you start your binge." The war hero replied "Well, I set-up two boilermakers, I drink one and wash it down with a beer, and I drink the other and wash it down with a beer, and then I'm off." Erickson replied: "Okay, you will leave this office, you will proceed to the nearest bar, you will order two boilermakers, and after the first one you will say something about that bastard therapist; after picking up the second one you will say something about this bastard Milton Erickson, may he rot in hell. Goodbye, the session is over" (Keeney, 2002, p. 4). The therapeutic intention is to shatter the "I am a suffering hero" mindset focusing on drinking, as well as to implant a continuous internal dialogue with the therapist associated with the drinking process.

Another type of addressee for paradoxical interventions may be emotionally disturbed adolescents. An example (from Sheras & Jackson, 1978): Much larger and heavier 15-year-old boy Willie is constantly picking on a smaller 14-year-old boy, Richie, who is quite frail in comparison, and who comes from a strict religious background that forbids fighting. There is a very real danger that Richie could be badly hurt. Willie is also violating the school's rule of "No physical or verbal abuse."

The therapist suggested the following contract, which was to be followed for two weeks:

We, the undersigned, hereby agree:

(1) To show absolutely no friendly gesture, nor make any friendly comment to each other during our entire stay.
(2) To save up our anger at each other until the specified time we have set aside. This is to take place in the presence of the staff.

For agreeing to do the above, we will be granted an opportunity to:

- Be protected.

---

[2] Milton Hyland Erickson was a well-known American psychiatrist and psychotherapist in the first half of the twentieth century, whose work was documented by others as he did not leave any written reports.

- Be granted other privileges and/or benefits that the staff can provide or arrange through the school.

The outcome was that the destructive behaviors decreased, though they were not totally eliminated. Moreover, the boys demonstrated new friendly behaviors (Sheras & Jackson, 1978).

Paradoxical interventions may also be used for peacemaking. In the case of the Israeli–Palestinian conflict, paradoxical thinking was applied to exposing individuals to amplified messages reflecting their societal beliefs. In other words, the participants' convictions were exaggerated to an absurd level. In the context of an insurmountable, protracted conflict, this paradoxical intervention led to attitude moderation, even among the most adamant participants (Hameiri et al., 2018).

The following example of counseling marital problems through paradoxical interventions comes from the author's own practice, and it demonstrates the significance of humor: A young woman complained that, on the one hand, she and her partner had just got married, feeling love for each other. On the other hand, they were experiencing a field of disagreement: She loves dancing but her husband does not; instead, he is fond of reading books. When they were invited to a dance parties, her husband refused to go, and that disappointed her.

It seemed that there were no deeper emotional mechanisms involved: they simply differed when confronted with a reading–dancing choice. However, if this were to remain unaddressed for a longer time, it could potentially grow into a significant problem.

The counselor considered inviting them both for a few marital sessions, but he realized that they did talk openly to one another about this issue; hence, the marital session would not, in this situation, provide added value. Instead, there was a good opportunity for a paradoxical assignment.

The suggestion was that the next time there was an opportunity to go dancing, the wife should tell her husband that it is okay to go, as he will be welcome to read while they danced. At the party, she should suggest to her husband that he stand up with his book in his hand, placing his arms around her and holding the book behind her back, so that he could enjoy reading while they danced. Simultaneously, she would hold a book behind his back, and they would both dance and read together. To help her see how this could work, the counselor played a simulation game with her, with them both dancing while peeking at books held behind the back of the other.

The woman laughed for the rest of the session and took home the idea of reading while dancing to share with her husband. They both had fun at home, making light of the previously heavy problem. Thereafter, whenever the dance–read problem appeared, they both laughed, remembering the counselor's weird assignment.

At the marital level, the curative mechanism was replacing the previously separate dwelling on unmet needs with shared and bonding joy in remembering a funny idea. On the individual level, humor enabled the gaining of some psychological distance to one's own emotions by looking at oneself and the situation from outside the box (Praszkier, 2019).

Gestalt and the Paradoxical Theory of Change

In Gestalt therapy, the goal is to achieve a client's awareness, which includes knowing the environment, taking responsibility for choices, self-knowledge, self-acceptance, and the ability to establish contact with others. Awareness is seen here as both the content and the process, both of which progress to deeper levels as the therapy proceeds (Yontef, 1993).

The founder of Gestalt therapy, Fritz Perls, believed that the ultimate goal of psychotherapy is the achievement of a degree of integration that facilitates its own development (Perls, 1992). Perls highlighted the significance of phenomenological experience (Crocker, 1999; Latner, 2000; Yontef, 1993), reflected in his concept by shifting the patient's awareness from interpretations to experiencing the "here and now." Along these lines, rather than talking about a patient's critical person (e.g., a parent), a Gestalt therapist might ask him or her to imagine this person in the present (e.g., as if sitting opposite them on an empty chair), or imagining that the therapist is the parent; in both situations, the patient is asked to talk directly to that person, in the present (Melnick & Nevis, 2005; Yontef, 1993).

Gestalt therapy may be perceived as a paradoxical theater, wherein everything may play a role. For example, a Gestalt therapist might notice something about a nonverbal behavior or tone of voice; the therapist might then guide the client to explore or exaggerate this nonverbal behavior and fully experience how this reverberates in their emotions.

An example of the latter comes from a group therapy session,[3] during which one of the participants, John, wanted to present his emotional problem. While doing so, he often stopped talking and looked up at the

---

[3] Facilitated by Eric Marcus, a Gestalt therapist from the USA.

ceiling. The therapist commented that he had noticed these looks and suggested that John imagine that this spot on the ceiling is saying something to him: "Be this place on the ceiling you are looking at, and talk to yourself." The therapist facilitated a role-changing dialogue between John playing the ceiling spot and John himself. It appeared that even when speaking about emotional problems, there is a compulsion to intellectualize instead of to feel, and looking at the ceiling represented a search for intellectualization. Furthermore, the patient gained insight into him having built a defense system against direct contact with his own feelings, seen as a threat. When asked who the person is that he associates with this threat, John mentioned his father and his early childhood. The therapist did not allow John to talk about this relationship in the past tense; instead, he placed an empty chair in front of John, asking him to imagine that his father was sitting there. Next, John took the place on this chair and spoke to himself, playing the role of his father, before changing place to his chair and replying to his imagined father. The dialogue continued until it resulted in a release of emotions and thus lead to further insights.

The Gestalt theory of change states that change occurs when one becomes what he or she is, not when he or she tries to become what he or she is not. Change is not possible when one pushes oneself to change; change happens only if one takes the time and effort to be what one is – to be fully immersed in one's current position. That is why the therapy flow is always brought to the "here and now," as illustrated in the example of John's session. Paradoxically, by rejecting the role of a "change agent," and instead suggesting experiencing the "how" of the "here and now," the Gestalt therapist makes meaningful and orderly change possible. In other words, the Gestalt therapist rejects the role of a changemaker, for his strategy is to encourage the patient to fully experience where and what he or she is (especially in one's mind and imagination) and, in this way, paradoxically open up an avenue for change (Beisser, 1970).

Paradoxical Intention

Paradoxical intention (PI) is a psychotherapeutic technique intended for patients with severe anxiety disorders, and was coined in 1959 by Victor Frankl (Frankl, 2006). It is a cognitive technique that involves persuading a patient to engage in their most feared behavior, thereby rehearsing the anxiety-inducing pattern (Ascher & Efran, 1978; Sutton, 2022).

For example, patients with stagefright would be asked to imagine performing and augmenting the associated feelings of anxiety. Similarly, a person who is afraid of blushing in front of others would be assigned a task to try to blush even more during such encounters (Ascher, 2002; Sutton, 2022).

In the case of hard-to-treat insomnia, there may be a recommendation to try to remain awake as long as possible, rather than attempting to fall asleep (Ascher & Efran, 1978; Espie, 2011). Additionally, PI works with stuttering patients: Instead of traditional suggestions to combat stuttering, the PI technique indicates its enhancement (e.g., looking in the mirror and stammering as much as possible). In this way, the patient gains control over their stammering, the first step of which is through its augmentation (Frankl, 1985, 2006).

The curative factor of PI may relate to the control mechanisms: Symptoms such as stage fright, blushing, or stammering may be out of a patient's control, completely overwhelming and absorbing emotional and cognitive reactions. Intentionally increasing these symptoms automatically restores control over them. Being able to augment blushing means that there is a mechanism for controlling its level. Based on the regained control, the patient may then try to use this new ability in the opposite way – that is, to decrease the symptoms.

PI may also be applied to family therapy. An example from the author's own family therapy practice: During several family sessions (mother, father, teenage son, and a younger daughter), it became apparent that the mother is overcontrolling the other family members. Addressing this problem head-on would make the mother feel hurt and, as a result, defensive. The therapist decided to apply a paradox intention technique, without labeling the issue as a problem of control. The recommendation was that, until the next session, the mother should make meticulous notes on what the other family members were doing. The primary intention was to provide space for the mother to reflect on her controlling behavior. The secondary intention was to create a situation whereby the mother delegated control to someone else – namely, the therapist, as she is following his recommendations and, in this way, relinquishing control. Moreover, the therapist expected that while making these notes, she would most probably explain to the rest of the family that she is doing this because of the therapist's assignment, conveying between the lines a message that "It is not me controlling you." Indeed, in the next session the mother and the other family members united in complaining about this burdensome task and praising, in unison, an anticontrolling style. Consequently, during subsequent sessions, it turned out that the family was self-modifying their relationships.

The Distance Hypothesis: Paradoxes Open an Outside-the-Box Perspective

In exploring the mechanisms that foster individual change through paradoxical interventions, there seems to be an open space for deeper-level interpretations. One hypothesis is that paradoxes induce neuroplasticity and openness to novel perspectives on one's own problems, possibly by developing some distance from one's own problems by enabling an outside-the-box point of view. The following provides an elaboration of the distance hypothesis.

The question is how spatial or temporal distance reflects in the level of creativity. To test the hypothesis that spatial distance enhances creative thinking, a study was conducted. Subjects were randomly divided into three groups: The first was told that the following story happened nearby, the second that it occurred far away, and the third was a control group with no spatial indication. All three groups heard the same story:

> A prisoner wanted to escape from a high storey of a jail. He found a rope, but it was only half as long as needed to reach the ground safely. He divided the rope in half, tied the two parts together, and safely escaped.

The subjects were asked how could he have done this. Finding the solution required creative thinking, as "dividing the rope" is commonly understood as cutting it into two pieces, which is not at all helpful for escape. To find an alternative solution, the subjects needed to realize that instead of cutting the rope in half, the prisoner untangled the rope longitudinally and tied the two strands together, achieving enough length to reach the ground.

The study revealed that those participants who envisioned the story happening far away performed significantly better than those thinking that it was just around the corner, and also better than the control group with no indication of distance (Jia et al., 2009; Shapira & Liberman, 2009). The conclusion confirmed the hypothesis that spatial distance augments creativity.

Similarly, studies on the role of temporal distance in creative thinking confirmed that performing tasks whilst imagining that they are happening in the distant future prompts higher-level creativity than being convinced that the task is performed in the present time (Liberman et al., 2002).

These studies suggest that paradoxes create a distance that induces a more creative approach, especially to one's own problems in the psychotherapeutic process. Interestingly, the diversity of experiences, along with temporal and spatial distance, may also augment neuroplasticity and thus increase openness to embracing new perspectives (Fischer, 2005).

CHAPTER 17

Life and Paradoxes

There are numerous paradoxical situations in life and work. This chapter provides several related examples and, where available, research results. It also presents the paradoxical benefits of chaos.

Paradoxes Are Natural

> Life is a preparation for the future; and the best preparation for the future is to live as if there were none.
> Albert Einstein (Satish, 2022)

Paradoxes are an inevitable part of people's life. For example, people desire freedom of choice, yet the more options they have, the less comfortable they feel. This is called the paradox of choice: On the one hand, there is no real freedom without choice; on the other hand, choice-induced paralysis may occur, indicating diminished rather than enhanced freedom. This situation is evident when individuals are offered too many options for a product, resulting in discomfort. Another example is when a doctor presents a sick patient with various treatment options, accompanied by a list of their limitations, benefits, and risks. The patient may feel overwhelmed by the array of choices and is likely to seek advice from the doctor, effectively delegating their freedom of choice. Experiments have shown that an excessive number of choices rarely makes people better off (Schwartz, 2004, 2015). In one of these experiments, the subjects ($N = 24$) had to choose the best result for a given query within 30 seconds, from a pool of either few or many items. It was found that choosing from fewer items (six items) resulted in higher satisfaction and greater confidence in the correctness of one's choice than choosing from a larger pool (24 items) (Oulasvirta et al., 2009).

The relationship paradox pertains to independence and establishing satisfactory relationships: Attachment theory (Cassidy, 2016) suggests that being able to trust and depend on certain people (e.g., parents and friends) creates a secure base and a gateway to increased independence in establishing relationships (Levy, 2021). The paradox lies in the idea that the more attached you are, the better off you are at being independent.

The paradox of inquiry (also known as the Learner or Meno's paradox) was mentioned by Plato in a dialogue between Socrates and Meno, where Meno indicates that if you know what you are looking for, inquiry is unnecessary (White, 1976). This is currently presented as the paradox of inquiry: If you do not know what you are looking for, inquiry is impossible. Therefore, inquiry is either unnecessary or impossible. The paradox also relates to connecting the act of searching to the event of finding, similar to how we describe the ideas of knowledge and ignorance as opposite and unrelated (Arfini, 2023).

Some authors also mention the group relationship paradox, referring to the balance between opposites: competition and cooperation (Gnyawali et al., 2016). Conflicts between individuals or factions within a group often create seemingly contradictory situations, causing even the best teams to sometimes get stuck. As a constructive way out, paradoxical suggestions are sometimes prescribed for dynamic action and performance, such as inviting a success-oriented group to risk failure or suggesting going down a dead-end to stimulate the group to revolt and focus on moving ahead (Smith & Berg, 1987).

The Paradox of the Positive Role of Chaos

The predominant view is that tight schedules, organization, neatness, and consistency are the keys to success. Based on case studies, the book *A Perfect Mess: The Hidden Benefits of Disorder* documents the opposite: That moderately messy systems are more efficient in using resources, generate better solutions, and are more resilient than neat ones (Abrahamson & Freedman, 2007). Nonlinear dynamical systems analysis confirms that chaotic complex systems (see Chapter 4) often demonstrate flexibility and adaptability, as well as order achieved through self-organization (Schuldberg, 1999).

It has also been documented, via an experiment, that chaos instigates creativity. The experiment verified the conjecture that order in the environment supports traditional and conventional thinking, whereas disorder supports novel and atypical paths. The subjects were placed in a waiting room; one randomly selected group waited in a neat and orderly room, and the other group in a messy and disorderly setting. This resulted in the participants from the disorderly room being significantly more creative than the participants in the orderly one (Vohs et al., 2013).

On a larger-scale operational level, an intriguing report on the competition between an orderly and a messy pharmaceutical company is as follows. The first one (Big Pharma) was stable, and competently and traditionally managed. The latter (Paris Jussieu) was going through a period of reconstruction and displacement (due to asbestos removal). Employees were dislodged from their offices and moved to interim, and shifting, workplaces. Thus, they repeatedly changed locations, meeting new colleagues each time.

Paradoxically, the firm experiencing chaos lodged more patents and published more papers than the stable one. Paris Jussieu staff were more likely to collaborate with their new neighbors, learning about their ideas, and – through the new encounters and inspirations – initiating new mutual projects and publications (Catalini, 2017; Lindsay, 2015). Due to the chaos, with employees shuffled to new places and randomly meeting associates from various departments and of diverse management levels (i.e., people they would not have otherwise met in a stable situation), the company initiated creative activities and generated novel ideas. It turns out that due to accidental (chaotic) meetings, employees who were usually isolated in their stable offices got "booster shots" of creative inspiration (Lindsay, 2015). Diving into the phenomenon of encountering various coworkers in diverse settings (colocation), Christian Catalin from the Sloan MIT School of Management documented that colocation is significant for the rate, direction, and quality of scientific collaboration (Catalini, 2017).

Drawing from this experience, there emerged a new approach to designing workspaces, fostering random connections between less familiar or unknown coworkers. One example is arranging the central space around a coffee machine, prompting staff to sit, sip coffee, and meet randomly with colleagues from different departments and different management levels. Paradoxically, companies promote chaotic meetings and chats during work time, as this yields a significant return. This solution, called "Coffee Machine Syndrome," becomes a source of new inspirations and cooperation (Eagle, 2004).

These chaos-to-order inspirations may drive current leaders to facilitate connections, colocation, inclusion, and working together (Dauer, 2020). Especially noteworthy is that the well-known Visa International was driven by a new organizational form, termed by Dee Hock, the founding CEO, as "chaordic" – that is, simultaneously chaotic and orderly. In his book *Birth of the Chaordic Age*, Hock credited the worldwide success of Visa to its chaordic structure (Hock, 2000).

Another example of paradoxically positive implications of chaos comes from the battlefield (during the first Gulf War), where the traditional top-down structure was replaced by decentralized management: General Stanley McCrystal believed that if soldiers interacting on the ground were free to come up with bottom-up decisions, they would be better able to handle situations as they arose. A more "chaotic" organization would be nimbler. General McChrystal discarded centuries of conventional military management traditions and, during the war, remade the Task Force into a nimble network. Criticized for causing chaos, General McCrystal documented that this shift was significantly successful (McChrystal, 2015).On a lighter note, following Albert Einstein's saying "If a cluttered desk is a sign of a cluttered mind, of what, then, is an empty desk a sign?",[1] one may want to have a look at the article *The Famous Creatives That Had a Messy Desk and Why You Should Too*, which features photos of what Albert Einstein's, Mark Twain's, and Steve Job's desks really looked like.[2]

The Paradox of Synchronization

Chaos and synchronization are closely related (Eroglu et al., 2017; Tang et al., 1983). Indeed, the synchronization of chaotic dynamics has attracted academic attention (Parlitz et al., 2007). For the lay-reader (i.e., the nonmathematician), this may be visible in some video documentations – for example, how chaotic puppies organize themselves into perfect sync,[3] or infants synchronize a body-language dialogue.[4]

Synchronization is defined as the coordination of events to operate a system in unison; it is a pervasive concept relevant to diverse domains in physics, biology, and the social sciences (Ramseyer & Tschacher, 2006). Sync can be considered if the properties of two subsystems (interacting parts of a larger system) agree in time (Brown & Kocarev, 2000).

Synchronization is, by itself, an intriguing phenomenon; it has engaged well-known scientists such as Albert Einstein, Henri Poincaré, Niels Bohr, and Norbert Wiener (see Strogatz, 2003), as well as lay-observers, in

---

[1] See Burkus, D. (2016). When To Say Yes To The Messy Desk. *Forbes*. Retrieved from: www.forbes.com/sites/davidburkus/2014/05/23/when-to-say-yes-to-the-messy-desk/. Accessed July 3, 2024.
[2] See www.canva.com/learn/creative-desks/. Accessed October 13, 2023.
[3] See www.youtube.com/watch?v=oY8-IzPo1lw. Accessed October 24, 2023.
[4] See www.youtube.com/watch?v=bHcXWNyxeTg. Accessed October 24, 2023.

watching how elegantly metronomes synchronize,[5] birds form a V-shaped flock,[6] and audiences clap in rhythm.[7]

Systems as diverse as clocks, metronomes, blinking fireflies, singing crickets, cardiac pacemaker cells, firing neurons, menstrual cycles, coupled lasers, and applauding audiences exhibit a tendency to operate in synchrony (Pikovsky et al., 2003; Strogatz, 2003). This phenomenon is universal and relates to inanimate matter, as well as to biological systems, including brains, individuals, groups, and families. Interestingly, it may have been the blinking-in-unison fireflies that triggered the first interest in sync; for example, one of the first articles on the synchronization of these blinking insects appeared in 1917 in the journal *Science* (Laurent, 1917).

Similarly, human sync is of interest to scientists, especially how minds, individuals, and groups synchronize, as well as the results of this process. Synchronization among humans seems to be an avenue to "the possible," as it facilitates synchronized actions (Fitzpatrick et al., 2016), better communication and social coherence (De Vignemont & Singer, 2006), increased task performance (Barsade, 2002), and better cooperation (Wiltermuth & Heath, 2009).

The paradox is that probably only unorganized, chaotic systems can generate higher-order synchronization – for example, blinking fireflies, self-organizing V-shaped flocks of birds, or strangers in an audience, each different, eventually catching a common clapping rhythm. On the contrary, well-orchestrated systems tend to repeat their preset patterns rather than transform into new sync.

Artificial Intelligence and Its Paradoxes

Artificial intelligence (AI) paradoxes were first mentioned by Hans Moravec, a professor at the Robotics Institute of Carnegie Mellon University in Pittsburgh, USA. He wrote as early as 1988 that research documented that for AI, the hard problems are easy and the easy problems are hard (Moravec, 1990). In other words, tasks that are easy for humans to perform (e.g., motor or social skills, or activities such as those gained as babies and toddlers – perception, communication, movement, etc.) are difficult for machines to replicate, whereas tasks that are difficult for humans (e.g., performing mathematical calculations or large-scale data analysis) are relatively easy for machines to accomplish (Arora, 2023; Jeevanandam, 2022).

---

[5] See, for example, www.youtube.com/watch?v=W1TMZASCR-I&t=6s. Accessed April 30, 2021.
[6] See www.youtube.com/watch?v=9l_uDJL-WAo. Accessed April 30, 2021.
[7] See www.youtube.com/watch?v=GRRtdpiyQMo. Accessed April 30, 2021.

Indeed, babies and toddlers learn through chaotic trials: being unexpectedly hugged, burning their fingers on a candle, swallowing a piece of a toy, being suddenly tickled by a loved uncle, having their bucket taken by another child in the sandpit, falling, experiencing fear of a monster, playing "peek-a-boo" with mom, and so forth. It is impossible to simulate this random and chaotic sequence of events. However, they all stimulate brain plasticity, and, in a feedback loop, a higher level of neuroplasticity fosters cognitive and affective development. Later, encounters and communication with others are largely random as well. The feedback we receive from these encounters contributes to our perception of the world and ourselves in a gene/environment or heritability/malleability interplay (Sauce & Matzel, 2018). In this vein, it is a chaotic process that builds up our neuronal processes, and – in this way – our identity. Moravec's paradox accurately states that these random processes are too difficult for AI.

There are other AI paradoxes mentioned in the literature. However, the caveat is that AI, being a trendy topic, generates various seemingly attractive speculations, albeit many of them, in fact, obvious.[8] Therefore, a critical distance is recommended regarding the following:

- On the one hand, AI aims to increase automation; on the other hand, it also requires more human involvement to reflect on the insights generated (automation paradox).
- AI generates job losses; however, it also creates new jobs – for example, providing the necessary support systems for those newly unemployed (transition paradox).
- AI takes over the creative process; however, it also offers new creative opportunities (creativity paradox). This may include AI support of our writings as opposed to generating fake news.
- AI can be used both for the public good and for harm, authoritarianism, and aggression (Michael et al., 2023).

This is probably an open issue as, while AI develops, more related paradoxes will likely emerge. One intriguing path is analyzing how traditional philosophy influences AI progress. For example, following Heidegger's thinking, one may reflect that if a computer is based on representations of the current state of the world, and something in the world changes, how does the program determine which of its represented facts can be assumed to have stayed the same and which might need to be updated (the so-called "frame problem") (Dreyfus, 2007).

---

[8] Citing Professor Jacek Koronacki, mathematician and AI expert (private correspondence).

Discussion and Summary

Paradoxes are not only quip puns (see examples in the Introduction). They often come from philosophy and are present in the academic literature (see Chapter 1). However, they can also serve as action-drivers. Elaborating on the concept of possibilitivity (i.e., perceiving insurmountable challenges as doable; see Chapter 7), Chapter 15 presented various examples of transcending the impossible in the field of social activities. Chapter 16 provided an overview of applications of paradoxical interventions in psychotherapy. Chapter 17 demonstrated paradoxes in life, including the astounding paradox that chaos may play a positive role in various settings.

It is worth mentioning that, in line with this section's various examples, chaos theory has been efficiently applied to explaining various phenomena in the natural sciences, such as in psychology (Ayers, 1997) and AI.

Finally, chaos and synchronization are, paradoxically, interrelated. Chaos can foster an ambience for the emergence of a higher order. Additionally, there seems to be an overall tendency to synchronize, both for inanimate matter and for living nature.

CHAPTER 18

Précis

> How wonderful that we have met with a paradox. Now we have some hope of making progress.
>
> Niels Bohr (Moore, 1966)

Paradoxes may be perceived as the core of philosophy, blending their amplified form, as well as their radical essence, while engaging with the seemingly obvious. Being paradoxical often impacts both meaning in life and the meaning of life (Smilansky, 2022).

This book is a journey through the meaning and essence of paradoxes, the way our minds deal with them (i.e., paradoxical or Janusian thinking), and how societal dynamics sometimes generate unpredictable, astounding phenomena. It delves into the mind's specific characteristics that enable perceiving insurmountable challenges as doable and, furthermore, how this way of thinking contributes to peacemaking. Moreover, it analyzes the paradoxical aspects of creativity, demonstrating the mechanisms that foster divergent thinking and neuroplasticity and the role of joy, while the dynamical approach to paradoxes is also considered. Finally, it presents paradoxes in action: How to predict the unpredictable, the essence and examples of changers-for-good, as well as how paradoxes are harnessed in psychotherapeutic processes, and how they occur in various life situations (e.g., how chaos turns into order and AI and its paradoxes).

The specificity of this book is that it stands as an exploration of the paradox phenomenon on various levels: philosophical, psychological, sociological, dynamical, and neuroscientific. It does so through literature and research reviews, illustrated by multiple and diverse case studies.

This book seems to be the first step in this kind of interdisciplinary approach to the phenomenon of paradoxes and paradoxical thinking. There are many more paradoxical occurrences to explore, a few examples of which are provided here.

The Paradox of Generosity

A comprehensive US-based study based on a survey (N = 2,000), plus in-depth interviews ($N > 60$), revealed a significant link between generosity and living a better life: More generous people are happier, suffer fewer illnesses and injuries, live with a greater sense of purpose, and experience less depression. These positive outcomes are especially related to generosity practiced regularly (random acts of kindness are not enough) (Smith & Davidson, 2014). The title of this book – *Giving We Receive, Grasping We Lose* – reveals the paradox of giving: The more we give, the more we have.[1] This paradox of generosity, as well as the following paradox of happiness, seems worthy of further study.

Paradox of Happiness

Happiness, if pursued directly and deliberately, turns out to be self-deceptive, as it undermines meaning. Instead, it is recommended to participate in meaningful activities and relationships. The paradox of happiness says that striving for happiness undermines happiness; instead, doing meaningful things and having meaningful relationships fosters happiness as an indirect result (Martin, 2012; Zerwas & Ford, 2021). The paradox of happiness also relates to groups, such as a community or a society: They are plausibly less happy if happiness is their core collective ultimate objective, as compared to when other values comprise their collective objectives (Eggleston, 2013).

The Importance of Recognizing Paradoxes

Identifying and embracing paradoxes is not only an exercise of our mind. An openness and a propensity to paradoxes may be a source of inspiration and a fulcrum for novel and successful actions. This tendency, called *paradoxicality* (see Chapter 2) may augment creativity and neuroplasticity (Part 5). There seems to be an importance for paradoxicality: Realizing and highlighting paradoxes fosters unique opportunities to acquire new knowledge and challenge truths assumed thus far (Hsiung, 2022; Pascual-Leone, 2010).

---

[1] One of the examples is Oseola McCarty's story; see https://underthrow.substack.com/p/the-giving-paradox?utm_source=profile&utm_medium=reader2. Accessed November 4, 2023.

The aim whilst writing this academic book was to keep it as simple as possible, being inspired by Albert Einstein's saying, "If you cannot explain it simply, you do not understand it well enough."[2]

I also aimed to open avenues beyond logical reasoning (see Chapter 13) – again, being inspired by Albert Einstein, who said that logic will get you from A to B, imagination will take you everywhere (Coleman, 2013).

The Wonder

Paradoxes generally arouse surprise and wonder. The latter is perceived as a special starting point for philosophy (Haralambous & Nielsen, 2013), seemingly because it is a transformational state of mind in which we become aware of an expanded field of possibility (Glăveanu, 2023). The wonder of paradoxicality is an apparent impossibility that requires courage to face (Heaton, 2014). It is left to the reader's reflection whether this author is right in holding that the wonder of paradoxicality can have the power to drive human development (Heaton, 2014).

On a more personal note, thirty-five years ago, as a psychotherapist, I wrote a pamphlet titled "On Philosophy of Wonder."[3] The conclusion was that encountering extraordinary human situations is always a wonder, and as such, it becomes a key to understanding, instead of relying on routine interpretations based on therapeutic ideologies.

Concluding Paradox

Finally, pushing eighty years of age, I always keep in mind Mark Twain's paradoxical saying: "Age is an issue of mind over matter: if you do not mind, it does not matter."

---

[2] There are some doubts as if this was really Albert Einstein's saying, or maybe Richard Fenman's? See, for example, https://skeptics.stackexchange.com/questions/8742/did-einstein-say-if-you-cant-explain-it-simply-you-dont-understand-it-well-en. Accessed July 18, 2024.
[3] Praszkier, R. (1989). *On Philosophy of Wonder*. TPD 124.

References

Aaron, D. B., Kelly, M. S., Trapp, N. T., Stern, A. P., Press, D. Z., & Pascual-Leone, A. (2018). Noninvasive brain stimulation: Challenges and opportunities for a new clinical specialty. *Neuropsychiatry, 30*(3), 173–179. https://doi.org/10.1176/appi.neuropsych.17110262.

Abaza, M. (2011). Revolutionary moments in Tahrir Square. *Global Dialogue.* https://globaldialogue.isa-sociology.org/articles/revolutionary-moments-in-tahrir-square. Accessed March 31, 2023.

Abbott, L. F., & Nelson, S. B. (2000). Synaptic plasticity: Taming the beast. *Nature Neuroscience, 3*(11), 1178–1183. https://doi.org/10.1038/81453.

Abraham, A. (2018). *The Neuroscience of Creativity.* Cambridge University Press.

Abrahamson E., & Freedman D. H. (2007). *A Perfect Mess: The Hidden Benefits of Disorder.* Little, Brown.

Ackermann, R. (1991). Super pragmatic paradoxes. In I. Mahalingam & B. Carr (Eds.) *Logical Foundations: Essays in Honor of D. J. O'Connor*, pp. 3–10. Palgrave Macmillan. https://doi.org/10.1007/978-1-349-21232-3_1.

Aharon, I., Etcoff, N., Ariely, D., Chabris, C. F., O'Connor, E., & Breiter, H. C. (2001). Beautiful faces have variable reward value: fMRI and behavioral evidence. *Neuron, 32*(3), 537–551. https://doi.org/10.1016/s0896-6273(01)00491-3.

Ahmad, W., Kutan, A. M., & Gupta, S. (2021). Black swan events and COVID-19 outbreak: Sector level evidence from the US, UK, and European stock markets. *International Review of Economics & Finance, 75*, 546–557. https://doi.org/10.1016/j.iref.2021.04.007.

Akhtar, M. (2008). What is self-efficacy? Bandura's 4 sources of efficacy beliefs. *Positive Psychology.* http://positivepsychology.org.uk/self-efficacy-definition-bandura-meaning/. Accessed May 27, 2023.

Alenina, N., & Klempin, F. (2015). The role of serotonin in adult hippocampal neurogenesis. *Behavioural Brain Research, 15*(277), 49–57. https://doi.org/10.1016/j.bbr.2014.07.038.

Alexander, A. (2011). Egypt's Muslims and Christians join hands in protest. *BBC News.* www.bbc.com/news/world-middle-east-12407793. Accessed April 2, 2023.

Allagui, I., & Kuebler, J. (2011). The Arab Spring and the role of ICTs. *International Journal of Communication, 5*, 1435–1442.

Alonso, R. (2010). Counter-narratives against ETA's terrorism in Spain. In National Coordinator for Counterterrorism (Eds.) *Countering Violent Extremist Narratives*, pp. 20–35. www.clingendael.org/sites/default/files/pdfs/Countering-violent-extremist-narratives.pdf. Accessed March 26, 2023.

Amabile, T. M. (1996). *Creativity in Context: Update to the Social Psychology of Creativity*. Westview Press.

Anderson, S. C., Branch, T. A., Cooper, A. B., & Dulvy, N. K. (2017). Black-swan events in animal populations. *PNAS, 114*(12), 3252–3257. https://doi.org/10.1073/pnas.1611525114.

Andrews, K. T. (2004). *Freedom Is a Constant Struggle*. University of Chicago Press.

Antipova, T. (2021). Coronavirus pandemic as black swan event. In T. Antipova (Ed.) *Integrated Science in Digital Age. ICIS 2020. Lecture Notes in Networks and Systems, vol. 136*. Springer. https://doi.org/10.1007/978-3-030-49264-9_32.

Arancegui, M. N., Querejeta, M. J. A., & Montero, E. M. (2011). Smart specialization strategies: The case of the Basque Country. Basque Institute of Competitiveness. 2011-R07. https://citeseerx.ist.psu.edu/document?repid=rep1&type=pdf&doi=7be908fc3ca0a065120465da5d3b4db8f09e4026. Accessed March 27, 2023.

Arfini, S. (2023). Serendipity and ignorance studies. In S. Copeland, W. Ross, & M. Sand (Eds.) *Serendipity Science*, pp. 125–143. Springer. https://doi.org/10.1007/978-3-031-33529-7_7.

Argomaniz, J. (2019). *Civil Action and the Dynamics of Violence*. Oxford University Press.

Aristotle (2016). *Metaphysics*. Hackett Publishing Company.

Aristotle (2018). *Physics VI*. Hackett Publishing Co.

Arora, A. (2023). Moravec's paradox and the fear of job automation in health care. *The Lancet, 402*(10397), 180–181. https://doi.org/10.1016/S0140-6736(23)01129-7.

Ascher, L. M. (2002). Paradoxical intention. In M. Hersen & W. Sledge (Eds.) *Encyclopedia of Psychotherapy*, pp. 331–338. Academic Press.

Ascher, L. M., & Efran, J. S. (1978). Use of paradoxical intention in a behavioral program for sleep onset insomnia. *Journal of Consulting and Clinical Psychology, 46*(3), 547–550. https://doi.org/10.1037//0022-006x.46.3.547.

Ash, T. G. (2002). *The Polish Solidarity*. Yale University Press.

Ashkenas, R., & Bodell, L. (2013). Nice managers embrace conflict, too. *Harvard Business Review*. https://hbr.org/2013/10/nice-managers-embrace-conflict-too. Accessed June 19, 2023.

Askenasy, J., & Lehmann, J. (2013). Consciousness, brain, neuroplasticity. *Frontiers in Psychology, 4*. https://doi.org/10.3389/fpsyg.2013.00412.

Astrain, L. N., & Stephens, M. (2013). *The Basques: Their Struggle for Independence*. Welsh Academic Press.

Avetisov, V., Gorsky, A., Maslov, S., Nechaev, S., & Valba, O. (2018). Phase transitions in social networks inspired by the Schelling model. *Physical Review E, 98*, 032308. https://doi.org/10.1103/PhysRevE.98.032308.

Ayers, S. (1997). The application of chaos theory to psychology. *Theory & Psychology, 7*(3), 373–398. http://dx.doi.org/10.1177/0959354397073005.

Bach-y-Rita, E. (1980). Neuroplasticity and the Feldenkrais method. *Feldenkrais Centre Vancouver*. https://feldenkraisvancouver.com/wp-content/uploads/2016/07/5-ARTICLESFeldenkraisMethodandNeuroplasticity.pdf. Accessed August 27, 2023.

Backman, M. E., & Tuckman, B. W. (1972). Review of *Remote Associates* Test by Sarnoff A. Mednick, Martha T. Mednick. *Journal of Educational Measurement*, 9(2), 161–162. http://www.jstor.org/stable/1433810.

Baixauli, E. (2017). Happiness: Role of dopamine and serotonin on mood and negative emotions. *Open Access Emergency Medicine*, 7(2).

Bakke, D. W. (2006). *Joy at Work: A Revolutionary Approach To Fun on the Job*. Pear Press.

Ballard, I. C., Murty, V. P., Carter, R. M., MacInnes, J. J., Huettel, S. A., & Adcock, R. A. (2011). Dorsolateral prefrontal cortex drives mesolimbic dopaminergic regions to initiate motivated behavior. *The Journal of Neuroscience*, 31(28), 10340–10346. https://doi.org/10.1523/JNEUROSCI.0895-11.2011.

Bandura, A. (1977). Self-efficacy: Toward a unifying theory of behavioral change. *Psychological Review*, 84(2), 191–215. https://doi.org/10.1037/0033-295X.84.2.191.

Bandura, A. (1982). Self-efficacy mechanism in human agency. *American Psychologist*, 37(2), 122–147. https://doi.org/10.1037/0003-066X.37.2.122.

Bardis, P. D. (1983). Irenometer: A scale for the measurement of attitudes toward peace. *South African Journal of Sociology*, 15(3), 122–123. https://doi.org/10.1080/02580144.1984.10428993.

Barnett, B. M. (1993). Invisible southern Black women leaders in the Civil Rights Movement: The triple constraints of gender, race, and class. *Gender & Society*, 7(2), 162–182. https://doi.org/10.1177/089124393007002002.

Barron, C., & Barron, A. (2013). *The Creativity Cure: A Do-It-Yourself Prescription for Happiness*. Scribner.

Barsade, S. G. (2002). The ripple effect: Emotional contagion and its influence on group behavior. *Administrative Science Quarterly*, 47(4), 644–675. https://doi.org/10.2307/3094912.

Bar-Tal, D. (2007). Sociopsychological foundations of intractable conflicts. *American Behavioral Scientist*, 50(11), 1430–1453. https://doi.org/10.1177/0002764207302462.

Bar-Tal, D., Hameiri, B., & Halperin, E. (2021). Paradoxical thinking as a paradigm of attitude change in the context of intractable conflict. *Advances in Experimental Social Psychology*, 63, 129–187. https://doi.org/10.1016/bs.aesp.2020.11.003.

Bartoli, A. (2021). Glimmers of hope for peace in South Sudan: The role of Sant'Egidio in peace processes. https://kroc.nd.edu/news-events/events/2021/11/11/glimmers-of-hope-for-peace-in-south-sudan-the-role-of-santegidio-in-peace-processes/. Accessed April 27, 2024.

Bartoli, A., Bui-Wrzosinska, L. & Nowak, A. (2010). Peace is in movement: A dynamical systems perspective on the emergence of peace in Mozambique. *Peace and Conflict: Journal of Peace Psychology*, 16(2), 211–230. https://doi.org/10.1080/10781911003691609.

Basadur, M., & Hausdorf, P. (1996). Measuring divergent thinking attitudes related to creative problem solving and innovation management. *Creativity Research Journal*, *9*(1), 21–32. https://doi.org/10.1207/s15326934crj0901_3.

Batty, M. (2008). Discontinuities, tipping points, and singularities: The quest for a new social dynamic. *Environment and Planning B: Planning and Design*, *35*(3), 379–380. https://doi.org/10.1068/b3503ed.

Baumann, O., & Stieglitz, N. (2014). Rewarding value-creating ideas in organizations: The power of low-powered incentives. *Strategic Management*, *35*(3), 358–375. https://doi.org/10.1002/smj.2093.

Beaty, R. E., Benedek, M., Silvia, P. J., & Schacter, D. L. (2016). Creative cognition and brain network dynamics. *Trends in Cognitive Sciences*, *20*(2), 87–95. https://doi.org/10.1016/j.tics.2015.10.004.

Beisser, A. (1970). The paradoxical theory of change. In J. Fagan, & I. L. Shepherd (Eds.) *Gestalt Therapy Now: Theory, Techniques, Applications*, pp. 77–80. Science & Behavior Books.

Benedek, M., Beaty, R., Jauk, E., Koschutnig, K., Fink, A., Silvia, P. J., Dunst, B., & Neubauer, A. C. (2014). Creating metaphors: The neural basis of figurative language production. *NeuroImage*, *90*(100), 99–106. https://doi.org/10.1016/j.neuroimage.2013.12.046.

Bennett, N., Wise, C., Woods, P. A., & Harvey, J. A. (2003). *Distributed Leadership*. National College of School Leadership, Nottingham. Full text available at www.researchgate.net/publication/42793697_Distributed_Leadership_A_Review_of_Literature.

Bennett, W. L., & Segerberg, A. (2012). The logic of connective action. *Information, Communication & Society*, *15*(5), 739–768. https://doi.org/10.1080/1369118X.2012.670661.

Berliner, D. (2016). How our contradictions make us human and inspire creativity. *AEON*. https://aeon.co/ideas/how-our-contradictions-make-us-human-and-inspire-creativity. Accessed May 9, 2023.

Berliner, D. (2017). Contradictions: From the intrapersonal to the social, and back. *Journal of Ethnographic Theory*, *7*(2), 45–49. https://doi.org/10.14318/hau7.2.007.

Berra, Y. (2010). *The Yogi Book*. Workman Publishing Company.

Bertagnoli, L. (2022). Divergent thinking: What it is, how it works. *BuiltIn*. https://builtin.com/career-development/divergent-thinking. Accessed July 10, 2023.

Betts, S. C., Laud, R., & Kretinin, A. (2018). Social entrepreneurship: A contemporary approach to solving social problems. *Global Journal of Entrepreneurship*, *2*(1), 31–40.

Beversdorf, D. Q. (2013). Pharmacological effects on creativity. In O. Vartanian & A. S. Bristol (Eds.) *Neuroscience of Creativity*, pp. 151–173. The MIT Press.

Boden, M. A. (2004). *The Creative Mind: Myths and Mechanisms*. Routledge.

Boden, M. A. (2013). Creativity as a neuroscientific mystery. In O. Vartanian, & A. S. Bristol (Eds.) *Neuroscience of Creativity*, pp. 3–18. The MIT Press.

Boecker, H., Sprenger, T., Spilker, M. E., Henriksen, G., Koppenhoefer, M., Wagner, K., J., Valet, M., Berthele, A., & Tolle, T. R. (2008). The runner's high: Opioidergic mechanisms in the human brain. *Cerebral Cortex*, *18*(11), 2523–2531. https://doi.org/10.1093/cercor/bhn013.

Bohdanova, T. (2014). Unexpected revolution: The role of social media in Ukraine's Euromaidan uprising. *European View*, *3*, 133–142. https://doi.org/10.1007/s12290-014-0296-4.

Bolden, R. (2011). Distributed leadership in organizations: A review of theory and research. *International Journal of Management Reviews*, *13*(4), 423–451. https://doi.org/10.1111/j.1468-2370.2011.00306.x.

Boler, M., Macdonald, A., Nitsou, C., & Harris, A. (2014). Connective labor and social media: Women's roles in the 'leaderless' Occupy movement. *The International Journal of Research into New Media Technologies*, *20*(4), 438–460. https://doi.org/10.1177/1354856514541353.

Bonetto, E., Pichot, N., Pavani, J.-B., & Adam-Troïan, J. (2021). The paradox of creativity. *New Ideas in Psychology*, *60*(100820). https://doi.org/10.1016/j.newideapsych.2020.100820.

Bornstein, D. (1998). Changing the World on a Shoestring. *The Atlantic Monthly*, *281*(1), 34–39. www.theatlantic.com/magazine/archive/1998/01/changing-the-world-on-a-shoestring/377042/. Accessed September 11, 2023.

Bornstein, D. (2004). *How to Change the World. Social Entrepreneurs and the Power of New Ideas*. Oxford University Press.

Breiter, H. C., Aharon, I., Kahneman, D., Dale, A., & Shizgal, P. (2001). Functional imaging of neural responses to expectancy and experience of monetary gains and losses. *Neuron*, *30*(2), 619–639. https://doi.org/10.1016/s0896-6273(01)00303-8.

Breithaupt, F. (2018). The bad things we do because of empathy. *Interdisciplinary Science Reviews*, *43*(2), 166–174. https://doi.org/10.1080/03080188.2018.1450928.

Broccoli, E., Canegallo, V., Santoddì, E., Cavarra, M., & Fabio, R. A. (2021). Development and preliminary evaluation of the Peace Attitudes Scale. *Peace and Conflict: Journal of Peace Psychology*, *27*(3), 512–517. https://doi.org/10.1037/pac0000508.

Brown, A. S., & Gershon, S. (1993). Dopamine and depression. *Journal of Neural Transmission*, *91*, 75–109. https://doi.org/10.1007/BF01245227.

Brown, B. (2003). *The Private Revolution: Women in the Polish Underground Movement*. Hera Trust.

Brown, M. H., & Hosking, D. M. (1986). Distributed leadership and skilled performance as successful organization in social movements. *Human Relations*, *39*(1). https://doi.org/10.1177/001872678603900104.

Brown, R., & Kocarev, L. (2000). A unifying definition of synchronization for dynamical systems. *Chaos*, *10*(2), 344–349. https://doi.org/10.1063/1.166500.

Buckwalter, W., Rose, D., & Turri, J. (2018). Impossible Intentions. https://philarchive.org/archive/BUCII. Accessed May 25, 2023.

Buechler, S. M. (1995). New social movement theories. *The Sociological Quarterly*, *36*(3), 441–464. https://doi.org/10.1111/j.1533-8525.1995.tb00447.x.

Buechler, S. M. (2011). *Understanding Social Movements: Theories from the Classical Era to the Present*. Paradigm Publishers.
Burrows, M. (1996). Neurotransmitters, neuromodulators and neurohormones. In M. Burrows, *The Neurobiology of an Insect Brain*, pp. 168–228. Oxford University Press.
Cannon, W. B. (1963). *The Wisdom of the Body*. W. W. Norton & Co.
Carriere, K. R. (2018). "We Are Book Eight": Dialoging the collective imagination through literary fan activism. *Culture & Psychology*, 24(4), 529–544. https://doi.org/10.1177/1354067X18796805.
Carver, C. S., & Scheier, M. F. (2014). Dispositional optimism. *Trends in Cognitive Sciences*, 18(6), 293–299. https://doi.org/10.1016/j.tics.2014.02.003.
Carver, C. S., Scheier, M. F., & Segerstrom, S. C. (2010). Optimism. *Clinical Psychology Review*, 30(7), 879–89. https://doi.org/10.1016/j.cpr.2010.01.006.
Cassidy, J. (2016). The nature of a child's ties. In J. Cassidy, & P. R. Shaver (Eds.) *Handbook of Attachment: Theory, Research and Clinical Applications*, pp. 3–24. Guilford Press.
Castells, M. (2010). *The Power of Identity: The Information Age: Economy, Society, and Culture*. Wiley-Blackwell.
Catalini, C. (2017). Microgeography and the direction of inventive activity. *MIT Sloan Research Paper, 5190*(16). https://pubsonline.informs.org/doi/pdf/10.1287/mnsc.2017.2798. Accessed October 13, 2023.
Cavarra, M., Canegallo, V., Santoddì, E., Broccoli, E., & Fabio, R. A. (2020). Peace and personality: The relationship between the Five Factor model's personality traits and the Peace Attitude Scale. *Peace and Conflict: Journal of Peace Psychology*, 27(3), 508–511. https://doi.org/10.1037/pac0000484.
Chaney, W. H. (2007). *A Workbook for the Dynamic Mind*. Houghton-Brace.
Chen, K.-Y., Fine, L. R., & Huberman, B. A. (2003). Predicting the future. *Information Systems Frontiers*, 5(1), 47–61. https://doi.org/10.1023/A:1022041805438.
Chen, M.-H., Chang, Y.-Y., & Lo, Y.-H. (2015). Creativity cognitive style, conflict, and career success for creative entrepreneurs. *Journal of Business Research*, 68(4), 906–910. https://doi.org/10.1016/j.jbusres.2014.11.050.
Chermahini, S. A., & Hommel, B. (2010). The (b)link between creativity and dopamine: Spontaneous eye blink rates predict and dissociate divergent and convergent thinking. *Cognition*, 115(3), 458–65. https://doi.org/10.1016/j.cognition.2010.03.007.
Cherry, K. (2021). What is a mindset and why it matters. *VeryWell Mind*. www.verywellmind.com/what-is-a-mindset-2795025. Accessed June 7, 2023.
Chierchia, G., & Singer, T. (2017). The neuroscience of compassion and empathy and their link to prosocial motivation and behavior. In J. C. Dreher & L. Tremblay (Eds.) *Decision Neuroscience*, pp. 247–257. Elsevier. https://doi.org/10.1016/B978-0-12-805308-9.00020-8.
Chiu, C., Dweck, C. S., Tong, J. Y., & Fu, J. H. (1997). Implicit theories and conceptions of morality. *Journal of Personality and Social Psychology*, 73(5), 923–940. https://doi.org/10.1037/0022-3514.73.5.923.

Citri, A., & Malenka, R. C. (2007). Synaptic plasticity: Multiple forms, functions, and mechanisms. *Neuropsychopharmacology, 33*, 18–41. https://doi.org/10.1038/sj.npp.1301559.

Clark, M. (2012). *Paradoxes.* Routledge.

Clark, R. P. (1984). *The Basque Insurgents: ETA, 1952–1980.* University of Wisconsin Press.

Coleman, J. S. (2013). "Logic will get you from A to B. Imagination will take you everywhere." Albert Einstein. www.jpfirm.com/news-resources/logic-will-get-you-from-a-to-b-imagination-will-take-you-everywhere-albert-einstein/. Accessed July 18, 2024.

Coleman, P. T. (2003). Characteristics of protracted, intractable conflict: Toward the development of a metaframework–I. *Peace and Conflict: Journal of Peace Psychology, 9*(1), 1–37. https://doi.org/10.1207/S15327949PAC0901_01.

Coleman, P. T., Vallacher, R. R., Nowak, A., & Bui-Wrzosinska, L. (2007). Intractable conflict as an attractor: A dynamical systems approach to conflict escalation and intractability. *American Behavioral Scientist, 50*(11), 1454–1475. https://doi.org/10.1177/0002764207302463.

Collerton, D. (2013). Psychotherapy and brain plasticity. *Frontiers in Psychology, 4.* https://doi.org/10.3389/fpsyg.2013.00548.

Collins, G. (2000). Thinking the impossible: Derrida and the divine. *Literature and Theology, 14*(3), 313–334. https://doi.org/10.1093/litthe/14.3.313.

Comunello, F., & Anzera, G. (2012). Will the revolution be tweeted? *Islam and Christian–Muslim Relations, 23*(4), 453–470. https://doi.org/10.1080/09596410.2012.712435.

Conrad, B. (2018). The role of dopamine as a neurotransmitter in the human brain. *Enzo.* www.enzolifesciences.com/science-center/technotes/2018/november/the-role-of-dopamine-as-a-neurotransmitter-in-the-human-brain/. Accessed August 8, 2023.

Cooley, C. H. (1918). *Social Process.* Charles Scribner's Sons.

Cooper, B. (2018). Social paradoxes and meta-problems. *The Abs-Tract Organization.* https://medium.com/the-abs-tract-organization/social-paradoxes-and-meta-problems-9f47c2659383. Accessed September 11, 2023.

Cooper, R. A. (1981). Jeremy Bentham, Elizabeth Fry, and English prison reform. *Journal of the History of Ideas, 42*(4), 675–690. https://doi.org/10.2307/2709127.

Costandi, M. (2016). *Neuroplasticity.* The MIT Press.

Cozolino, L. (2017). *The Neuroscience of Psychotherapy: Healing the Social Brain.* Norton & Company.

Crocker, S. (1999). *A Well-Lived Life: Essays in Gestalt Therapy.* Gestalt Press.

Cropley, A., & Cropley, D. (2007). Resolving the paradoxes of creativity: An extended phase model. *Cambridge Journal of Education, 38*(3), 355–373. https://doi.org/10.1080/03057640802286871.

Csikszentmihályi, M. (1997a). *Creativity: Flow and the Psychology of Discovery and Intention.* Harper Perennial.

References

Csikszentmihályi, M. (1997b). Happiness and Creativity. *The Futurist*, *31*(5). www.proquest.com/openview/7124e880d8ed7c86b0e0ca581ef9bcca/1?pq-origsite=gscholar&cbl=47758. Accessed September 3, 2023.

Cuevas, J. (2019). Neurotransmitters and their life cycle. *Reference Module in Biomedical Sciences*, 1–7. https://doi.org/10.1016/B978-0-12-801238-3.11318-2.

Cunha, M. P., Rego, A., Berti, M., & Simpson, A. C. (2022). Understanding pragmatic paradoxes: When contradictions become paralyzing and what to do about it. *Business Horizons*, *66*(4), 453–462. https://doi.org/10.1016/j.bushor.2022.09.004.

Curry, H. B. (2010). *Foundations of Mathematical Logic*. Dover Publishing.

Czyżewski, K. (2006). *The Borderland Foundation: A Living Experiment in Cross-cultural Relations*. Boston University, Institute for Human Sciences.

Czyżewski, K. (2020). The culture of coexistence in the longue duree: On practicing the ethos of the borderland. *The Bridge: The Magazine of Academia Balcanica Europeana*, 6. https://bridgemagazineonline.com/krzysztof-czyzewski-the-culture-of-coexistence-in-the-longue-duree/. Accessed June 12, 2023.

Dallyn, S. (2017). Cryptocurrencies as market singularities: The strange case of Bitcoin. *Journal of Cultural Economy*, *10*(5), 462–473. https://doi.org/10.1080/17530350.2017.1315541.

Darbellay, F., Moody, Z., Sedooka, A., & Steffen, G. (2014). Interdisciplinary research boosted by serendipity. *Creativity Research Journal*, *26*(1), 1–10. https://doi.org/10.1080/10400419.2014.873653.

Dauer, J. (2020). *Creative culture: Human-centered interaction, design, & inspiration*. Lead Hand Books.

Davis, G. A. (1993). Personalities of creative people. *R&D Innovator*, *2*(4). www.winstonbrill.com/bril001/html/article_index/articles/1-50/article34_body.html. Accessed July 3, 2023.

De Vignemont, F., & Singer, T. (2006). The empathic brain: How, when and why? *Trends in Cognitive Sciences*, *10*(10), 435–441. https://doi.org/10.1016/j.tics.2006.08.008.

de Vries, H. B., & Lubart, T. I. (2018). Scientific creativity: Divergent and convergent thinking and the impact of culture. *Journal of Creative Behavior*, *53*(2), 145–155. https://doi.org/10.1002/jocb.184.

Derrida, J. (1991). *Given Time*. University of Chicago Press.

Derrida, J. (1995). *The Gift of Death*. University of Chicago Press.

Deutsch, M. (1973). *The Resolution of Conflict: Constructive and Destructive Processes*. Yale University Press.

Devanne, H., & Allart, E. (2019). Boosting brain motor plasticity with physical exercise. *Clinical Neurophysiology*, *49*(2), 91–93. https://doi.org/10.1016/j.neucli.2019.01.003.

Diditwister (2012). Uncovering Spanish state terrorism: GAL and the "Dirty War" against ETA. http://diditwister.wordpress.com/2012/10/10/uncovering-spanish-state-terrorism-gal-and-the-dirty-war-against-eta. Accessed March 26, 2023.

Dinsdale, M. (2023). Paradox vs contradiction: What's the difference? *ProWritingAid*. https://prowritingaid.com/paradox-vs-contradiction. Accessed June 17, 2023.

Doidge, N. (2007). *The Brain that Changes Itself: Stories of Personal Triumph from the Frontiers of Brain Science*. Penguin Books.

Doidge, N. (2016). *The Brain's Way of Healing: Remarkable Discoveries and Recoveries from the Frontiers of Neuroplasticity*. Penguin Books.

Drayton, W. (2002). The citizen sector: Becoming as entrepreneurial and competitive as business. *California Management Review, 44*(3), 120–132. https://doi.org/10.2307/41166136.

Drayton, W. (2005). Where the real power lies. *Alliance, 10*(1), 29–30. www.alliancemagazine.org/feature/where-the-real-power-lies/. Accessed September 11, 2023.

Dreyfus, H. L. (2007). Why Heideggerian AI failed and how fixing it would require making it more Heideggerian. *Philosophical Psychology, 20*(2), 247–268. https://doi.org/10.1080/09515080701239510.

Drucker, P. F. (2001). *Management Challenges For the 21st Century*. Harper Business.

Du, J., Reznikov, L. R., Price, M. P., Zha, X., Lu, J., Moninger, T. O., Wemmie, J. A., & Welsh, M. J. (2014). Protons are a neurotransmitter that regulates synaptic plasticity in the lateral amygdala. *PNAS, 111*(24), 8961–8966. https://doi.org/10.1073/pnas.1407018111.

Duncker, K. (1945). On problem-solving. *Psychological Monographs, 58*(5), i–113. https://doi.org/10.1037/h0093599.

Dunn, P. A., & Rogers, D. K. (2000). Feldenkrais sensory imagery and forward reach. *Perceptual and Motor Skills, 91*(3), 755–757. https://doi.org/10.2466/pms.2000.91.3.755.

Dweck, C. S. (2000). *Self-Theories: Their Role in Motivation, Personality, and Development*. Psychology Press.

Dweck, C. S. (2006). *Mindset: The New Psychology of Success*. Random House.

Dysthe, K., Krogstad, H. E., & Müller, P. (2008). Oceanic rogue waves. *Annual Review of Fluid Mechanics, 40*(1), 287–310. https://doi.org/10.1146/annurev.fluid.40.111406.102203.

Eagle, N. (2004). Can serendipity be planned? *MIT Sloan Management Review, 46*(1), 10–14.

Edmonds, B. (2010). Computational modelling and social theory – The dangers of numerical representation. In E. Mollona (Ed.) *Computational Analysis of Firm Organizations and Strategic Behaviour*, pp. 36–68. Routledge.

Eggleston, B. (2013). Paradox of happiness. *The International Encyclopedia of Ethics*, pp. 3794–3799. Blackwell Publishing.

Elkington, J., & Hartigan, P. (2008). *The Power of Unreasonable People: How Social Entrepreneurs Create Markets That Change the World*. Harvard Business Review Press.

Elst, O. F. V., Foster, N. H. D., Vuust, P., Keller, P. E., & Kringelbach, M. L. (2023). The neuroscience of dance: A conceptual framework and systematic

review. *Neuroscience & Biobehavioral Reviews, 150*, 105197. https://doi.org/10.1016/j.neubiorev.2023.105197.
Érdi, P. (2008). *Complexity Explained*. Springer.
Eroglu, D., Lamb, J. S. W., & Pereira, T. (2017). Synchronization of chaos and its applications. *Contemporary Physics, 58*(3), 207–243. https://doi.org/10.1080/00107514.2017.1345844.
Espiau, G. I. (2011). Social Innovation in the Basque Region. *Social Innovation Community*. www.siceurope.eu/network/community-led-innovation/social-innovation-basque-region. Accessed March 24, 2023.
Espie, C. A. (2011). Paradoxical intention therapy. In Michael Perlis, Mark Aloia, & Brett Kuhn (Eds.), *Behavioral Treatments for Sleep Disorders*, pp. 61–70. Academic Press.https://doi.org/10.1016/B978-0-12-381522-4.00006-7.
EuskoBarómetro (2009). Universidad del País Vasco. www.ehu.eus/documents/1457190/1525260/eb-2009-05.pdf/b4975fd1-92ef-4580-9106-ff20c97f54f5?t=1382534231000. Accessed April 22, 2023.
Evans, O. G. (2024). Dopamine function in the brain. *Simply Psychology*. www.simplypsychology.org/the-role-of-dopamine-as-a-neurotransmitter-in-the-human-brain.html. Accessed July 18, 2024.
Fast Company (2005). *Fast Company the Rules of Business: 55 Essential Ideas to Help Smart People (and Organizations) Perform at Their Best*. Crown Business.
Fauconnier, G., & Turner, M. (2003). *The Way We Think*. Basic Books.
Feldenkrais, M. (1980). Mind and body. Moshé Feldenkrais – His Life, His Work & More. www.feldenkraismethod.com/wp-content/uploads/2014/11/Mind-and-Body-Moshe-Feldenkrais.pdf. Accessed August 27, 2023.
Feldenkrais, M. (2002). *The Potent Self: A Study of Spontaneity and Compulsion*. North Atlantic Books.
Feldenkrais, M. (2005). *Body and Mature Behavior: A Study of Anxiety, Sex, Gravitation, and Learning*. Frog Books.
Festinger, L. (1957). *A Theory of Cognitive Dissonance*. Stanford University Press.
Findlay, C. S., & Lumsden, C. J. (1988). The creative mind: Toward an evolutionary theory of discovery and innovation. *Journal of Social and Biological Structures, 11*(1), 3–55. https://doi.org/10.1016/0140-1750(88)90025-5.
Fink, A., & Benedek, M. (2013). The creative brain: Brain correlates underpinning the generation of original ideas. In O. Vartanian, A. S. Bristol, & J. C. Kaufman (Eds.) *Neuroscience of Creativity*, pp. 207–231. The MIT Press.
Fischer, G. (2005). Distances and diversity: Sources for social creativity. *Proceedings of the 5th Conference on Creativity & Cognition*, 128–136. https://doi.org/10.1145/1056224.1056243.
Fitzpatrick, P., Frazier, J. A., Cochran, D. M., Mitchell, T., Coleman, C., & Schmidt, R. C. (2016). Impairments of social motor synchrony evident in autism spectrum disorder. *Frontiers in Psychology, 7*, 1323. https://doi.org/10.3389/fpsyg.2016.01323.
Flaherty, A. W. (2005). Frontotemporal and dopaminergic control of idea generation and creative drive. *The Journal of Comparative Neurology, 493*(1), 147–153. https://doi.org/10.1002/cne.20768.

Flay, B. R. (1978). Catastrophe theory in social psychology: Some applications to attitudes and social behavior. *Behavioral Science*, 23(4), 335–350. https://doi.org/10.1002/bs.3830230404.

Fletcher, J., & Olwyler, K. (1997). *Paradoxical Thinking. How to Profit from Your Contradictions*. Berrett-Koehler.

Fligstein, N. (2013). Understanding stability and change in fields. *Research in Organizational Behavior*, 33, 39–51. https://doi.org/10.1016/j.riob.2013.10.005.

Flores, P. J. (2014). Group psychotherapy and neuroplasticity. In R. Grossmark, & F. Wright (Eds.) *The One and the Many*, pp. 168–187. Routledge.

Förster, J., Friedman, R. S., & Liberman, N. (2004). Temporal construal effects on abstract and concrete thinking: Consequences for insight and creative cognition. *Journal of Personality and Social Psychology*, 87(2), 177–189. https://doi.org/10.1037/0022-3514.87.2.177.

Forsyth, J. K., Bachman, P., Mathalon, D. H., & Asarnow, R. F. (2015). Augmenting NMDA receptor signaling boosts experience-dependent neuroplasticity in the adult human brain. *PNAS*, 112(50), 15331–15336. https://doi.org/10.1073/pnas.1509262112.

Foster, S. C. (1974). *Stephen Foster Song Book. Original Sheet Music of 40 Songs.* Dover Publications.

Fox, K., & Stryker, M. (2017). Integrating Hebbian and homeostatic plasticity: Introduction. *Philosophical Transactions of the Royal Society B*, 372(1715), 20160413. https://doi.org/10.1098/rstb.2016.0413.

Frank, D. L. (2008). Neuroplasticity: Bridging psychoanalysis and neuroscience. *The Psychoanalytic Quarterly*, 77(3), 921–938. https://doi.org/10.1002/j.2167-4086.2008.tb00370.x.

Frankl, E. V. (1985). Paradoxical intention. In G. R. Weeks (Ed.) *Promoting Change through Paradoxical Therapy*, pp. 99–110. Dow Jones-Irwin.

Frankl, E. V. (2006). *Man's Search for Meaning*. Beacon Press.

Franklin, E. (1996). *Dance Imagery for Technique and Performance*. Human Kinetics.

French, R. P. (2016). The fuzziness of mindsets: Divergent conceptualizations and characterizations of mindset theory and praxis. *International Journal of Organizational Analysis*, 24(4), 673–691. https://doi.org/10.1108/IJOA-09-2014-0797.

Friszke, A. (2006). Regional Mazovian Executive Committee: Origin, structure and activity. In A. Friszke (Ed.) *Underground Solodarity 1981–1989*, pp. 405–487. Institute for Social Studies, Polish Academy of Science.

Fromm, E. (1990). *The Sane Society*. Holt Paperbacks.

Fry, E. G. (2018). *Observations on the Visiting, Superintendence, and Government of Female Prisoners*. Franklin Classics Trade Press.

Fuller, S. (2018). Advantages & disadvantages for using role play as a training method. *Bizfluent.com*. https://bizfluent.com/info-12027484-advantages-disadvantages-using-role-play-training-method.html. Accessed April 23, 2023.

Gaiarsa, J. L., Caillard, O., & Ben-Ari, Y. (2002). Long-term plasticity at GABAergic and glycinergic synapses: Mechanisms and functional significance. *Trends in Neurosciences, 25*(11), 564–570. https://doi.org/10.1016/S 0166-2236(02)02269-5.

Gardner, M. (1962). A New Prediction Paradox. *The British Journal for the Philosophy of Science, 13*(49), 51.

Gelman, A., King, G., & Boscardin, J. (1998). Estimating the probability of events that have never occurred: When is your vote decisive? *Journal of the American Statistical Association, 93*(441), 1–9. https://doi.org/10.1080/01621459.1998.10474082.

Gerrow, K., & Triller, A. (2010). Synaptic stability and plasticity in a floating world. *Current Opinion in Neurobiology, 20*(5), 631–639. https://doi.org/10.1016/j.conb.2010.06.010.

Ghosh, S. K. (2018). Happy hormones at work: Applying the learnings from neuroscience to improve and sustain workplace happiness. *NHRD Network Journal, 11*(4). https://doi.org/10.1177/2631454118806139.

Gingell, S. (2020). How does psychotherapy change our brains? *Psychology Today*. www.psychologytoday.com/intl/blog/what-works-and-why/202011/how-does-psychotherapy-change-our-brains. Accessed September 27, 2023.

Glăveanu, V. P. (2018a). Epilogue: Creativity as immersed detachment. *Journal of Creative Behavior, 53*(2), 189–192. https://doi.org/10.1002/jocb.242.

Glăveanu, V. P. (2018b). Creativity and wonder. *Journal of Creative Behavior, 53* (2), 171–177. https://doi.org/10.1002/jocb.225.

Glăveanu, V. P. (2020). *The Possible: A Sociocultural Theory*. Oxford University Press.

Gleick, J. (2008). *Chaos: Making a New Science*. Penguin Books.

Gnyawali, D. R., Madhavan, R., He, J., & Bengtsson, M. (2016). The competition–cooperation paradox in inter-firm relationships: A conceptual framework. *Industrial Marketing Management, 53*, 7–18. https://doi.org/10.1016/j.indmarman.2015.11.014.

Gold, T., & Hermann, B. (2003). *The Role and Status of DoD Red Teaming Activities*. Defense Science Board. https://doi.org/10.21236/ADA430100

Goldstein, J. (1999). Emergence as a construct: History and issues. *Emergence: Complexity and Organization, 1*(1), 49–72. https://doi.org/10.1207/s15327000em0101_4.

Goodwin, P., & Wright, G. (2010). The limits of forecasting methods in anticipating rare events. *Technological Forecasting and Social Change, 77*(3), 355–368. https://doi.org/10.1016/j.techfore.2009.10.008.

Goodwyn, J., Jasper, J. M., & Polletta, F. (2004). Emotional dimensions of social movements. In D. A. Snow, S. A. Soule, H. Kiersi, & M. C. Cammon (Eds.) *The Blackwell Companion to Social Movements*, pp. 416–432.

Granovetter, M. S. (1973). The strength of weak ties. *The American Journal of Sociology, 78*(6), 1360–1380.

Granovetter, M. S. (1983). The strength of weak ties: A network theory revisited. *Sociological Theory, 1*(1), 201–233. https://doi.org/10.2307/202051.

Greco, A., & Heucher, K. (2022). A paradox approach to navigating the tensions of ethnographic research. *Academy of Management Proceedings* (1st ed., vol. 2022). https://doi.org/10.5465/AMBPP.2022.17934abstract.

Gruber, H. E. (1988). The evolving systems approach to creative work. *Creativity Research Journal*, *1*(1), 27–51. https://doi.org/10.1080/10400418809534285.

Guilford, J. P. (1950). Creativity. *American Psychologist*, *5*(9), 444–454. https://doi.org/10.1037/h0063487.

Guilford, J. P. (1957). Creative abilities in the arts. *Psychological Review*, *64*(2), 110–118. https://doi.org/10.1037/h0048280.

Gusfield, J. R. (1966). Functional areas of leadership in social movements. *Sociological Quarterly*, *7*(2), 137–156. https://doi.org/10.1111/j.1533-8525.1966.tb01684.x.

Gutting, G. (2013). *Thinking the Impossible: French Philosophy Since 1960*. Oxford University Press.

Guzman-Marin, R., Bashir, T., Suntsova, N., Szymusiak, R., & McGinty, R. (2007). Adult hippocampal neurogenesis is reduced by sleep fragmentation in the adult rat. *Neuroscience*, *148*(1), 325–333. https://doi.org/10.1016/j.neuroscience.2007.05.030.

Habermas, J. (1985). *The Theory of Communicative Action* (v.2). Beacon Press.

Halperin, E. (2016). *Emotions in Conflict: Inhibitors and Facilitators of Peace Making*. Routledge.

Hameiri, B., Bar-Tal, D., & Halperin, E. (2018). Paradoxical thinking interventions: A paradigm for societal change. *Social Issues and Policy Review*, *13*(1), 36–62. https://doi.org/10.1111/sipr.12053.

Hameiri, B., Porat, R., Bar-Tal, D., Bieler, A., & Halperin, E. (2014). Paradoxical thinking as a new avenue of intervention to promote peace. *Proceedings of the National Academy of Sciences*, *111*(30), 10996–11001. https://doi.org/10.1073/pnas.1407055111.

Hamel, J. (1992). On the status of singularity in sociology. *Current Sociology*, *40*(1), 99–119. https://doi.org/10.1177/001139292040001008.

Hammer, J. (2007). Peace at Last? Smithsonian.com, People & Places. www.smithsonianmag.com/history/peace-at-last-142666835. Accessed July 18, 2024.

Hammonds, K. H. (2005). A lever long enough to move the world. *Fast Company*, 90. www.fastcompany.com/magazine/90/open_ashoka.html. Accessed September 11, 2023.

Han, H. (2014). *How Organizations Develop Activists: Civic Associations and Leadership in the 21st Century*. Oxford University Press.

Han, H., McKenna, E., & Oyakawa, M. (2021). *Prisms of the People: Power & Organizing in Twenty-First-Century America*. University of Chicago Press.

Handy, C. (1995). *The Age of Paradox*. Harvard Business School Press.

Harmon, C., & Pava, P. (1981). *Towards a Concept of Normative Incrementalism: One Prospect for Purposeful Non-Synoptic*. University of Pennsylvania.

Harry, B., Sturges, K. M., & Klingner, J. K. (2005). Mapping the process: An exemplar of process and challenge in grounded theory analysis. *Educational Researcher*, *34*(2), 3–13. https://doi.org/10.3102/0013189X034002003.

Hauksson, K. M. (2023). Paradoxes in the workplace: How to challenge your thinking and grow. *LinkedIn*. www.linkedin.com/pulse/paradoxes-workplace-how-challenge-your-thinking-grow-hauksson/?trk=article-ssr-frontend-pulse_more-articles_related-content-card. Accessed January 29, 2024.

Hawkes, C. H. (1992). Endorphins: The basis of pleasure? *Journal of Neurology, Neurosurgery and Psychiatry*, 55(4), 247–250. https://doi.org/10.1136/jnnp.55.4.247.

Hazy, J. K., & Ashley, A. S. (2011). Unfolding the future: Bifurcation in organizing form and emergence in social systems. *Emergence: Complexity & Organization*, 13(3), 57–79.

Hedman, C. G. (1970). Intending the impossible. *Philosophy*, 45(171), 33–38. www.jstor.org/stable/3749522.

Heracleous, L. (2020). *Janus Strategy*. Kindle Direct Publishing.

Heracleous, L., & Robson, D. (2020). Why the "paradox mindset" is the key to success. *BBC Worklife*. www.bbc.com/worklife/article/20201109-why-the-paradox-mindset-is-the-key-to-success. Accessed June 14, 2023.

Heras, H. A. (2014). Collaboration patterns and product innovation in the Basque Country. Does foreign ownership matter? *Journal of Entrepreneurship, Management and Innovation*, 10(3), 29–56. https://doi.org/10.7341/20141032.

Herrera, D. (2004). Mondragón: A for-profit organization that embodies Catholic social thought. *Review of Business*, 25(1), 56–68.

Hock, D. W. (2000). *Birth of the Chaordic Age*. Berrett-Koehler.

Hockenbury, D. H., & Hockenbury, S. E. (2011). *Discovering Psychology*. Worth Publishers.

Hockenbury, D., Nolan, S. A., & Hockenbury, S. E. (2016). *Discovering Psychology*. Worth Publishers.

Hollender, J. (2011). A visit to Mondragon: People before profits. *Jeffrey Hollender*. www.jeffreyhollender.com/a-visit-to-mondragon-people-before-profits. Accessed March 24, 2023.

Hołyst, J., Kacperski, K., & Schweitzer, F. (2000). Phase transitions in social impact models of opinion. *Physica A: Statistical Mechanics and Its Applications* 285(1), 199–210. https://doi.org/10.1016/S0378-4371(00)00282-X.

Hötting, K., & Röder, B. (2013). Beneficial effects of physical exercise on neuroplasticity and cognition. *Neuroscience & Biobehavioral Reviews*, 37(9), 2243–2257. https://doi.org/10.1016/j.neubiorev.2013.04.005.

Hsiung, M. (2022). From paradoxicality to paradox. *Erkenntnis: An International Journal of Scientific Philosophy*, 1(25). https://doi.org/10.1007/s10670-022-00640-9.

Hughes, J. R. (1958). Post-tetanic potentiation. *Physiological Reviews*, 38(1), 91–113. https://doi.org/10.1152/physrev.1958.38.1.91.

Hynes, M., & Sharpe, S. (2009). Affected with joy: Evaluating the mass actions of the anti-globalization movement. *Borderlands*, 8(3), 1–21.

Ingram, A. E., Lewis, M. W., & Gartner, W. B. (2016). Paradoxes and innovation in family firms: The role of paradoxical thinking. *Entrepreneurship Theory and Practice*, 40(1). https://doi.org/10.1111/etap.12113.

Islam, M. S. (2021). Soccer performance connected with happy hormones: A review. *Journal of Specific Sport Science*, 1(1), 31–36.

Jacobs, B. L., van Praag, H., & Gage, F. H. (2000). Adult brain neurogenesis and psychiatry: A novel theory of depression. *Molecular Psychiatry, 5*, 262–269. https://doi.org/10.1038/sj.mp.4000712.

Jäncke, L. (2009). The plastic human brain. *Restorative Neurology and Neuroscience, 27*(5), 521–538. https://doi.org/10.3233/RNN-2009-0519.

Jeevanandam, N. (2022). AI concepts for beginners – What is true about Moravec's Paradox? *INDIAai.* https://indiaai.gov.in/article/what-is-true-about-moravec-s-paradox. Accessed December 18, 2023.

Jia, L., Hirt, E. R., & Karpen, S. C. (2009). Lessons from a faraway land: The effect of spatial distance on creative cognition. *Journal of Experimental Social Psychology, 45*(5), 1127–1131. https://doi.org/10.1016/j.jesp.2009.05.015.

Johansson, B. B. (2004). Brain plasticity in health and disease. *The Keio Journal of Medicine, 53*(4), 231–246. https://doi.org/10.2302/kjm.53.231.

Johnson, N. (2009). *Simply Complexity: A Clear Guide to Complexity Theory.* OneWorld Publications.

Johnston, M. V. (2009). Plasticity in the developing brain: Implications for rehabilitation. *Developmental Disabilities Research Reviews, 15*(2), 94–101. https://doi.org/10.1002/ddrr.64.

Kandel. E., Koester, J. D., Mack, S. H., & Siegelbaum, S. (2021). *Principles of Neural Science.* McGraw Hill.

Kang, S. H., Kim, J., Kim, I., Moon, Y. A., Park, S., & Koh, S.-B. (2022). Dance intervention using the Feldenkrais method improves motor, and non-motor symptoms and gait in Parkinson's disease: A 12-month study. *Journal of Movement Disorders, 15*(1), 53–57. https://doi.org/10.14802/jmd.21086.

Kaplan, E. P. (2020). *Paradox Psychology: It's Not What You Think.* Ramot Press.

Karpik, L. (2010). *Valuing the Unique: The Economics of Singularities.* Princeton University Press.

Kaufman, S. B. (2010). Why creative folks blink a lot. *Psychology Today.* http://www.psychologytoday.com/blog/beautiful-minds/201004/why-creative-folks-blink-lot. Accessed July 12, 2023.

Kavada, A. (2015). Creating the collective: Social media, the Occupy Movement and its constitution as a collective actor. *Information, Communication & Society, 18*(8), 872–886. https://doi.org/10.1080/1369118X.2015.1043318.

Keeney, B. P. (2002). *Aesthetics of Change.* The Guilford Press.

Kelman, H. C. (1990). Interactive problem-solving: A social-psychological approach to conflict resolution. In J. W. Burton & F. Dukes (Eds.) *Conflict: Readings in Management and Resolution* (pp. 199–215). Macmillan.

Kendall, D. (2005). *Sociology in Our Times.* Cengage Learning.

Kennedy, J. J. (2023). How neuroplasticity affects creativity. *Psychology Today.* www.psychologytoday.com/intl/blog/brain-reboot/202306/how-neuroplasticity-affects-creativity. Accessed August 12, 2023.

Kenney, P. (2001). Framing, political opportunities, and civic mobilization in the eastern European revolutions: A case study of Poland's freedom and peace movement. *Mobilization, 6*(2), 193–210. https://doi.org/10.17813/maiq.6.2.5r33j8553677u806.

Kenney, P. (2002). *A Carnival of Revolution: Central Europe 1989.* Princeton University Press.

Kenton, W. (2023). Financial crisis: Definition, causes, and examples. *Investopedia*. www.investopedia.com/terms/f/financial-crisis.asp. Accessed March 10, 2023.

Khosrokhavar, F. (2015). The civil sphere and the Arab Spring. In P. Kivisto & G. Sciortino (Eds.) *Solidarity, Justice, and Incorporation: Thinking through The Civil Sphere*, pp. 142–171. Oxford University Press.

Khuzaima, A. (2014). The passion and the power of individuals. *Breath of the Hearth*. https://breathoftheheart.wordpress.com/2014/03/24/the-passion-and-the-power-of-individuals/, Accessed July 10, 2024.

Killian, L. M. (1984). Organization, rationality and spontaneity in the Civil Rights Movement. *American Sociological Review*, 49(6), 770–783. https://doi.org/10.2307/2095529.

Kimball, S. R. (2014). Rapping the Arab Spring. *World Policy Journal*, 30(4), 79–86. https://doi.org/10.1177/0740277513517650.

King, G., & Zeng, L. (2001). Logistic regression in rare events data. *Political Analysis*, 9(2), 137–163. https://doi.org/10.1093/oxfordjournals.pan.a004868.

King, M. L. (2001). *The Autobiography of Martin Luther King, Jr*. Grand Central Publishing.

Klein, G. (2016). Mindsets: What they are and why they matter. *Psychology Today*. www.psychologytoday.com/us/blog/seeing-what-others-dont/201605/mindsets. Accessed June 25, 2024.

Klein, M. O., Battagello, D. S, Cardoso, A. R., Hauser, D. N., Bittencourt, J. C., & Correa, R. G. (2018). Dopamine: Functions, signaling, and association with neurological diseases. *Cellular and Molecular Neurobiology*, 39, 31–59. https://doi.org/10.1007/s10571-018-0632-3.

Klein, P. (2015). *A Handbook of Test Construction: Introduction to Psychometric Design*. Routledge.

Klein, S. B. (2014). Sameness and the self: Philosophical and psychological considerations. *Frontiers in Psychology*, 5(29). https://doi.org/10.3389/fpsyg.2014.00029.

Kolb, B., & Whishaw, I. Q. (1998). Brain plasticity and behavior. *Annual Review of Psychology*, 49, 43–64. https://doi.org/10.1146/annurev.psych.49.1.43.

Konrath, S., Corneille, O., Bushman, B. J., & Luminet, O. (2014). The relationship between narcissistic exploitativeness, dispositional empathy, and emotion recognition abilities. *Journal of Nonverbal Behavior*, 38(1), 129–143. https://doi.org/10.1007/s10919-013-0164-y.

Krešimir, Š, Bolčević, F., & Medved, V. (2017). Exercises based on neuroplasticity principles increase mobility in elite senior football players. *8th International Scientific Conference on Kinesiology, Opatija, Croatia*. https://priordanpokret.hr/wp-content/uploads/2019/08/Sos-Kinesiology-Opatija-2017-1.pdf. Accessed August 30, 2023.

Kruger, J., & Dunning, D. (1999). Unskilled and unaware of it: How difficulties in recognizing one's own incompetence lead to inflated self-assessments. *Journal of Personality and Social Psychology*, 77(6), 1121–1134. https://doi.org/10.1037/0022-3514.77.6.1121.

Kubik, J. (1994). *The Power of Symbols Against the Symbols of Power*. Penn State University Press.

Kulisevsky, J., Pagonabarraga, J., & Martinez-Corral, M. (2009). Changes in artistic style and behaviour in Parkinson's disease: Dopamine and creativity. *Journal of Neurology*, *256*(5), 816–819. https://doi.org/10.1007/s00415-009-5001-1.

Kuo, M.-F., Paulus, W., & Nitsche, M. A. (2008). Boosting focally-induced brain plasticity by dopamine. *Cerebral Cortex*, *18*(3), 648–651. https://doi.org/10.1093/cercor/bhm098.

Kurzweil, R. (2005). *The Singularity Is Near: When Humans Transcend Biology*. Viking Penguin.

La Rosa, C., Parolisi, R., & Bonfanti, L. (2020). Brain structural plasticity: From adult neurogenesis to immature neurons. *Frontiers in Neuroscience*, *14*. https://doi.org/10.3389/fnins.2020.00075.

Langman, L. (2013). Occupy: A new social movement. *Current Sociology*, *61*(4), 510–524. https://doi.org/10.1177/0011392113479749.

Latner, J. (2000). The theory of Gestalt therapy. In E. Nevis (Ed.) *Gestalt Therapy: Perspectives and Applications*, pp. 13–56. Gestalt Press.

Laurent, P. (1917). The supposed synchronal flashing of fireflies. *Science*, *45*(1150), 44. https://doi.org/10.1126/science.45.1150.44.b.

Lederach, J. P. (1996). *Preparing for Peace: Conflict Transformation across Cultures*. Syracuse University Press.

Lederach, J. P. (2003). *The Little Book of Conflict Transformation*. Good Books.

Lederach, J. P. (2005). *The Moral Imagination: The Art and Soul of Building Peace*. Oxford University Press.

Levy, S. R., Stroessner, S. J., & Dweck, C. S. (1998). Stereotype formation and endorsement: The role of implicit theories. *Journal of Personality and Social Psychology*, *74*(6), 1421–1436. https://doi.org/10.1037/0022-3514.74.6.1421.

Levy, T. (2021). The dependency paradox in relationships. *Evergreen Psychotherapy Center*. https://evergreenpsychotherapycenter.com/the-dependency-paradox-in-relationships/. Accessed October 6, 2023.

Leypoldt, G. (2014). Singularity and the literary market. *New Literary History*, *45*(1), 71–88. https://doi.org/10.1353/nlh.2014.0000.

Li, L., Scaglione, A., Swami, A., & Zhao, Q. (2012). Phase transition in opinion diffusion in social networks. *IEEE International Conference on Acoustics, Speech and Signal Processing (ICASSP)*, Kyoto, Japan, 3073–3076. https://doi.org/10.1109/ICASSP.2012.6288564.

Liberman, N., Sagristano, M. D., & Trope, Y. (2002). The effect of temporal distance on level of mental construal. *Journal of Experimental Social Psychology*, *38*(6), 523–534. https://doi.org/10.1016/S0022-1031(02)00535-8.

Lieberman, J. N. (1965). Playfulness and divergent thinking: An investigation of their relationship at the kindergarten level. *The Journal of Genetic Psychology*, *107*(2), 219–224. https://doi.org/10.1080/00221325.1965.10533661.

Li-Hua, R. (2014). Embracing contradiction. In *Competitiveness of Chinese Firms*, pp. 87–104. Palgrave Macmillan. https://doi.org/10.1057/9781137309303_5.

Lindsay, G. (2014). Engineering serendipity. *Aspen Ideas Festival*. https://medium.com/aspen-ideas/engineering-serendipity-941e601a9b65#.eicshe5kn. Accessed July 10, 2023.

Lindsay, G. (2015). How to engineer serendipity. *TIME*. http://time.com/3951029/engineer-serendipity/. Accessed October 11, 2023.

Liu, Y., Xu, S., & Zhang, B. (2019). Thriving at work: How a paradox mindset influences innovative work behavior. *The Journal of Applied Behavioral Science, 56*(3), 347–366. https://doi.org/10.1080/13537119908428572.

Llera, F. J. (1999). Basque polarization: Between autonomy and independence. *Nationalism and Ethnic Politics, 5*(3–4), 101–120. https://doi.org/10.1080/13537119908428572.

Llera, F. J., Mata, J. M., & Irvin, C. L. (1993). ETA: From secret army to social movement – the post-Franco schism of the Basque nationalist movement. *Terrorism and Political Violence, 5*(3), 106–134. https://doi.org/10.1080/09546559308427222.

Lomranz, J., & Benyamini, Y. (2016). The ability to live with incongruence: Aintegration – the concept and its operationalization. *Journal of Adult Development, 23*, 79–92. https://doi.org/10.1007/s10804-015-9223-4.

Longbine, D. F. (2012). *Red Teaming: Past and Present*. School of Advanced Military Studies.

Longo, G. (2018). How future depends on past and rare events in systems of life. *Foundations of Science, 23*, 443–474. https://doi.org/10.1007/s10699-017-9535-x.

Loyer, B. (1998). Basque Nationalism Undermined by ETA. *Le Monde Diplomatique*, http://mondediplo.com/1998/02/08basque. Accessed March 26, 2023.

MacLean Jr., W. E., Lewis, M. H., Bryson-Brockmann, W. A., Ellis, D. N., Arendt, R. E., & Baumeister, A. A. (1985). Blink rate and stereotyped behavior: Evidence for dopamine involvement? *Biological Psychiatry, 20*(12), 1321–1326. https://doi.org/10.1016/0006-3223(85)90117-9.

MacNair, R. M. (2012). *The Psychology of Peace: An Introduction*. Praeger.

Madan, A. (2024). *Sowing Ideas to Growing Business: Decoding Entrepreneurial Lessons from the Plant World*, Part 3: Creativity. Notion Press.

Maddux, J. E. (2011). Self-Efficacy: The Power of Believing You Can. In S. J. Lopez & C. R. Snyder (Eds.) *Oxford Handbook of Positive Psychology*, pp. 335–343. Oxford University Press.

Madsen, O. J. (2014). Transgression. In T. Teo (Eds.) *Encyclopedia of Critical Psychology*, pp. 2002–2004. Springer. https://doi.org/10.1007/978-1-4614-5583-7_319.

Mair, J., & Martí, I. (2006). Social entrepreneurship research: A source of explanation, prediction, and delight. *Journal of World Business, 41*, 36–44.

Mair, J., Robinson, J., & Hockerts, K. (2006). Introduction. In J. Mair, J. Robinson, & K. Hockerts (Eds.) *Social Entrepreneurship*, pp. 1–13. Palgrave Macmillan.

Malhotra, S., & Sahoo, S. (2017). Rebuilding the brain with psychotherapy. *Indian Journal of Psychiatry, 59*(4), 411–419. https://doi.org/10.4103/0019-5545.217299.

Mannucci, P. V., & Shalley, C. E. (2022). Embracing multicultural tensions: How team members' multicultural paradox mindsets foster team information elaboration and creativity. *Organizational Behavior and Human Decision Processes*, *173*(2), 104191. https://doi.org/10.1016/j.obhdp.2022.104191.

Manz, C. C., Shipper, F., & Stewart, G. L. (2009). Everyone a team leader: Shared influence at W. L. Gore & Associates. *Organizational Dynamics*, *38*(3), 239–244. https://doi.org/10.1016/j.orgdyn.2009.04.006.

Mapes, J. J. (2003). *Quantum Leap Thinking*. Sourcebooks.

Markman, A. (2022). The role of contradictions in creativity. *Psychology Today*. www.psychologytoday.com/intl/blog/ulterior-motives/202207/the-role-contradictions-in-creativity. Accessed June 19, 2023.

Marko, M., Michalko, D., & Riečanský, I. (2018). Remote associates test: An empirical proof of concept. *Behavior Research Methods*, *51*, 2700–2711. https://doi.org/10.3758/s13428-018-1131-7.

Markuartu, J. J. I. (2012). *The Basque Case: A Comprehensive Model for Sustainable Human Development*. Universidad del País Vasco.

Martin, M. W. (2012). Paradoxes of happiness. In M. W. Martin (Eds.) *Happiness and the Good Life*, pp. 91–106. Oxford University Press.

Martin, R. (2016). Dancing in the spring: Dance, hegemony, and change. In G. Morris & J. R. Giersdorf (Eds.) *Choreographies of 21st Century Wars*, pp. 207–230. Oxford University Press.

Martin, R. L. (2009). *The Opposable Mind: How Successful Leaders Win Through Integrative Thinking*. Harvard Business Review Press.

Martin, R. L., & Osberg, S. (2007). Social entrepreneurship: The case for definition. *Stanford Social Innovation Review*, Spring 2007, 29–39.

Marx, G. (2023). *Groucho And Me*. Must Have Books

Mason, L., Peters, E., Williams, S. C., & Kumari, V. (2017). Brain connectivity changes occurring following cognitive behavioral therapy for psychosis predict long-term recovery. *Translational Psychiatry*, *7*(1), e1001. https://doi.org/10.1038/tp.2016.263.

Mason, M. (2007). Exploring "the impossible": Jacques Derrida, John Caputo and the philosophy of history. *Rethinking History*, *10*(4), 501–522. https://doi.org/10.1080/13642520600816106.

Masys, A. J. (2012). Black swans to grey swans: Revealing the uncertainty. *Disaster Prevention and Management*, *21*(3), 320–335. https://doi.org/10.1108/09653561211234507.

McAdam, D. (1999). *Political Process and the Development of Black Insurgency, 1930–1970*. The University of Chicago Press.

McAdams, D. P. (2001). The psychology of life stories. *Review of General Psychology*, *5*(2), 100–122. https://doi.org/10.1037/1089-2680.5.2.100.

McChrystal, S. (2015). *Team of Teams: New Rules of Engagement for a Complex World*. Portfolio.

McClelland, D. C. (1967). *The Achieving Society*. The Free Press.

McEwen, B. S. (2016). In pursuit of resilience: Stress, epigenetics, and brain plasticity. *Annals of the New York Academy of Science*, *1373*(1), 56–64. https://doi.org/10.1111/nyas.13020.

McIntyre, D. A. (2009). Memo To Congress: "Buy Land, They Ain't Making Any More Of It." *Time*. https://time.com/archive/6905241/memo-to-congress-buy-land-they-aint-making-any-more-of-it/. Accessed July 17, 2024.

McKirahan, R. (2001). Zeno's dichotomy in Aristotle. *Philosophical Inquiry*, 23(1–2), 1–24. https://doi.org/10.5840/philinquiry2001231/216.

Mednick, S. (1962). The associative basis of the creative process. *Psychological Review*, 69(3), 220–232. https://doi.org/10.1037/h0048850.

Melnick, J., & Nevis, S. M. (2005). Gestalt therapy methodology. In A. L. Woldt, & S. M. Toman (Eds.) *Gestalt Therapy, History, Theory, and Practice*, pp. 101–116. Sage Publications.

Merens, W., Van der Does, W., & Spinhoven, P. (2007). The effects of serotonin manipulations on emotional information processing and mood. *Journal of Affective Disorders*, 103(1–3), 43–62. https://doi.org/10.1016/j.jad.2007.01.032.

Merzenich, M. M., Tallal, P., Peterson, B., Miller, S., & Jenkins, W. M. (1999). Some neurological principles relevant to the origins of – and the cortical plasticity-based remediation of – developmental language impairments. In J. Grafman & Y. Christen (Eds.) *Neuronal Plasticity: Building a Bridge from the Laboratory to the Clinic. Research and Perspectives in Neurosciences*, pp. 169–187. Springer. https://doi.org/10.1007/978-3-642-59897-5_12.

Miall, H. (2004). Conflict transformation: A multi-dimensional task. *Berghof Handbook for Conflict Transformation*. http://kar.kent.ac.uk/289/1/miall_hand book.pdf. Accessed October 9, 2021.

Michael, K., Abbas, R., & Roussos, G. (2023). AI in cybersecurity: The paradox. *IEEE Transactions on Technology and Society*, 4(20), 104–109. https://doi.org/10.1109/TTS.2023.3280109.

Michalko, M. (2012). Janusian thinking: Get creative ideas by imagining two opposites or two contradictory ideas. *The Creativity Post*. www.creativitypost.com/article/janusian_thinking. Accessed June 20, 2023.

Miller, E., & Smarick, K. (2011). ETA ceasefires by the numbers. *College Park, MD: START*. www.start.umd.edu/sites/default/files/publications/local_attach ments/ETACeasefires.pdf. Accessed February 1, 2024.

Miron-Spektor, E., Emich, K. J., Argote, L., & Smith, W. K. (2022). Conceiving opposites together: Cultivating paradoxical frames and epistemic motivation fosters team creativity. *Organizational Behavior and Human Decision Processes*, 171(5), 104–153. https://doi.org/10.1016/j.obhdp.2022.104153.

Miron-Spektor, E., Ingra, A., Keller, J., Smith, W. K., & Lewis, M. W. (2017). Microfoundations of organizational paradox: The problem is how we think about the problem. *Academy of Management Journal*, 61(1). https://doi.org/10.5465/amj.2016.0594.

Misztal, B. (1992). Between the state and solidarity: One movement, two interpretations – the Orange Alternative Movement in Poland. *The British Journal of Sociology*, 43(1), 55–78. https://doi.org/10.2307/591201.

Mohaupt, F., & Ziegler, R. (2014). Toilets before independence: David Kuria and Ecotact. In R. Ziegler, L. Partzsch, J. Gebauer, M. Henkel, J. Lodemann, &

F. Mohaupt (Eds.) *Social Entrepreneurship in the Water Sector*, pp. 34–57. Edward Elgar Publishing.

Monday, H. R., Younts, T. J., & Castillo, P. O. (2018). Long-term plasticity of neurotransmitter release: Emerging mechanisms and contributions to brain function and disease. *Annual Review of Neuroscience, 8*(41), 299–322. https://doi.org/10.1146/annurev-neuro-080317-062155.

Moore, R. (1966). *Niels Bohr*. Knopf.

Moravec, H. (1990). *Mind Children: The Future of Robot and Human Intelligence*. Harvard University Press.

Morris, A. (2006). Freedom is a constant struggle: The Mississippi Civil Rights Movement and its legacy by Kenneth T. Andrews. *Contemporary Sociology, 35*(4), 413–415. https://doi.org/10.1177/009430610603500.

Mort, G. S., Weerawardena, J., & Carnegie, K. (2006). Social entrepreneurship: Towards conceptualization. *Journal of Philanthropy and Marketing, 8*(1), 76–88. https://doi.org/10.1002/nvsm.202.

Mozdzierz, G. J., Macchitelli, F. J., & Lisiecki, J. (1976). The paradox in psychotherapy: An Adlerian perspective. *Journal of Individual Psychology, 32*(2), 169–184.

Müller, P., Rehfeld, K., Schmicker, M., Hökelmann, A., Dordevic, M., Lessmann, V., Brigadski, T., Kaufmann, J., & Müller, N. G. (2017). Evolution of neuroplasticity in response to physical activity in old age: The case for dancing. *Frontiers in Aging Neuroscience, 9*. https://doi.org/10.3389/fnagi.2017.00056.

Mumford, M. D. (2003). Where have we been, where are we going? Taking stock in creativity research. *Creativity Research Journal, 15*(2–3), 107–120. https://doi.org/10.1080/10400419.2003.9651403.

Myers, L. K. (2016). Application of neuroplasticity theory through the use of the Feldenkrais Method® with a runner with scoliosis and hip and lumbar pain: A case report. *Journal of Bodywork and Movement Therapies, 20*(2), 300–309. https://doi.org/10.1016/j.jbmt.2015.06.003.

Nafday, A. M. (2009). Strategies for managing the consequences of black swan events. *Leadership and Management in Engineering, 9*(4), 191–197. https://doi.org/10.1061/(ASCE)LM.1943-5630.0000036.

Nascimento, M. de M. (2021). Dance, aging, and neuroplasticity: An integrative review. *Behavior, Cognition and Neuroscience, 27*(4), 372–381. https://doi.org/10.1080/13554794.2021.1966047.

Nederhof, A. J. (1985). Methods of coping with social desirability bias: A review. *European Journal of Social Psychology, 15*(3), 263–280. https://doi.org/10.1002/ejsp.2420150303.

Nelson, T. (2020). The story of Georgia Gilmore: This Montgomery, Alabama cook helped fund the civil rights movement. *Southern Living*. www.southernliving.com/culture/georgia-gilmore-civil-rights. Accessed March 23, 2023.

Nietzsche, F. (1997). *Twilight of the Idols*. Hackett Publishing Company.

Noelle-Neumann, E. (1974). The spiral of silence: A theory of public opinion. *Journal of Communication*, 24(2), 43–51. https://doi.org/10.1111/j.1460-2466.19 74.tb00367.x.
Noelle-Neumann, E., & Petersen, T. (2004). The spiral of silence and the social nature of man. In L. L. Kaid (Eds.) *Handbook of Political Communication Research*, pp. 339–356. Routledge.
Nordquist, R. (2019). Definition and examples of conceptual blending. *ThoughtCo*. www.thoughtco.com/what-is-conceptual-blending-cb-1689780. Accessed June 20, 2023.
Nowak, A., & Vallacher, R. R. (1998). *Dynamical Social Psychology*. The Guildford Press.
Nowak, A., & Vallacher, R. R. (2005). Information and influence in the construction of shared reality. *IEEE: Intelligent Systems*, 1, 90–93.
Nowak, A., & Vallacher, R. R. (2018). Nonlinear societal change: The perspective of dynamical systems. *The British Journal of Social Psychology*, 58(1), 105–128. https://doi.org/10.1111/bjso.12271.
Oakley, T. V. (1998). Conceptual blending, narrative discourse, and rhetoric. *Cognitive Linguistics*, 9(4), 321–360. https://doi.org/10.1515/cogl.1998.9.4.321.
Olson, A. K., Eadie, B. D., Ernst, C., & Christie, B. R. (2006). Environmental enrichment and voluntary exercise massively increase neurogenesis in the adult hippocampus via dissociable pathways. *Hippocampus*, 16(3), 250–260. https://doi.org/10.1002/hipo.20157.
Onuch, O. (2014). Social Networks and Social Media in Ukrainian "Euromaidan" Protests. *The University of Manchester*. https://research.manchester.ac.uk/en/publications/social-networks-and-social-media-in-ukrainian-euromaidan-protests. Accessed March 29, 2023.
Onuch, O. (2015a). Maidans Past and Present: Comparing the Orange Revolution and the Euromaidan. In D. R. Marples, & F. V. Mills (Eds.) *Ukraine's Euromaidan: Analyses of a Civil Revolution*, pp. 27–56. Ibidem Press.
Onuch, O. (2015b). EuroMaidan protests in Ukraine: Social media versus social networks. *Problems of Post-Communism*, 62(4). https://doi.org/10.1080/10758216.2015.1037676.
Osa, M. (2003). *Solidarity and Connections: Networks of Polish Opposition*. University of Minnesota Press.
Oulasvirta, A., Hukkinen, J. P., & Schwartz, B. (2009). When more is less: The paradox of choice in search engine use. *Proceedings of the 32nd international ACM SIGIR conference on Research and Development in Information Retrieval*, 516–523. https://doi.org/10.1145/1571941.1572030.
Oya, S., Aihara, K., & Hirata, Y. (2014). Forecasting abrupt changes in foreign exchange markets: Method using dynamical network marker. *New Journal of Physics*, 16(115015). https://doi.org/10.1088/1367-2630/16/11/115015.
Parlitz, U., Junge, L., & Kocarev, L. (1999). Chaos synchronization. In H. Nijmeijer, & T. Fossen (Eds.) *New Directions in Nonlinear Observer Design. Lecture Notes in Control and Information Sciences*, 244, pp. 511–525. Springer. https://doi.org/10.1007/BFb0109942.

Pascual-Leone, A. (2010). The importance of recognizing paradoxes. *European Journal of Neuroscience*, 32, 1030–1031. https://doi.org/10.1111/j.1460-9568.2010.07441.x.

Pascual-Leone, A., Amedi, A., Fregni, F., & Merabet, L. B. (2005). The plastic human brain cortex. *Annual Review of Neuroscience*, 28, 377–401. https://doi.org/10.1146/annurev.neuro.27.070203.144216.

Pascual-Leone, A., Freitas, C., Oberman, L., Horvath, J. C., Halko, M., Eldaief, M., Bashir, S., Vernet, M., Shafi, M., Westover, B., Vahabzadeh-Hagh, A. M., Rotenberg, A. (2011). Characterizing brain cortical plasticity and network dynamics across the age-span in health and disease with TMS-EEG and TMS-fMRI. *Brain Topography*, 24(3–4), 302–315. https://doi.org/10.1007/s10548-011-0196-8.

Pellis, S., & Pellis, V. (2009). *The Playful Brain: Venturing to the Limits of Neuroscience*. Oneworld Publications.

Pena-López, A., Sánchez-Santos, J. M., & Novo, J. A. (2013). The singularities of social capital in family business. In K. X. Smyrnios, P. Z. Poutziouris, & S. Goel (Eds.) *Handbook of Research on Family Business*, pp. 205–235. Edward Elgar Publishing.

Peng, K., & Nisbett, R. E. (1999). Culture, dialectics, and reasoning about contradiction. *American Psychologist*, 54(9), 741–754.

Peredo, A. M., & McLean, M. (2006). Social entrepreneurship: A critical review of the concept. *Journal of World Business*, 41(1), 56–65. https://doi.org/10.1016/j.jwb.2005.10.007.

Pereira, F. C. (2007). *Creativity and Artificial Intelligence: A Conceptual Blending Approach*. Mouton de Gruyter.

Perica, R. (2010). The dancing imagination: How does imaginative imagery facilitate movement qualities in dance training and performance? *Edith Cowan University*. https://ro.ecu.edu.au/theses_hons/1407. Accessed August 30, 2023.

Perkins, D. N. (1988). Creativity and the quest for mechanism. In R. J. Sternberg & E. E. Smith (Eds.) *Psychology of Human Thought*, pp. 309–336. Cambridge University Press.

Perls, F. S. (1992). *Ego, Hunger and Aggression*. The Gestalt Journal Press.

Petzinger, G. W., Fisher, B. W., McEwen, S., Beeler, J. A., Walsh, J. P., & Jakowec, M. W. (2013). Exercise-enhanced neuroplasticity targeting motor and cognitive circuitry in Parkinson's disease. *The Lancet*, 2(7), 716–772. https://doi.org/10.1016/S1474-4422(13)70123-6.

Pheng, L. S. (1995). Lao Tzu's Tao Te Ching and its relevance to project leadership in construction. *International Journal of Project Management*, 13(5), 295–302. https://doi.org/10.1016/0263-7863(95)00021-H.

Pikovsky, A., Rosenblum, M., & Kurths, J. (2003). *Synchronization: A Universal Concept in Nonlinear Science*. Cambridge University Press.

Piotrowski, C., Keller, J. W., & Ogawa, T. (1993). Projective techniques: An international perspective. *Psychological Reports*, 72(1), 179–182. https://doi.org/10.2466/pr0.1993.72.1.179.

Plonka, L. (2021). Creativity: Thinking while moving. In S. Elgelid, & C. Kresge (Eds.) *The Feldenkrais Method: Learning Through Movement*, pp. 109–116. Handspring Publishing.
Plutarch (2013). *Theseus*. CreateSpace Independent Publishing Platform.
Porter, M. E., Ketels, C. H. M., & Miller, K. K. (2004). *Basque Country: Strategy for Economic Development*. Harvard Business School.
Potonik, K., Verwaeren, B., & Nijstad, B. (2022). Tensions and paradoxes in creativity and innovation. *Journal of Work and Organizational Psychology*, *38*(3), 149–163. https://doi.org/10.5093/jwop2022a19.
Powers, R. (2010). Use it or lose it: Dancing makes you smarter, longer. *Stanford Dance*. https://socialdance.stanford.edu/syllabi/smarter.htm. Accessed June 30, 2024.
Praszkier, R. (2013). Social entrepreneurs open closed worlds: The transformative influence of weak ties. In A. Nowak, K. Winkowska-Nowak, & D. Bree (Eds.) *Complex Human Dynamics, From Mind to Societies*, pp. 111–129. Springer.
Praszkier, R. (2018a). *Empowering Leadership of Tomorrow*. Cambridge University Press.
Praszkier, R. (2018b). *What Makes Profound and Peaceful Social Transitions? A Case of Solidarity: The Polish Underground Movement*. iASK Polányi Centre Publications, II.2018/WP01.
Praszkier, R. (2019a). Leaders' portfolio: psycho-social mechanisms augmenting creativity. *Journal of Positive Management*, *9*(1), 18–40. https://doi.org/10.12775/JPM.2018.134.
Praszkier, R. (2019b). *Working Wonders: How to Make the Impossible Happen*. Cambridge University Press.
Praszkier, R. (2021). Possibilitivity. In V. P. Glăveanu (Eds.) *The Palgrave Encyclopedia of the Possible*, pp. 1058–1064. Palgrave Macmillan. https://doi.org/10.1007/978-3-319-98390-5_202-1.
Praszkier, R. (2023a). Three-dimensional delineation of changers-for-good: From practice to conceptualization. *Possibility Studies and Society*, *1*(3), 361–379. https://doi.org/10.1177/27538699231177149.
Praszkier, R. (2023b). The empassion scale: Introduction, validation, and application. *Polish Psychological Forum*, *1*(28), 37–55. https://doi.org/10.34767/PFP.2023.01.03.
Praszkier, R., & Bartoli, A. (2014). The role of civil society in the peace process of the Basque Country. *International Journal of Peace Studies*, *19*(2), 69–93. https://doi.org/10.13140/RG.2.1.2417.6809.
Praszkier R., & Munnik, P. (2021). Social entrepreneurship. In V. P. Glăveanu (Eds.) *The Palgrave Encyclopedia of the Possible*, pp. 1508–1517. Palgrave Macmillan. https://doi.org/10.1007/978-3-319-98390-5_218-1.
Praszkier, R., & Munnik, P. (2022). Peace-oriented mindset. In V. P. Glăveanu (Eds.) *The Palgrave Encyclopedia of the Possible*, pp. 974–982. Palgrave Macmillan. https://doi.org/10.1007/978-3-319-98390-5_264-2.

Praszkier, R., Munnik, P., & Zabłocka, A. (2021). Paradox mindset in management: Theory and measurement. *Journal of Positive Management*, *11*(1), 3–12. http://dx.doi.org/10.12775/JPM.2020.001.

Praszkier, R., & Nowak, A. (2012). *Social Entrepreneurship: Theory and Practice*. Cambridge University Press.

Praszkier, R., Nowak, A., & Coleman, P. (2010). Social entrepreneurs and constructive change: The wisdom of circumventing conflict. *Peace and Conflict: Journal of Peace Psychology*, *16*, 153–174. https://doi.org/10.1080/10781911003691633.

Praszkier, R. & Zabłocka, A. (2021). The perception of doability and how is it measured. *Mind & Society*, *20*(2). https://doi.org/10.1007/s11299-021-00284-2.

Praszkier, R., Zabłocka, A., & Munnik, P. (2023). Peace-oriented mindset and how to measure it. *Europe's Journal of Psychology*, *19*(3). https://doi.org/10.5964/ejop.10445.

Priest, G. (2003). *Beyond the Limits of Thought*. Clarendon Press.

Priest, G. (2007). What's so bad about contradictions? In G. Priest, J. C. Beall, & B. Armour-Garb (Eds.) *The Law of Non-Contradiction: New Philosophical Essays*, pp. 23–40. Clarendon Press.

Pugh, J. D., & Williams, A. (2014). Feldenkrais method empowers adults with chronic back pain. *Holistic Nursing Practice*, *28*(3), 171–183. https://doi.org/10.1097/HNP.0000000000000026.

Putnam, R. D. (1993). The prosperous community: Social capital and public life. *The American Prospect*, *13*, 35–42.

Putnam, R. D. (2000). *Bowling Alone. The Collapse and Revival of American Community*. Simon and Shuster.

Quine, W. V. O. (1976). *The Ways of Paradox and Other Essays*. Harvard University Press.

Quinn, R. E. (1998). *Paradox and Transformation: Toward a Theory of Change in Organization and Management*. Ballinger Pub Co.

Ramseyer, F., & Tschacher, W. (2006). Synchrony: A core concept for a constructivist approach to psychotherapy. *Constructivism in the Human Sciences*, *11*(1–2), 150–171.

Reckwitz, A. (2020). The Society of Singularities. In D. Bachmann-Medick, J. Kugele, & A. Nünning (Eds.) *Futures of the Study of Culture*, pp. 141–154. De Gruyter.

Reinecke, A., Thilo, K. V., Croft, A., & Harmer. C. J. (2018). Early effects of exposure-based cognitive behavior therapy on the neural correlates of anxiety. *Translational Psychiatry*, *8*(1), 225.

Relph, E. (2016). The Paradox of Place and the Evolution of Placelessness. In R. Freestone & E. Liu (Eds.) *Place and Placelessness Revisited*, pp. 20–34. Routledge.

Rescher, N. (2001). *Paradoxes: Their Roots, Range and Resolution*. Open Court.

Reziti, T. (2023). An individualized intervention, based on the Feldenkrais method, for multiple sclerosis symptoms: The neuroplasticity scale

assessment. *Journal of Neurology & Experimental Neuroscience*, 9(1), 7–17. https://doi.org/10.17756/jnen.2023-102.
Rifkind, G. & Yawanarajah, N. (2019). Preparing the psychological space for peacemaking. *New England Journal of Public Policy*, 31(1), 1–11.
Roberts, A. (2012). *Painting by Mouth: Art, Modernity and Disability: Bartram Hiles (1872–1927)*. Unpublished doctoral thesis, University of the Arts London, Falmouth University. https://repository.falmouth.ac.uk/3296/.
Rogers, C. (1995). *On Becoming a Person*. HarperOne.
Rose, J. (1980). *Elizabeth Fry*. Macmillan.
Rosenstein, B. (2022). The Peter Drucker approach to change. *Psychology Today*. www.psychologytoday.com/us/blog/the-peter-drucker-files/202202/the-peter-drucker-approach-change-0. Accessed February 24, 2023.
Rothenberg, A. (1971). The process of Janusian thinking and creativity. *Archives of General Psychiatry*, 24(3), 195–205. https://doi.org/10.5465/amj.2016.0594.
Rothenberg, A. (1996). The Janusian process in scientific creativity. *Creativity Research Journal*, 9(2–3), 207–231.
Rothenberg, A. (2011). The Janusian process in scientific creativity. *Creativity Research Journal*, 9(2–3), 207–231. https://doi.org/10.1080/00107530.1983.10746594.
Rotter, J. B. (1966). Generalized expectancies for internal versus external control of reinforcement. *Psychological Monographs: General and Applied*, 80(1), 1–28. https://doi.org/10.1037/h0092976.
Runco, M. A. (1991). Metaphors and creative thinking. *Creativity Research Journal*, 4(1), 85–86. https://doi.org/10.1080/10400419109534376.
Runco, M. A. (2007). *Creativity. Theories and Themes: Research, Development and Practice*. Elsevier Academic Press.
Rushing, W. (2009). *Memphis and the Paradox of Place: Globalization in the American South*. University of North Carolina Press.
Rusu, I. (2013). Dopamine, endorphins and epinephrine. *European Journal of Science and Theology*, 9(6), 1–3.
Sainsbury, R. M. (2009). *Paradoxes*. Cambridge University Press.
Saleh, Y. (2011). Egyptian revolution brings show of religious unity. *Reuters*. www.reuters.com/article/us-egypt-christians-idUSTRE71H6KA20110218. Accessed April 2, 2023.
Samson, K., & Nowak, A. (2010). Linguistic signs of destructive and constructive processes in conflict. *IACM 23rd Annual Conference Paper*, Boston, June 24–27, 2010. https://doi.org/10.2139/ssrn.1615028.
Santarnecchi, E., Bossini, L., Vatti, G., Fagiolini, A., La Porta, P., Di Lorenzo, G., Siracusano, A., Rossi, S., & Rossi, A. (2019). Psychological and brain connectivity changes following trauma-focused CBT and EMDR treatment in single-episode PTSD patients. *Frontiers in Psychology*, 10(129). https://doi.org/10.3389/fpsyg.2019.00129.
Sasmita, A. O., Kurvilla, J., & Ling, A. P. K. (2018). Harnessing neuroplasticity: Modern approaches and clinical future. *International Journal of Neuroscience*, 128(11), 1061–1077. https://doi.org/10.1080/00207454.2018.1466781.

Satish, S. (2022). Making the horse fly. *The Economic Times.* https://economictimes.indiatimes.com/opinion/speaking-tree/making-the-horse-fly/articleshow/95646065.cms?from=mdr. Accessed July 18, 2024.

Sauce, B., & Matzel, L. D. (2018). The paradox of intelligence: Heritability and malleability coexist in hidden gene-environment interplay. *Psychological Bulletin, 144*(1), 26–47. https://doi.org/10.1037/bul0000131.

Savage, C. W. (1967). The paradox of the stone. *Philosophical Review, 76*(1), 74–79.

Sawyer, R. K. (2007). *Social Emergence. Societies as Complex Systems.* Cambridge University Press.

Schelling, T. C. (2006). *Micromotives and Macrobehavior.* W. W. Norton.

Scheve, T. (2014). What are endorphins? *How Stuff Works?* http://science.howstuffworks.com/life/endorphins1.htm. Accessed July 12, 2023.

Schilit, W. K., & Locke, E. A. (1982). A study of upward influence in organizations. *Administrative Science Quarterly, 27*(2), 304–316. https://doi.org/10.2307/2392305.

Schlaug, G. (2006). The brain of musicians. A model for functional and structural adaptation. *Annals of the New York Academy of Sciences, 930*(1), 281–299. https://doi.org/10.1111/j.1749-6632.2001.tb05739.x.

Schlaug, G. (2015). Musicians and music making as a model for the study of brain plasticity. *Progress in Brain Research, 217,* 37–55. https://doi.org/10.1016/bs.pbr.2014.11.020.

Schuldberg, D. (1999). Chaos Theory and Creativity. In M. A. Runco, & S. R. Pritzker (Eds.) *Encyclopedia of Creativity,* pp. 259–272. Academic Press.

Schwartz, B. (2004). *The Paradox of Choice.* Harper Perennial.

Schwartz, B. (2012). *Rippling: How Social Entrepreneurs Spread Innovation Throughout the World.* Jossey-Bass.

Schwartz, B. (2015). The Paradox of Choice. In S. Joseph (Eds.) *Positive Psychology in Practice: Promoting Human Flourishing in Work, Health, Education, and Everyday Life,* pp. 121–138. Wiley.

Scott, A. (1990). *Ideology and the New Social Movements.* Unwin Hyman.

Seltzer, L. F. (1986). *Paradoxical Strategies in Psychotherapy: A Comprehensive Overview and Guidebook.* John Wiley & Sons.

Semler, R. (2004). *The Seven-Day Weekend: Changing the Way Work Works.* Portfolio.

Sen, P. (2007). Ashoka's big idea: Transforming the world through social entrepreneurship. *Futures, 39*(5), 534–553. https://doi.org/10.1016/j.futures.2006.10.013.

Senge, P. M. (2006). *The Fifth Discipline: The Art & Practice of The Learning Organization.* Doubleday.

Shapira, O., & Liberman, N. (2009). Why thinking about distant things can make us more creative. *Scientific American.* www.scientificamerican.com/article/an-easy-way-to-increase-c/#comments. Accessed July 3, 2024.

Shelton, C. D. (2013). *Brain Plasticity: Rethinking How the Brain Works.* Choice PH.

Shepherd, B. (2005), The use of joyfulness as a community organizing strategy. *Peace & Change, 30*(4), 435–468. https://doi.org/10.1111/j.1468-0130.2005.00328.x.
Sheras, P. L., & Jackson, S. R. (1978). Paradox as an intervention strategy with emotionally disturbed adolescents. Paper presented at the Annual Convention of the American Psychological Association, Toronto, Canada, August 1978.
Shevsky, D. (2022). Euromaidan revolution in Ukraine. In J. A. Goldstone, L. Grinin, & A. Korotayev (Eds.) *Handbook of Revolutions in the 21st Century. Societies and Political Orders in Transition*, pp. 851–863. Springer. https://doi.org/10.1007/978-3-030-86468-2_32.
Shore, J. J. (1981). Use of paradox in the treatment of alcoholism. *Health & Social Work, 6*(1), 11–20. https://doi.org/10.1093/hsw/6.1.11.
Short, S. E., Afremov, J., & Overby, L. (2001). Using mental imagery to enhance children's motor performance. *The Journal of Physical Education, Recreation and Dance, 72*(2), 19–23. https://doi.org/10.1080/07303084.2001.10605829.
Shultz, J. (2022). G.K. Chesterton: The Prince of Paradox. Fairmont State University Library. https://library.fairmontstate.edu/news/1/GK-Chesterton-The-Prince-of-Paradox. Accessed July 17, 2024.
Simonton, D. K. (2017). Domain generated-creativity: On producing original, useful and surprising combinations. In J. C. Kaufman, V. P. Glăveanu , & J. Baer (Eds.) *The Cambridge Handbook of Creativity Across* Domains, pp. 41–62. Cambridge University Press.
Simpson, K. (2019). Through "mouth painting," disabled Aurora artist creates portraits that defy his limitations. *The Denver Post*. www.denverpost.com/2018/01/13/disabled-aurora-artist-paints-with-mouth/. Accessed August 14, 2023.
Sleesman, D. J. (2019). Pushing through the tension while stuck in the mud: Paradox mindset and escalation of commitment. *Organizational Behavior and Human Decision Processes, 155*(C), 83–96. https://doi.org/10.1016/j.obhdp.2019.03.008.
Smilansky, S. (2022). Paradoxes and Meaning in Life. In I. Landau (Eds.) *The Oxford Handbook of Meaning in Life*, pp. 475–491. Oxford University Press.
Smith, C., & Davidson, H. (2014). *The Paradox of Generosity: Giving We Receive, Grasping We Lose*. Oxford University Press.
Smith, K. K., & Berg, D. N. (1987). *Paradoxes of Group Life: Understanding Conflict, Paralysis, and Movement in Group Dynamics*. Jossey-Bass.
Smug, D., Ashwin, P., & Sornette, D. (2018). Predicting financial market crashes using ghost singularities. *PLOS ONE*. https://doi.org/10.1371/journal.pone.0195265.
Snyder & S. J. Lopez (Eds.) *The Handbook of Positive Psychology*. Oxford University Press.
Sokal, A. (1996). Transgressing the boundaries: Towards a transformative hermeneutics of quantum gravity. *Social Text, 46–47*, 217–252. https://doi.org/10.2307/466856.
Solnyshkov, D., & Malpuech, G. (2022). Love might be a second-order phase transition. *Physics Letters A, 445*, 128245. https://doi.org/10.1016/j.physleta.2022.128245.

Song, H., Stevens, C. F., & Gage, F. H. (2002). Neural stem cells from adult hippocampus develop essential properties of functional CNS neurons. *Nature Neuroscience, 5*(5), 438–445. https://doi.org/10.1038/nn844.

Sornette, D. (2017). *Why Stock Markets Crash: Critical Events in Complex Financial Systems.* Princeton University Press.

Spencer, A. T., & Croucher, S. M. (2008). Basque nationalism and the spiral of silence. An analysis of public perceptions of ETA in Spain and France. *International Communication Gazette, 70*(2), 137–153. https://doi.org/10.1177/1748048507086909.

Sprouse-Blum, A. S., Smith, G., Sugai, D., & Don Parsa, F. (2010). Understanding endorphins and their importance in pain management. *Hawaii Medical Journal, 69*(3), 70–71.

Squazzoni, F., Jager, W., & Edmonds, B. (2013). Social simulation in the social sciences: A brief overview. *Social Science Computer Review, 32*(3), 279–294. https://doi.org/10.1177/0894439313512975.

Stein, M. I. (1953). Creativity and culture. *Journal of Psychology, 36*(2), 311–322. https://doi.org/10.1080/00223980.1953.9712897.

Stein, M. I. (1974). *Stimulating Creativity, vol. 1.* Academic Press.

Steinhelfer, T. (2011). Occupy movement holds dance party in America's heartland. *People's World.* www.peoplesworld.org/article/occupy-movement-holds-dance-party-in-america-s-heartland/. Accessed April 18, 2023.

Sternberg, R. J., & Lubart, T. I. (1991). An investment theory of creativity and its development. *Human Development, 34*(1), 1–31. https://doi.org/10.1159/000277029.

Sternberg, R. J., & Lubart, T. I. (2004). The concept of creativity: Prospects and paradigms. In Robert J. Sternberg (Eds.) *Handbook of Creativity,* pp. 3–15. Cambridge University Press.

Stevens, F., & Taber, K. (2021). The neuroscience of empathy and compassion in pro-social behavior. *Neuropsychologia, 159*(107925), 3–10. https://doi.org/10.1016/j.neuropsychologia.2021.107925.

Stodd, J., & Reitz, E. A. (2017). Black swans: Disruption of power. *Interservice/Industry Training, Simulation, and Education Conference (I/ITSEC),* 17174, 1–12.

Stone, D. N. (2002). Overconfidence in initial self-efficacy judgments: Effects on decision processes and performance. *Organizational Behavior and Human Decision Processes, 59*(3), 452–474. https://doi.org/10.1006/obhd.1994.1069.

Stoppler, M. C. (2014). Endorphins: Natural pain and stress fighters. *MedicineNet.com.* www.medicinenet.com/script/main/art.asp?articlekey=55001. Accessed August 2, 2023.

Strogatz, S. (2003). *Sync: How Order Emerges from Chaos in the Universe, Nature, and Daily Life.* Hyperion.

Sussmann, H. J., & Zahler, R. S. (1978). Catastrophe theory as applied to the social and biological sciences: A critique. *Synthese, 37*(2), 117–216. https://doi.org/10.1007/bf00869575.

Sutcliffe, A., & Wang, D. (2012). Computational modelling of trust and social relationships. *Journal of Artificial Societies and Social Simulation, 15*(1), 3.
Sutcliffe, A., Wang, D., & Dunbar, R. (2012). Social relationships and the emergence of social networks. *Journal of Artificial Societies and Social Simulation, 15*(4), 3.
Sutton, J. (2022). How does paradoxical intention really work in therapy? *PositivePsychology.* https://positivepsychology.com/paradoxical-intent/. Accessed September 24, 2023.
Swann, W. B., Pelham, B. W., & Chidester, T. R. (1988). Change through paradox: Using self-verification to alter beliefs. *Journal of Personality and Social Psychology, 54*(2), 268–273. https://doi.org/10.1037//0022-3514.54.2.268.
Sztompka, P. (1993). *The Sociology of Social Change.* Blackwell Publishers.
Takeuchi, H., Osono, E., & Shimizu, N. (2008). The contradictions that drive Toyota's success. *Harvard Business Review.* https://hbr.org/2008/06/the-contradictions-that-drive-toyotas-success. Accessed June 23, 2023.
Taleb, N. N. (2010). *The Black Swan: Second Edition: The Impact of the Highly Improbable.* Random House.
Tang, Y., Mees, A., & Chua, L. (1983). Synchronization and chaos. *IEEE, 30*(9), 620–626. https://doi.org/10.1109/TCS.1983.1085409.
Taylor, J. C., Lashman, R., & Helling, P. (1994). *Practical Problem-Solving Skills in the Workplace.* American Management Association.
Teixeira-Machado, L., Araújo, F. M., Cunha, F. A., Menezes, M., Menezes, T., & DeSantana, J. M. (2015). Feldenkrais method-based exercise improves quality of life in individuals with Parkinson's disease: A controlled, randomized clinical trial. *Alternative Therapies, 21*(1), 8–14. https://doi.org/10.1016/j.jpain.2015.01.471.
Teixeira-Machado, L., Arida, R. M., & Mari, J. D. J (2019). Dance for neuroplasticity: A descriptive systematic review. *Neuroscience & Biobehavioral Reviews, 96*, 232–240. https://doi.org/10.1016/j.neubiorev.2018.12.010.
Thalberg, I. (2006). Intending the impossible. *Australasian Journal of Philosophy, 40*(1), 49–56. https://doi.org/10.1080/00048406212341031.
Theofilatos, A., Yannis, G., Kopelias, P., & Papadimitriou, F. (2016). Predicting road accidents: A rare-events modeling approach. *Transportation Research Procedia, 14*, 3399–3405. https://doi.org/10.1016/j.trpro.2016.05.293.
Tourish, D. (2005). Critical upward communication: Ten commandments for improving strategy and decision making. *Long Range Planning, 38*(5), 485–503. https://doi.org/10.1016/j.lrp.2005.05.001.
Tourish, D., & Robson, P. (2003). Critical upward feedback in organisations: Processes, problems and implications for communication management. *Journal of Communication Management, 8*(2), 150–167. https://doi.org/10.1108/13632540410807628.
Trach, N. (2016). "Together we are power!": Identities and values in Euromaidan slogans. *Władza Sądzenia, 8*, 95–107.
Tsarev, D., Trofimova, A., Alodjants, A., & Khrennikov, A. (2019). Phase transitions, collective emotions and decision-making problem in heterogeneous

social systems. *Scientific Reports, 9*, 18039. https://doi.org/10.1038/s41598-019-5 4296-7.
Turner, M. (1998). *The Literary Mind.* Oxford University Press.
Tyszka, J. (2009). The Orange alternative: Street happenings as social performance in Poland under Martial Law. *New Theatre Quarterly, 14*(56), 311–323. https://doi.org/10.1017/S0266464X00012392.
Tzu-Wei, L., Sheng-Feng, T., & Yu-Min, K. (2018). Physical exercise enhances neuroplasticity and delays Alzheimer's disease. *Brain Plasticity, 4*(1), 95–110. https://doi.org/10.3233/BPL-180073.
Uranga, M. G. (2002). *Basque Economy: From Industrialization to Globalization.* University of Nevada Press.
Vallacher, R. R., & Nowak, A. (2007). Dynamical social psychology: Finding order in the flow of human experience. In A. W. Kruglanski, & E. T. Higgins (Eds.) *Social Psychology: Handbook of Basic Principles,* pp. 734–758. Guilford Publications.
Vallacher, R. R., Coleman, P. T., Nowak, A., & Bui-Wrzosinska, L. (2010). Rethinking intractable conflict: The perspective of dynamical systems. *American Psychologist, 65*(4), 262–278. https://doi.org/10.1007/978-1-4419-9994 -8_4.
Van Andel, P. (1994). Anatomy of the unsought finding: Serendipity: Origin, history, domains, traditions, appearances, patterns and programmability. *British Journal for the Philosophy of Science, 45*(2), 631–648.
Van Praag, H., Kempermann, G., & Gage, F. (1999). Running increases cell proliferation and neurogenesis in the adult mouse dentate gyrus. *Nature Neuroscience, 2,* 266–270. https://doi.org/10.1038/6368.
Van Praag, H., Schinder, A. F., Christie, B. R., Toni, N., Palmer, T. D., & Gage, F. H. (2002). Functional neurogenesis in the adult hippocampus. *Nature, 415*(6875), 1030–1034. https://doi.org/10.1038/4151030.
Van Zomeren, M., Postmes T., & Spears R. (2008). Toward an integrative social identity model of collective action: A quantitative research synthesis of three socio-psychological perspectives. *Psychological Bulletin, 134*(4), 504–535.
Vohs, K. D., Redden, J. P., & Rahinel, R. (2013). Physical order produces healthy choices, generosity, and conventionality, whereas disorder produces creativity. *Psychological Science, 24*(9), 12. https://doi.org/10.1177/0956797613480186.
Von Goethe, J. W., & Eckermann, J. P. (2014). *Conversations of Goethe with Johann Peter Eckermann.* Ravenio Books.
Voss, P., Thomas, M. E., Cisneros-Franco, J. M., & de Villers-Sidani, É. (2017). Dynamic brains and the changing rules of neuroplasticity: Implications for learning and recovery. *Frontiers in Psychology, 4*(8), 1657. https://doi.org/10.338 9/fpsyg.2017.01657.
Wang, J., & Liu, F. (2023). Experiencing tensions, paradoxical thinking and college students' creativity. *Asia Pacific Education Review.* https://doi.org/10.1 007/s12564-023-09858-w.
Weeks, G. R., & L'Abate, L. (1982). *Paradoxical Psychotherapy.* Routledge.

Wel, M. (2020). Why blind compassion is dangerous. *Psychology Today.* www.psychologytoday.com/us/blog/urban-survival/202012/why-blind-compassion-is-dangerous. Accessed September 21, 2023.

Wertheimer, M. (1959). *Productive Thinking.* Harper & Brothers Publishers.

White, N. (1976). *Plato on Knowledge and Reality.* Hackett.

Whyte, W. (1991). *Making Mondragón: The Growth and Dynamics of the Worker Cooperative Complex.* Cornell University Press.

Wilensky, U. (1999). *NetLogo.* Center for Connected Learning and Computer-Based Modeling. Evanston, IL: Northwestern University. http://ccl.northwestern.edu/netlogo/. Accessed June 23, 2024.

Wilkinson, S. T., Holtzheimer, P. E., Gao, S., Kirwin, D. S., & Price, R. B. (2019). Leveraging neuroplasticity to enhance adaptive learning: The potential for synergistic somatic-behavioral treatment combinations to improve clinical outcomes in depression. *Biological Psychiatry, 85*(6), 454–465. https://doi.org/10.1016/j.biopsych.2018.09.004.

Williams, J., & Bond, J. (2002). *Eyes on the Prize: America's Civil Rights Years, 1954–1965.* Penguin Books.

Wilson, M. I., & Corey, K. E. (2012). The role of ICT in Arab spring movements. *Network and Communication Studies, 26*(3/4), 343–356. https://doi.org/10.4000/netcom.1064.

Wilson, M. P., Pepper, D., Currier, G. W., Holloman, G. H., & Feifel, D. (2012). The psychopharmacology of agitation: Consensus statement of the American Association for Emergency Psychiatry Project BETA Psychopharmacology Workgroup. *Western Journal of Emergency Medicine, 13*(1), 26–34. https://doi.org/10.5811/westjem.2011.9.6866. PMC 3298219.

Wiltermuth, S. S., & Heath, C. (2009). Synchrony and cooperation. *Psychological Science, 20*(1), 1–5. https://doi.org/10.1111/j.1467-9280.2008.02253.x.

Wolsfeld, G., Segev, E., & Sheafer, T. (2013). Social media and the Arab Spring: Politics comes first. *The International Journal of Press/Politics, 18*(2), 115–137. https://doi.org/10.1177/1940161212471716.

Woodworth, P. (2003). *Dirty War, Clean Hands: ETA, the GAL and Spanish Democracy.* Yale University Press.

Wright, S. C., Taylor, D. M., & Moghaddam, F. M. (1990). Responding to membership in a disadvantaged group: From acceptance to collective protest. *Journal of Personality and Social Psychology, 58*(6), 994–1003. https://doi.org/10.1037/0022-3514.58.6.994.

Wurth, K. B. (2018). The creativity paradox: An introductory essay. *Journal of Creative Behavior, 53*(2), 127–132. https://doi.org/10.1002/jocb.231.

Wynn, L. T. (1991). The dawning of a new day. The Nashville sit-ins, February 13–May 10, 1960. *Tennessee Historical Quarterly, 50*(1), 42–54.

Yang, A., Abbass, H. A., & Sarker, R. (2006). Characterizing warfare in red teaming. *IEEE Explore, 8971846.* https://doi.org/10.1109/TSMCB.2005.855569.

Yanpallewar, S. U., Fernandes, K., Marathe, S. V., Vadodaria, K. C., Jhaveri, D., Rommelfanger, K., Ladiwala, U., Jha, S., Muthig, V., Hein, L., Bartlett, P., Weinshenker, D., & Vaidya, V. A. (2010). α2-adrenoceptor blockade accelerates the neurogenic, neurotrophic, and behavioral effects of chronic antidepressant treatment. *Journal of Neuroscience, 30*(3), 1096–1109. https://doi.org/10.1523/JNEUROSCI.2309-09.2010.

Yau, S., Gil-Mohapel, J., Christie, B. R., & So, K. (2014). Physical exercise-induced adult neurogenesis: A good strategy to prevent cognitive decline in neurodegenerative diseases? *BioMed Research International, 403120*. https://doi.org/10.1155/2014/403120.

Yeo, R., & Dopson, S. (2018). Getting lost to be found: The insider–outsider paradoxes in relational ethnography. *Qualitative Research in Organizations and Management, 13*(4), 333–355. https://doi.org/10.1108/QROM-06-2017-1533.

Yontef, G. (1993). *Awareness, Dialogue, and Process, Essays on Gestalt Therapy*. The Gestalt Journal Press.

Yunus, M. (2008). *Banker To the Poor: Micro-Lending and the Battle Against World Poverty*. PublicAffairs.

Zabłocka, A., Praszkier, R, Petrushak, E., & Kacprzyk-Murawska, M. (2016). Measuring the propensity for building social capital depending on ties-strength. *Journal of Positive Management, 7*(4), 19–39. https://doi.org/10.12775/JPM.2016.020.

Zeeman, E. C. (1976). Catastrophe theory. *Scientific American, 234*(4), 65–83.

Zenke, F., Gerstner, W., & Ganguli, S. (2017). The temporal paradox of Hebbian learning and homeostatic plasticity. *Current Opinion in Neurobiology, 43*, 166–176. https://doi.org/10.1016/j.conb.2017.03.015.

Zerwas, F. K., & Ford, B. Q. (2021). The paradox of pursuing happiness. *Current Opinion in Behavioral Sciences, 39*, 106–112. https://doi.org/10.1016/j.cobeha.2021.03.006.

Zheng, X., Sun, J., & Zhong, T. (2010). Study on mechanics of crowd jam based on the cusp-catastrophe model. *Safety Science, 48*(10), 1236–1241. https://doi.org/10.1016/j.ssci.2010.07.003.

Zubar, N., & Ovcharenko, V. (2017). Beyond Maidan Nezalezhnosti. *Kolegium Europy Wschodniej im. Jana Nowaka-Jeziorańskiego, 01*(25), 38–45.

Index

"intelligent" risk, 8
"Solidarity," 33, 46

Achilles, 1, 16
Africa, 88, 99
Artificial Intelligence (AI), 2, 142, 143, 145
aintegration, 21
American Psychological Association's (APA), 22
Apuyo, Collins, 5, 100
Arab Spring, 49, 50, 52, 53, 54, 55
Aristotle, 12, 16, 17, 28
Ashoka, 5, 90, 119
attractor, 38, 39, 121, 123, 124, 125, 127, 128

Bakke, Dennis W., 8
Bandura, Albert, 66
Bangladesh, 6, 125, 126, 127
Banksy, 4
Basque, 33, 44, 45, 46, 52, 53, 55
Berra, Yogi, 3, 16
bifurcation, 36, 37, 41
big idea, 42, 53, 56
Birth of the Chaordic Age, 141
black swan events, 2, 11, 30, 33, 34, 35, 52, 57, 60
Blackstock, Cindy, 124, 125, 127, 128
body, 17, 88, 96, 105, 108, 110, 111, 141
Bohr, Niels, 22, 141, 145
bonding, 53
Bornstein, David, 6
bottom-up initiatives, 41, 42, 52, 55
BP Deepwater Horizon, 34
brain, 38, 94, 100, 101, 102, 103, 104, 105, 107, 108, 109, 110, 111, 112, 113, 129, 130, 143
brain plasticity, 94, 100, 102, 107, 129, 143
bridging, 53, 54
British, 72, 118, 119, 122, 125
business, 2, 5, 6, 7, 8, 21, 31, 57, 71, 77, 78, 100, 110, 126
butterfly effect, 33, 36, 41, 52

Canada, 124
causations, 40
challenges, 2, 12, 16, 65, 68, 69, 70, 72, 77, 79, 84, 96, 117, 124, 144, 145
changemaking-for good (C4 G), 117
changers-for-good, 116, 117, 145
chaos, 36, 40, 62, 64, 138, 139, 140, 141, 144, 145, 149, 157, 177
Chesterton, Gilbert Keith, 1
Chhetri, Lucky, 122, 127
Churchill, Winston, 3
Civil Rights Movement, 33, 42, 43, 44, 52, 53, 54
Coffee Machine Syndrome, 140
cognitive behavioral therapy (CBT), 130
Colombia, 73, 99
compassion, 117, 118
complex systems, 40, 139
complexity, 21, 40, 58, 64
conceptual blending, 20
conflict, 5, 19, 39, 59, 79, 82, 83, 84, 85, 86, 88, 89, 92, 133
conflict resolution, 83, 88, 162
conflict transformation, 83, 84, 92
constructive tension, 20
contradictions, 4, 8, 9, 10, 12, 14, 15, 16, 18, 19, 20, 21, 22, 23, 24, 25, 26, 28, 130
contradictory, 10, 11, 15, 16, 20, 21, 22, 24, 25, 26, 27, 95, 101, 139
convergent thinking, 97, 98
cooperation, 33, 38, 50, 53, 56, 61, 86, 89, 91, 139, 140, 142
coordination, 56, 141
corporate social responsibility (CSR), 7
creative thinking, 60, 97, 137
creativity, 7, 8, 12, 19, 20, 21, 22, 23, 24, 25, 26, 60, 69, 73, 94, 95, 96, 97, 98, 100, 104, 109, 110, 139, 143, 145, 146
culture, 1, 20, 34, 42, 44, 51, 54, 71, 89, 123, 124, 125, 127, 128
cusp catastrophe, 30, 33, 35, 36, 41, 52, 59
Czyżewski, Krzysztof, 90

dancing, 50, 54, 110, 111, 112, 113, 126, 133
distance, 15, 36, 60, 96, 134, 137, 143, 162, 164
divergent thinking, 94, 97, 98, 99, 100, 108, 110, 111, 127, 145
diversity, 2, 87, 137, 157
dopamine, 104, 105, 107, 111, 113
Drayton, William, 119
Drucker, Peter, 31
Dweck, Carol, 66
dynamical, 2, 32, 33, 34, 35, 36, 39, 41, 57, 121, 123, 128, 139, 145
dynamics, 11, 25, 33, 35, 36, 37, 38, 40, 54, 57, 58, 59, 60, 61, 82, 83, 88, 127, 128, 141, 145

Einstein, Albert, 93, 138, 141, 147
Embracing Contradictions, 19
emergence, 51, 144, 161, 177
empassion, 117
Empassion Scale (ES), 117
empathy, 72, 73, 117, 118, 122
endorphinergic system, 105
endorphins, 104, 105, 113
equilibrium, 35, 36, 38, 123, 128
ETA, 44, 45, 46, 52
ethnographic, 7
Eubulides of Miletus, 17
Euromaidan, 50, 51, 52, 53, 54, 55
exceeding oneself, 74, 76, 77

feedback loops, 40, 54, 130
Feldenkrais approach, 108, 109, 110
Feldenkrais, Moshé, 108
First Nation, 124, 127, 128
Freud, Sigmund, 129, 131
Fromm, Erich, 64
Fry, Elizabeth, 118, 119, 127
functional compensatory plasticity, 102

Germany, 99
Gestalt therapy, 134
Gilmore, Georgia, 43, 44
Glăveanu, Vlad, 64, 96, 98, 159, 171, 175
Goethe, Wolfgang von, 9, 19
Google Lab, 8
Green teaming, 59, 60
Gulf War, 141

Habermas, Jürgen, 42
happy hormones, 111
Hasan, Munir, 125, 126, 127, 128
Hebbian plasticity, 103
here and now, 134, 135
Heroic Failure, 8
Himalayas, 71, 122, 127

hindsights, 34, 60
Hock, Dee, 140, 141
Hoffman, Frank, 69, 99
horizontal communication, 54
human sync, 142
humor, 20, 131, 133, 134
Hurricane Katrina, 34

impossibility, 64
impossible, xi, 1, 4, 5, 6, 11, 12, 47, 53, 64, 65, 67, 68, 69, 70, 74, 75, 79, 97, 98, 115, 116, 117, 119, 139, 143, 144
Influence of Contradictions Questionnaire, 26
innovation, 7, 8, 10, 11, 21, 46, 96, 127
Institute of Advanced Studies Kőszeg (iASK), xi
Intending the Impossible, 74, 76, 77
interdisciplinary, 2, 98, 145

Janusian thinking, 21, 22, 28, 145
joy, 8, 9, 48, 51, 54, 55, 107, 110, 111, 113, 126, 128, 134, 145
Joy at Work, 8

Kenya, 5, 70, 71, 88, 120
Khan, Arif, 5, 39
King, Martin Luther, 43
Kuria, David, 120, 121, 127

Lao Tzu, 1
Lennon, John, 3
Lewis, Lorenzo, 123, 124, 127, 128
locus of control, 66, 79

market, 6, 9, 33, 34, 35, 40, 41, 48, 58, 59, 60, 71, 100
Marks, Groucho, 3
Martin Luther King, 55
Maxwell, James Clerk, 32
McClelland, David, 67
McCrystal, Stanley, 141
metaphors, 20, 107, 110, 113
mindset, 10, 24, 25, 26, 69, 84, 91, 104, 123, 132
MIT School of Management, 140
Moravec, 142, 143

Need for achievement, 67
Nepal, 70, 71, 72, 75, 76, 122, 123, 128
network, 20, 41, 51, 53, 55, 56, 71, 77, 89, 102, 141
networking, 54, 56
networks, 25, 33, 42, 46, 47, 50, 51, 54, 58, 62, 101, 109
neurogenesis, 102, 105, 106
neurogenesis plasticity, 101, 106, 113, 130
neurohormones, 104, 111, 113
neuronal connections, 108, 109, 111, 113

Index

neuroplasticity, 11, 12, 100, 101, 102, 103, 106, 107, 108, 109, 110, 111, 112, 113, 129, 130, 143, 145, 146
neuroscience, 2, 11, 12, 34, 110, 111, 117, 129, 145
neurotransmitters, 103, 104, 111, 113
New Social Movement, 42, 56

Occupy, 54, 55, 56
Optimism, 67
Orange Alternative, 48
oxymoron, 57, 61

Pakistan, 5, 39
paradox, 1, 10, 14, 15, 16, 17, 19, 22, 24, 25, 26, 61, 64, 65, 68, 69, 82, 83, 89, 90, 95, 101, 110, 113, 116, 118, 127, 131, 136, 138, 139, 143, 144, 145, 146
paradox of generosity, 146
paradox of happiness, 146
paradox psychology, 131
paradoxes, 1, 2, 4, 7, 8, 9, 10, 11, 12, 13, 14, 15, 16, 18, 19, 22, 24, 25, 28, 64, 65, 79, 93, 95, 97, 107, 108, 111, 115, 116, 117, 119, 120, 129, 130, 138, 142, 143, 144, 145, 146
paradoxical intention (PI), 130, 131, 132, 133, 135, 144
paradoxical thinking, 2, 11, 14, 22, 23, 24, 25, 28, 84, 94, 95, 107, 113, 133, 145
paradoxicality, 2, 19, 146, 147
Parks, Rosa, 43, 52
Paz, Yehudah, 83
peacebuilding, 23, 82, 83, 84, 88
peacemaker, 85
peacemaking, 79, 82, 84, 86, 92, 133, 145
Peace-Oriented Mindset (POM), 82
Peace-Oriented Mindset (POM) Questionnaire, 82, 85, 92
Perception of Doability Questionnaire, x, 70, 71, 86, 92
Perls, Fritz, 131, 134
phase transition, 30, 33, 38, 41, 49, 50, 52
Plato, 139
Plutarch, 17
Poland, xi, 46, 47, 53, 54, 90, 91
Popper, Karl, 17
possibilitivity, 69, 70, 73, 79, 84, 85, 144
possibility, 34, 73
possible, xi, 10, 26, 33, 41, 57, 58, 59, 62, 64, 69, 70, 85, 86, 88, 96, 97, 99, 107, 115, 117, 129, 135, 136, 142, 147
predicting unpredictable, 57
prediction, 57, 165
Procter & Gamble, 8
Properties of Networks, 53
psychoanalysis, 129
psychotherapy, 2, 12, 116, 129, 130, 134, 144

Radio Solidarity, 47
rare events, 35
Red teaming, 59
Rogers, Carl, 131
Rotter, Julian, 66
Russell, Bernard, 10

Schelling simulation, 57
Schelling, Thomas C., 57
Schrödinger's cat, 1
Schwartz, Beverly, 7
science of paradox, 10
seemingly contradictory, 15
self-contradictory, 10, 11
self-efficacy, 66, 69, 79
serotonin, 105, 111, 113
Shaw, George Bernard, 6
singularity, 30, 31, 32, 33, 34, 36, 42, 43, 46, 47, 50, 51, 52, 56, 58, 61, 98
sit-ins, 43, 44
small worlds, 53
social capital, 53
social entrepreneurs/entrepreneurship, 4, 5, 7, 8, 12, 116, 117, 119, 120
Social Movements, vi, ix, 40, 42, 52, 54, 57, 153, 159, 174
social psychology, 11, 34
societal transformations, 11
Socrates, 1, 14, 16, 139
solidarity, 49, 50, 52, 53, 54, 56
Sternberg, Robert, 96
synaptic plasticity, 102
synchronization, 141, 142, 144
synchronize, 141, 142, 144

Tahrir Square, 49, 50
Taleb, Nassim, 11, 34
TATA, 8
Thinking the Impossible, 74, 75, 77
Toyota, 25
Twain, Mark, 3, 141, 147

unpredictability, 34, 57
unreasonable, 6, 96
USA, 25, 42, 53, 55, 77, 89, 123, 124, 134, 142

weak ties, 53
Wiener, Norbert, 141
Wilde, Oscar, 2

Yunus, Mohammad, 6

Zeno of Elea, 1, 16, 17

For EU product safety concerns, contact us at Calle de José Abascal, 56–1°, 28003 Madrid, Spain or eugpsr@cambridge.org.

www.ingramcontent.com/pod-product-compliance
Ingram Content Group UK Ltd.
Pitfield, Milton Keynes, MK11 3LW, UK
UKHW022153100325
455882UK00026B/424